Challenge and Change in Indian Administration

Challenge and Change in Indian Administration

Edited by
P.S.N. Sinha

Commonwealth

Challenge and Change in Indian Administration

Edition : 2024

ISBN 81-7169-168-4

Published by :

COMMONWEALTH PUBLISHERS
4831/24, Prahlad Street,
Ansari Road, Darya Ganj,
New Delhi - 110002
Ph. : 23275511, 23257835
Fax : 91- 011- 23257835
e-mail : commonwealthbooks@gmail.com

Typesetting by :
Rishu Computers
Delhi

Printed at :
Roshan Offset Printers
Delhi

Preface

The areas of public administration and organisational management are too intricately linked in the prevailing situation of optimal efficiency and result-oriented delivery of schemes and programmes for the ultimate and assured benefit of the majority of the population in the conscious attempt by Government and its various departments and agencies to improve the quality of life. Goals and objectives are essential in the regime of planned social and economic development, especially for the poor and downtrodden. Implementation of goals and objectives call for related schemes and programmes, both at national and sectoral levels. The Five Year Plans are intended to achieve the desired degree of social and economic growth with justice and equity. These plans are necessarily geared to meet the needs of the millions of rural population who live in illiteracy and poverty. Administration of the numerous programmes meant to take the benefits and fruits of development to the target groups are therefore a massive task for both Central and State governments, on the one hand, and for the implementing agencies and instruments, including local and municipal authorities, on the other.

At the national level areas of concern and crucial importance can be identified as economic and monetary management, administration of public and utility services, urban planning and management, rural development programmes including those which are target-specific and region specific, management of foreign trade and international relations, and personnel administration in civil as well as armed and police forces establishments. The complex interrelationships among these areas of public administration need to be analysed and examined on a continual basis for monitoring of plan programme implementation. For instance, the constant surveillance of the vital public distribution system is as essential as a continuous monitoring of the government's tax revenues and public expenditure.

It has been recognised that it is the efficacy and dedication of administrative agencies assigned with specific development tasks that determines the pace, quality and extent of development effort in all spheres of social and economic activity. The intra-departmental and inter-departmental aspects of coordination are crucial in the development process. The building up of a viable administrative structure of development programme agency is another critical aspect. There are several other factors in the development process which determine the outcome of the elusive goal of all governments, that is, efficient and clean administration.

Combining the theories and principles of management with the tools, techniques and devices of administration, the government administration monolith is seen as a lumbering giant going about its daily chores quite clumsily and with enormous waste of time and energy. Apart from the numerous Central ministries and departments and their appendages all over the country, there are the departments, cells and units of the State governments, each with their own peculiar problems and dilemmas. While Centre-State relations at the political and economic level seem to determine the coordination, or lack of it, at other levels, including administrative and economic, the problems too are intricate and not easily amenable to perceived solutions.

One specific and persistent cause for concern has been the lack of quality and effectiveness in the services rendered by the public and utility services. Power generation, transmission and distribution is particularly noticeable in this context. Urban planning through development authorities is yet another in view of the visible evidence of growing slums, deteriorating municipal services, near-collapse public transport systems, increasingly difficult access to proper medical and health care services in public hospitals, loss of sense of direction in the critical sphere of uniform education and related opportunities in this respect, and above all the persisting ineffectiveness of women's development programmes in both city and village—all these would appear to point to a certain malaise in administration which calls for immediate and even drastic remedy. In spite of the numerous inquiry commissions and committees as well as the work study teams that have investigated the state of affairs in respect of the poor quality of services rendered by governmental and departmental public and utility services, the ills of poor administration have continued to eat into the finances as well as the efficiency of these services.

The origins, design and evolution of public administration in India is a subject that is as engrossing as the story of development that has taken place in the country since ancient times. A tribute also is in order to the British colonial administration from the late nineteenth century and upto the granting of independence, an era that bequeathed to India the steel frame of a bureaucracy that has proved itself both durable and indispensable, in spite of its various ills and stupendous tasks it is required to perform in constrained conditions at the best of times. From the British parliamentary enactments for the governance of the colonial dominion of India through the East India Company and subsequently the Viceroys and Governors-General of the British India government, to the present day amendments in Independent India, has been a long and hard trek across history in the country's search for administration of schemes and programmes that, unlike the British objective, are now rich with the potential of social and economic progress with equity and justice, with specific stress on the uplift of the millions of poor and downtrodden in rural and urban India.

The fact of challenge presented by the imperative of change and development in India is twofold in character: First, social and economic development must be so directed and channelled that the weakest sections of society also are provided the necessary opportunities for betterment and growth and, secondly, India has to keep pace with the rapidly changing world economic and political environment in order to continue its long quest for a rightful place in the comity of nations, in dignity and self-reliance. The inevitable march into the twenty-first century has already begun and it remains to be given the necessary impetus through an administrative resurgence induced by the correct social and economic development policies. The process was set in motion recently with the economic and monetary reforms set in motion by the newly inducted government at the Centre. Administration in India needs to change gears in a big way to prove equal to the formidable and critical challenge that faces the nation.

The primary objective of this collection of articles, papers, essays and extracts is to bring together what has been perceived as useful and relevant material for students as well as researchers. Since the materials are drawn from a variety of sources that are both governmental and individual, the points of views and content of ideas are bound to offer interesting insights to the reader. The articles etc. are published as well as unpublished and thus in book form in their collective effect are both useful and handy. The editor hopes that with the expertise and knowledge of the writers included in the publications, the individual as well as collective value and utility of the volumes are not diminished in any way.

The editor and publishers owe a debt of gratitude to the various institutions and organisations whose publications and reports have provided much of the material included in tne series. They are also thankful to the librarians and documentation personnel who assisted in identifying the papers and articles. It is our fervent hope that the reader will find some substantial material of utility and value in the present collections.

EDITOR

Contents

1

THE CHALLENGE OF DEVELOPMENT: ROLE OF ADMINISTRATIVE AGENCIES IN INDIA

AKHTAR ALI KHAN

In the initial phases of planning in the developing countries, it was believed that the main cause of poverty in these countries was the absence of growth due to a complex historical process and, therefore, the remedy lay in creating catelytic factors for rapid economic growth. In the first decade of development, no special attention was given to identify the poorest section of the population or to pin-point developmental programmes specially for ameliorating their living conditions. The under-current of development thinking during the period was that a substantial reduction in poverty will follow from growth over a period of time. It was thought that the benefits from overall growth would trickle down to those most in need. However, there is a definite evidence of some trends which suggest that even sustained growth can be accompanied by continuing abject poverty of the lowest deciles of population. There are indications in a large number of cases that a section of people may even be impoverished by development.

Courtesy: *Indian Journal of Politics*, AMU, Aligarh.

In India, as in other developing countries of South Asia and Latin America, the mass of poor people live in rural areas, and in fact, urban poverty is more or less an extension of rural poverty. It is only after late 1960s that concern about the rural poor has increasingly been expressed in India with the realization that in spite of appreciable increase in the index of overall agricultural output in the country, availability of food to the people has not increased. About 48 per cent of the rural population lived below the poverty line. It is an undisputed fact that India suffers from abject poverty both in qualitative and quantitative terms. Poverty hits one between the eyes and even the most insensitive amongst us cannot help feel the presence of poverty in its starkest form, hunger and squalor are conspicuous by their abundance around isolated cases of economic plenty.

Developmental Programmes Revisited

In order to meet the challenges of development planned efforts have been made. After Independence, various development programmes have been launched from time to time for the betterment of rural masses and their economy. In 1952, National Extention Scheme and Community Development Programme were launched as means for the all round development of rural areas. It aimed at the integration of policy and programmes. Continuous cooperation and active participation of the people in an organized manner were taken as prerequisites for the success of the programmes. Unfortunately, the desired level of participation could not be enlisted in these programmes. Mehta Committee on Panchayati Raj (1957) attributed the failure of the programme to the unrepresentative character of these local bodies. In 1969, 14 major Commercial Banks were nationalised and one of the objectives was to afford credit facilities to small farmer in the rural areas. The Minimum Needs Programme also aims at providing minimum requirements for rural areas. The theme of Integrated Rural Development (IRD) is to provide a package of development programmes pertaining to all aspects of rural economy and covering rural people in their entirely with the objective of removing difficulties in the way of better socio-economic life in rural areas by utilising the advancements in the field of science and technology in a single strategy. 'Habitat Movement' has also been conceived as a tool for the economic upliftment of the rural poor. The Food-For-Work Programme, now known as National Rural Employment Programme (NREP), was launched in 1976-77 with the objective of providing jobs to the rural unemployed and under-employed. The 5th of June, 1978[1] observed as 'World Environment Day' in New Delhi, was closely realised to the socio-economic upliftment of the rural poor. Lastly, a Rural Reconstruction Ministry has been set up at the Centre.[2]

Efforts have also been made through the Five-Year-Plans which were adopted as essential instruments of socio-economic change and development in India. The first-Five-Year-Plan was based on the idea of 'All round balanced development' followed by the Socialistic Pattern of Society' approach in the Second Five-Year-Plan. In the Third Five-Year-Plan emphasis was laid on increasing the national income and improving conditions of the rural masses. While the fourth five-year plan aimed at "growth with stability" the emphasis was laid on 'removal of poverty' in the Fifth Five-Year Plan. While the immediate objectives of development plans have varied from plan to plan in the light of prevailing economic situation, their major thrust has been to achieve economic growth and modernization coupled with social justice. The challenge of development has had a bearing on the character and role of the administration.

Causes of Failure

From an overview of administrative efforts for development it is clear that there has been no lack of effort on the part of the Government. Still after pressing into service a vast reservoir of talent and resources with remedial steps identified, the desired benefits could not accrue to the rural poor.

In order to find out the shortcomings of the developmental programmes so far launched, various committees like Mehta Committee, Rural Banking Enquiry Committee, Rural Survey

Credit Committee, K.R. Damle Working Group, Dantawala Committee and Ashok Mehta Committee etc. were set up. These Committees identified administrative, structural, procedural and institutional weaknesses and suggested specific remedies to enlist people's continuous cooperation and active participation for the success of development programmes.[3]

According to the Draft Sixth Five Year Plan (1978-83) the problems resulting in a significant gap in planning and implementation in the earlier plans have been broadly classified under various groups as follows:[4]

(a) Technical, administrative and managerial problems including lack of delegation of authority to subordinate organization levels, delays in issuing sanctions, approvals etc. and lack of specific assignment of responsibility and accountability for results:

(b) Inadequacy of data base and information system;

(c) Inadequate attention to inter-lankages, the lack of systems approach and poor monitoring and evaluation feel back system.

When a chain of administrative, organizational and practical changes have made very little impact on overall development of rural areas the whole situation warrants a fresh look, possibly from different angles, at the total socio-economic scene of the country.

While there are various factors responsible for a low development programmes requiring multi-disciplinary approach for their solution, we may classify them in two broad categories: (i) Policy perspective, and (ii) Implementation Perspective. The role of administrative agencies, being the main focus of the article we will concentrate mainly on the implementation perspective of developmental plans.

Implementation Perspective and Administrative Agencies

In view of the great diversity and varied intensity and magnitude of problems in Rural India, it will neither be desirable nor feasible to evolve a uniform formula for the entire country. These arrangements will have to have great amount of flexibility within a broad pattern to meet the specific problems of different areas. Administrative role for rural development in this paper is thus being kept in the form of a broad frame-work as it is obviously not possible to cover all the variations involved. Administration for all round rural development must take into account not only the socio-economic structure but also the mobilization and implementational capability of the apparatus involved, particularly from the view point of an effective delivery system and support in respect of the different aspects of rural development.

In the course of the implementation of a plan the administrative agencies have to face the following basic challenges which may be discussed in turn:

(1) Personnel development and boosting morale of the administrative agency entrusted with the responsibility of implementation of plans.

(2) Securing people's participation in the programme.

(3) Maintaining coordination and communication between the people and the administration.

The personnel involved in development programme forms its back-bone. For the efficient performance of the personnel it is essential that they should have the 'urge' to serve the rural masses and aptitude to mix with the have nots (rural poor). They must be goal-oriented with leadership qualities and adopt an analytical approach to the problem, identified. For this the present system of Personnel Administration needs a thorough overhaul with regard to the system of recruitment, training, placement and promotion that the candidates from rural background may have an equality of opportunity. After their entry into public services they should be trained accordingly to play a vital role in implementing the development programmes. If the personnel to be entrusted with the job of implementing the development programmes come only from the urban areas with urban taste in their life-styles, there is a latent danger for the success of a specific development programme.

In view of the scarceness of resources implicit in anti-poverty programmes three questions concerning their efficiency need consideration:

(a) to what extent are the field agencies equipped with necessary professional knowledge and competence?

(b) have they developed ways of tackling the numerous specific problems faced by the intended beneficiaries?; and

(c) have they acuqired effective means of discriminating new ideas and delivering inputs to the mass of rural poor rather than to a privileged few?

It is an established fact that the administrative machinery is not fully geared to take up the challenge of elimination of rural poverty because political leadership and bureaucracy often have a similar class background to landed farmers and tend to identify with their interests. Despite the fact that the Government departments have been carrying out the work of Welfare of the masses for the last three decades there is still a hiatus between the aspirations of rural poor and the competency of bureaucracy to deal with their problems. It is, therefore, necessary that steps should be taken for structural improvement of the administration through a concerted programme in inculcating professionalism and job effectiveness of the various functionaries involved in the development process. This will *inter-alia* include management training adjusted to place a premium on innovation and ability to improve performance within existing constraints.

However, adopting a sound recruitment and training system is not enough. The morale of the cadre should be maintained throughout the service. The majority of the personnel do not want to go to rural areas and scrve the masses because they have to put themselves into a lot of difficulties due to lack of essential services and civil amenities otherwise available to them in urban areas. However, the problem of optimum utilization of huge natural resources available in the countryside for rural development persists. In order to stimulate the persnnel for service in rural areas and for creating an urge and affording incentives for motivation to the personnel following suggestions are worth consideration.[5]

Essential amenities like drinking water and residential accommodation etc. must be provided on priority basis;
Children of personnel working in rural areas should be given preference for admission to various courses within the stipulated qualitative norms and also in allotment of hostel accommodation in educational institutions in urban areas;
Services of mobile dispensary must be provided in each village at least once in a week;
The Head of the Functional Department should personally meet the personnel working in rural areas to appraise himself of the specific difficulty the personnel are facing;
A period of five years service in rural areas should be considered a qualification for the grant of six months (but not more than two years) extention in service beyond normal age of retirement;

Once additional increment should be granted to each personnel for a period of ten years service in rural areas as an incentive;

Transfer cases should be strictly dealt with on the principle of 'first-come-first served';

Personnel matters pertaining to payment of wages, increment, leave, Provident Fund, re-imbursement, settlement of dues, if any, must be settled as quickly as possible;

On completion of 10 years service in rural areas each personnel should be awarded a 'Certificate of Service' on behalf of Union Ministry of Labour and Employment in recognition of his services to the rural masses;

Permission for prosecuting studies must be granted to the willing personnel immediately on receipt of such requests;

2 to 4 days special casual leave may be granted on the basis of remoteness and working conditions in the area;

Field Units of DAVP should strictly adhere to organising a programme for entertainment of village folks at least once in three months;

One copy of Employment News and National importance news papers should be supplied to each village panchayat;

Consideration should be given to the specific requests of the personnel for their place of posting; and

On completion of 2 years service in rural areas each personnel should be awarded a title, "Gram Sudharak" by the Governor of the State concerned in consultation with the Union Ministry of Labour and Employment. The title should normally be awarded on the Republic day.

In fact, the role of administration in a 'Welfare State' is different from that of a totalitarian state where it is merely an instrument of maintenance of law and order. In a welfare State they are the potent agent of social change and economic development. Unfortunately in the present social-political climate even the development functionaries are showing greater interest in regulatory functions. A proper attitude and morale is an essential pre-requisite for them.

When a decision is reached and it has to be executed, the administrator should bring into being a sense of social purpose among his staff of all ranks. Whatever major decision is reached, and whenever a particular piece of work has to be executed he should see to it that his men see what it is for and realise that it is a good and laudable purpose. They should be made to feel that it would be a service to society to bring it about. There is an often repeated story that brings this out. Some one saw stone-cutters at work in Guiody Raj Bhawan at Madras and he asked one of them, What are you doing?" He replied, "I am cutting stones, do you not see"? "What are you doing"? He asked the second man. His reply was, "Sir I am a poor man earning my living." To the same question, a third man answered "Sir, I am chiselling a Budha image." A fourth man replied' "Sir, we are building the Gandhi Mandapam to serve as a holy centre for prayer." It is this last man's feeling that must be impressed on all those who have to carry out anything decided upon.

Need for Decentralization

Among the important issues involved in different facets of district administration, the one principle of crucial importance is need for decentralization of administration because decentralization, besides operational autonomy for the field administrators which it involves, signifies meaningful participatory role for them. As has been already pointed out effective field administration requires an appropriate psychology of work, a high level of morale, commitment, and identification. It emanates from comprehension, at both emotive and intellectual levels, of various development activities in their inter relation, and partly from overall job satisfaction. A first step to such comprehension is the need on the part of the field administrators to participate in goal setting as well as in policy formation particularly when policies are spelt out in terms of concrete action programmes. Through such participation a clear perception of goals can occur to field administrators and the policies of the organization can be fully understood in both letter and spirit.[6] This must be made effective all along the line.

Appropriate financial and executive authority should also be delegated to them. The delegation of powers and simplification of rules and procedures has been duly stressed in Draft Sixth Plan (1978-83). It states that, "further simplification of rules and procedures and setting up of time limits or norms for completing various types of works, together with delegation of financial and administrative powers will be attempted by each Government agency so as to minimize the problems experienced at the citizen administrative contact points and enable the citizens to get full benefit of plan schemes.[7]

Securing Participation of the People

Effective implementation of any development programme depends on the people's continuous cooperation and active participation. It was realized within a few years of the working of the community Development Programme that one of the less successful aspects of the programme was in respect of evoking popular initiative. In January, 1957 the Government of India appointed a Study Team under the Chairmanship of Mr. Balwantrai Mehta to study and report on Community Development Projects and National Extension Service. The Mehta Study team offered two board directional thrusts: (1) it argued that there should be administrative decentralization for the effective implementation of the development programmes, and (ii) the decentralized administrative system should be under the control of elected bodies. It stated that, "development cannot progress without responsibility and power. Community Development can be real only when the community understand its problems, realizes its responsibility exercises the necessary powers through its chosen representatives and maintains a constant and intelligent of local administration. With this objective, he recommended an early establishment of Statutory local bodies and devolution to them of the necessary resources, power and authority.[8]

In fact, the programmes for the development of the rural poor are sought to be implemented in a framework of centralized planning and anministrative system. Most of such programmes are sponsored by the centre. Provision of funds leads to the determination of how they should be spent and what is the criterion of effectiveness. Such a concern of the Central agencies providing funds at least reduces local level initiative if it does not eliminate it completely. Consequently, Schemes do not necessarily reflect the needs of areas and people concerned. Administrators start to care more about financial targets than about the achievement of programme goals due to inflexible procedures.

Therefore, the first task is to bring project formulation and execution as close to the beneficiary as possible. As a matter of fact it is they who should become responsible for translating their aspirations into action for their own good. Unless this is done, programmes to help the rural poor will turn out to be simply a charity extended to the villagers instead a programme for self reliance with their full participation. Demands on the Governments will grow and the significance of their own group action and self help will be blurred, while on the other hand, effective participation at micro level can build up pressure to reorient policies at macro level in their favour.[9] So far the scheme and programmes have been formulated without associating them on the presumption that they are not aware of their needs and the means to improve their lot. Similarly, while implementing the government imposed schemes they are not taken into confidence and their grievances are not heard at an appropriate administrative level. It is, therefore, suggested that for ensuring the involvement of the rural poor, village level watch-dog committee should be set up to keep an eye on the implementation of the programmes. Moreover there are certain requirements at the local level for meaningful participation of the people:

(a) Professional expertise in order to formulate projects so that schemes are executed effectively;

(b) An adequate data base that can feed information for planning purposes to both the district as well as levels higher up;

(c) A systematic monitoring and evaluation system that can enable the district authorities to take corrective action in time, a concurrent evaluation system that can assess whather the local, identification of beneficiary groups and operational processes of project implementation are fulfilling the goals of the programme or not.

It may be useful to have a system of setting up various working groups to discuss in detail the programme of development to be taken up in different sectors on the basis of guidelines issued by the State, the overall priorities and the local requirements and potentialities. It will be necessary to ensure that at the district block levels, the plans do not turn out to be just a list of demands and these take into account the constraints involved. For this purpose, it may be necessary to develop some objective criteria particularly for the spread of infrastructure items and social services like education, health, roads etc. in terms of their existing locations spread and need for strengthening the same for integrated development. For all this proper arrangements for collection, maintenance and analysis of data both at district and block levels are obviously of vital importance. The objective analysis of data should also be made available to all concerned with the planning process for their enlightened participation and purposeful contribution.

Further in order to secure continuous cooperation and active participation of the people the personnel involved in the process of implementation of the development programmes must have the knowledge of the social system in which they operate and adopt the modulus operation for the success of programme. A healthy communication system is a prerequisite for that, several deficiencies of communication have been observed at the field level between the administrator and the public. It is futile to understand the problems of non-elite rural group through representative institutions as these institutions are dominated by powerful and elite sections of society. The field administrators must improve their contacts with the common people particularly those belonging to the weaker sections of the society. This may require not only additional changes suitably backed by institutional devices like organization of the rural poor and a vigilant press and an informed public opinion.

Need for Coordination

In Physiology the term coordination denotes the combined action of a number of muscles in a complex movement. In public administration, the definition is not different: coordination is the harmonious combined action of agents or functions towards a given objective.[10]

For an integrated rural development there is a need of synchronization of actions and horizontal coordination which is unfortunately lacking in our present administrative system. As the things stand today the District Collector is the Chief Coordinator and is the only person who gets to know about different sectoral plans and their complementarity. This awareness about complementarity of the programmes must percolate to other levels of officers at the local level so that interdependencies in a development programme could be better identified and appreciated.[11]

For effective coordination the District Collector should be assisted in his work by another officer of nearly similar rank with clear-cut responsibility for coordination at the district level. In the states like Maharashtra and Gujarat where effective democratic decentralization has taken place, such an arrangement already exists—an officer at district level under the Zila Parishad is in charge of all development work in the district. At the block level this responsibility should rest with Block Development Officer. He further proposes to set up formal coordination Committee at each level with the coordinating officers as Chairman. These Coordination Committees should comprise of all the top officers of various department at these levels as also the representatives of the Panchayati Raj and other institutions and agencies concerned with rural development in the respective areas.

Implementation of Plans at the Grass-Root Level

In 1977, the Department of Personnel and Administrative Reforms set up a working Group to look into the matter of administrative structure and procedure for decentralized development specially the multiplicity of functionaries at the village level. The Group reported that in some areas, there had been a proliferation of functionaries at village level and growth of multi-channels and parallel hierarchies at other levels.[12]

As it stands today, the farmer has to face the problem of multiplicity of authorities for getting his requirements such as seeds, fertilizers, pesticides, marketing facilities, credit etc. He has to obtain clearance and sanction from a number of officials which takes away his considerable time and money.

In view of the above mentioned difficulties of farmers, the Group recommended that as far as possible there should be three functionaries at the village level with non overlapping functions. The services may be classified and assigned to these functionaries.

The area of jurisdiction of village level functionaries should be decided in view of the number of families which will have to be attended to and also the distance to be covered.

The Group further recommended that there should be a single integrated service point which will cater to almost all the needs of the villagers. It proposed to establish integrated co-operative societies at the village level. This society should function both as a credit society and as a service society. It should supply inputs and marketing facilities to its members. In tribal areas it was expected to carry out barter trade till such time as the tribal economy becomes well monetised. The Group recommended that all the credit that is flowing in to the village through various financial agencies may be channelised through the integrated cooperative society. The dues of electricity board etc. could also be collected by the integrated society.

The measures suggested by the Group are worth consideration for effective administration of rural development programme.

Conclusion

There has been no dearth of well maning efforts on the part of the Government. Rural reconstruction programmes started about thirty-five years ago could be expected to achieve significant results provided adequatc institutions created for their implementation. There is a need for stimulating the bureaucracy with an urge to serve the rural areas and incentives required for motivating the field-level personnel should be provided by the Government. Besides, a happy relationship between the administration and beneficiaries is a necessary ingredient for translating the objectives of planning into effective action. Moreover, there is need to avoid the lack of delegated authority and the lop-sided approach to development and the fragmented linkages between policy making and implementation.

Development of the rural poor is a multi-dimensional notion. The sense of deprivation is not merely confined to essential commodities. Ultimately it is concerned with dignity of man and the whole processes and strategies of development have to be aimed at providing this sense of dignity to the rural poor.

REFERENCES

1. "The Man and his Environment", Hindustan Times, 6-6-1978, p. 3.

2. See B.L. Gulati, "Development of Rural Poor: Intentions and Implementations," Paper presented at the Annual Conference of Indian Institute of Public Administration, New Delhi, 1961.

3. *Ibid.*

4. Government of India, Planning Commission, Draft Sixth Five-Year Plan, 1978-83, p. 121.

5. See B.L. Gulati, *op. cit.*

6. Amal Ray, Organizational Aspects of Rural Development. The World Press, Calcutta, 1976, pp. 18-19.

7. Government of India, Planning Commission, Draft Sixth Five-Year Plan, 1978-83, p. 122.

8. Report of the Team for the Study of Community Projects and National extention Service, November, 1957.

9. Kuldeep Mathur, "Development of Rural Poor: Intentions and Implementations," Key-Paper read at the annual conference of the Indian Institute of Public Administration, New Delhi, 1980.

10. Dimock and Dimok, Public Administration, 4th Edition, Holt Rinchart and Winston Inc., p. 402.

11. T.N. Chaturvedi, "Perspectives of Administrative Reforms For Integrated Rural Development: India". Paper presented in the EROPA meeting held at Manila, February 20-21, 1980.

12. Personnel and Administrative Reforms. Report of the Working Group on Rationalization of Points of Contacts with Administration at the Village Level, New Delhi, 1977.

2

ORGANIZATIONAL CULTURE AND COMMITMENT TO WORK

S.R. JAISWAL

This study aims at examining the impact of Organizational Culture on the level of 'Commitment to work' based on data collected from 120 respondents drawn from Bokaro Steel Plant (a unit of SAIL). The findings of the study leads to author to come to the conclusion that organizational culture does influence the level of commitment to work significantly. The author also feels that better organizational culture where one's higher order needs are satisfied through autonomy, achievement, responsibility etc. leads to higher level of commitment and conversely an organization with coercive authority system affects the level of commitment negatively. Thus, the level of commitment can be raised considerably by developing a better organizational culture.

Organizational culture and its impact on various aspects of work-life have been analyzed by a number of social scientists both in the country and abroad. Survey of literature indicates that organizational culture affects the level of commitment to work considerably. The nature of this relationship was explored in the past. For the present study also it was proposed to examine the impact of organizational culture on commitment to work in the framework of Bokaro Steel Plant. For this the following hypothesis was made:

Hypothesis: "Organizational Culture has an impact on the commitment to work. In other words the level of commitment to work does vary with the variation in organisational culture."

Methodology

(*i*) *Questionnaire*: For measuring the impact of organizational culture on the level of commitment to work a questionnaire was developed which consists of two parts—Part I dealts with the background information of the respondents and Part II deals with the cultural variables in seven dimensions basis on Rensis Likert's Management Systems.

The four management systems represent four cultures—Autocratic, Benevolent-Autocratic, Consultative and Democratic and are arranged in the order A<B<C<D. This fact was not disclosed to the respondents at the time of administering the questionnaire. The respondents were given the following instructions:

"Four hypothetical organizations are presented separately. Please read the description carefully, assume yourself as an employee of these organizations and your present positional hierarchy similar in all the four. Please also assume that these organizations are identical in respect of working conditions, technology. promotional plans, wages, size of the firm, financial standing and none of the firms is likely to be wound up. Now, put your choice against the alternative of responses across all the four organizations. Answers are to be given on a five point scale with the following response alternatives:

1. To a very little extent

2. To a little extent
3. To some extent
4. To a great extent
5. To a very great extent.

The scale for measuring commitment was adopted from Berret's study on 'Individual and Organizational Objectives; A Study of Goal Integration Mechanism (1970) which was used and adopted in successive study (P. Singh, T. Mathew and G. Das). Details are given in Annexure—I.

(*ii*) *Sample*: The sample consists of 120 respondents from a public sector undertaking (Steel Plant). The universe was limited to 3497 executives stationed at Bokaro Steel City. They were selected on random sampling basis. They belong to four divisions of the plant *viz.* Work, Construction Services and Mines. 45 per cent of the respondents were from Works Division, 26 per cent from Construction, 23 per cent from Services and the remaining 6 per cent from Mines and Quarries. 116 of them were males and only 4 females. Majority of the respondents were graduate with minimum 10 years of experience on an average in the age group of 30-40. The Sample represents 4 per cent of the total population.

(*iii*) *Data Collection*: Data were collected over a period of four months. 160 questionnaires were prepared and administered out of which only 130 were selected for the study because others were found unfit for the purpose. The respondents were spread over the entire plant and main administrative building spread over a radious of 8 Kms. The respondents were personally explained the questionnaire by the researcher. The following two statements were used in the study to measure commitment:

1. To what exent the described organisation is effective in getting you involved in meeting its needs and achieving its objectives?

2. To what extent does the organisation described above meets your needs and goals as an individual?

The responses against both the statements were collected on a five point Likert type scale already mentioned.

The response alternatives were given weightage ranging from 1 to 5 (1 for 'to a very little extent' and 5 for 'to a very great extent' and intervening values for the intermediate alternatives. The response to the first alternative measures the degree of individual contribution to the organizational objectives and that for the second statement measures the organizational contribution to the pursuit of individual goals. Neither, however, measures commitment directly. For measuring commitment a special indexing scale was developed to combine the scores on both the items. The formulae is given in Appendix II.

(*iv*) *Scoring of Responses*: The responses scores, scores of 120 respondents across all the four organizations were collected and then tabulated on a specially designed proforma forming part of the instrument for this study. The scores were then converted into commitment index using Berret formulae. Based on a tally-bar chart a frequency table was drawn as given in Appendix III. The commitment scores was then clubbed into the three categories, low, medium and high. The low range was taken to be between 0.60 to 1.50, medium range between 1.67 to 3.00 and the high range between 3.60 to 5.00. A frequency distribution of the three was then drawn across the organizations as given in Table 2.1, to find the variation in the levels of commitment to work across the organizations. Mean and variance of the scores were then calculated as given in Table 2.2. To test the hypothesis 'Z' value was calculated for all the size combinations of mean commitment scores—AB, AC, BC, BD, AD and CD. Finally a frequency polygon was drawn to show the variation at a glance.

Limitations of the Study

Various definitions indicate the organizational culture includes values, modes, beliefs, customs, ideas, habits, behaviour, process, structure, technology and in fact anything and everything in the organizational system which affect the behaviour of individuals in the organization. It is however, not feasible to take into account the entire range of dimensions in a single study because of the limitations imposed by time and resources. As such for the purpose of this study organizational culture has been given an operational definition which refers to a set of attributes and mechanism which organisations adopt and utilize to deal with their members and environment. They include a set of systems—leadership styles, communication patterns, control systems, goal setting, delegation of authority, interaction influence mechanism, contron systems etc. which represent the process of formulating decisions and the pattern of organizational adoption.

Commitment which is another important variable in this study has been defined as the function of goal integration—integration of goals of individuals with the objectives of the organization—higher the level of goal congruence, higher the degree of commitment.

This study is limited to examining the coverted attitude as reflected in the response of the respondents and which affects the overt behaviour. Thus, it is a perception based study.

Data-Analysis and Findings

Table 2.1 represents the frequency distribution of the commitment responses across four organizations (A), (B), (C), and (D) representing for cultures—Autocratic, Benevolent-Autocratic Consultative and Democratic cultures. Responses have been clubbed on the basis of range of commitment—low, medium and high. The Analysis of the table indicates that in case of Autocratic and Benevolent-Autocratic organisations atleast 30 per cent of the response fall in the low range. The percentage of response in the case of Consultative organisation is 50 per cent and it is less than 40 per cent in the Democratic

TABLE 2.1

Table Showing Categories of Commitment Scores, Corresponding Range of Commitment and No. of Respondents Across each Category and Corresponding Percentage Across the Organizations

Commitment Score (Range)	*Organisations*							
	A		*B*		*C*		*D*	
	No. of responses	*Percentage*	*No. of responses*	*Percentage*	*No. of responses*	*Percentage*	*No. of responses*	*Percentage*
1	*2*	*3*	*4*	*5*	*6*	*7*	*8*	*9*
Low (0.60—1.50)	98	81.67	96	80.00	60	50.00	46	38.33
Medium (1.60—3.00)	19	15.83	21	17.50	38	31.67	45	37.50
High (3.60 – 5.00)	3	2.50	3	2.50	22	18.33	29	24.17
Total	120	100.00	120	100.00	120	100.00	120	100.00

set up. Thus, the low range of commitment shows a declining trend across the organisations from (A) to (D). In other words when the organisational culture varies from Autocratic to Benevolent-Autocratic and then to Consultative and then again to Democratic form, the low range of commitment goes on decreasing. As against this examination of high range of commitment scores indicates a reverse trend *i.e.*, the range of commitment scores have increasing trend across the organizations (A), (B), (C) and (D) being highest (24.17%) in Democratic organisation and lowest (2.50%) in Autocratic and Benevolent-Autocratic organisations. Thus, the high range of commitment goes on increasing across the organisations. Examination of medium range of commitment scores indicate a similar upward trend—15.83 per cent in (A), 17.50 per cent in (B), 31.67 per cent in (C) and 37.50 per cent in (D). Thus the findings of this table support the hypothesis that organisational culture has an impact on the level of commitment to work. In other words level of commitment to work does vary with a variation in organisational culture.

An important finding of this study is that even in democratic form of organizational culture a considerable percentage of commitment falls in low range (38.33%) and approximately and equivalent percentage in the medium range (37.50%). Thus the high range of commitment was only 24.14 per cent. It was also found that even in cases of Autocratic and Benevolent-Autocratic cultures there was high range of commitment (2.50). Thus, commitment is a matter of degree only. This finding is in line with the finding of Reynolds and Gregory, which indicates that some other factors also have influenced on the level of commitment to work. This fact has already been established by the findings of Sharma, Prabhu, Dayal, Singh *et al.* but this does not fall within the scope of this study. However, it indicates the need for a further study in the area so as to pin-point other valuable affecting commitment at the micro level.

Another important finding of this study is that when the

organisational culture varies from (A) to (B) there is no change in high range of commitment percentage but the moment it changes to (C), there is dramatic increase from 2.50 per cent to 18.33 per cent (nearly 8 times). It further increases to 24.17 per cent in (D) *i.e.*, approximately 11 times.

TABLE 2.2

Table Showing Mean and Variance of Commitment Across the Classified Organisations

	Organisations			
	Automatic	*Benevolent-Autocratic*	*Consul-tative*	*Democratic*
	(*A*)	(*B*)	(*C*)	(*D*)
Mean	1.196	1.246	1.966	2.269
Variance	0.521	0.561	1.444	1.754

Table 2.2 shows the mean and variance scores of commitment across the four organizations. The mean scores across the organisations (A), (B), (C) and (D) are in the progressive order 1.196, 1.246, 1.966 and 2.269. It is higest in the case of Dimocratic organisation and lowest in the Autocratic culture.

Similarly, variance also shows a progression from 0.521 to 1.754. Both the mean and variance scores are in the progressive order across the organisation A<B<C<D. Analysis of this Table also shows variation in commitment scores across the organisations.

Table 2.3 indicates that mean score of commitment is not statistically significant between organisations A and B as also C and D, the Z value being 0.526 and 1.756 respectively against the tabulated value of 1.96 (at 5% confidence level. Tne non-significant difference between organisations (A) and (B) as also

TABLE 2.3

Table Showing Organisational Z Values

X_A X_B	=0.526*
X_A X_C	=6.017
X_A X_D	=7.792
X_B X_C	=5.570
X_B X_D	=7.365
X_C X_D	=1.856*

$P < .05$

Z value to be significant at 5% level ≥ 1.96

*Not significant at 5% level.

between organisations (C) and (D) can be explained in terms of their cultures. Socio-psychological needs satisfaction in such organisations is not in fact, different substantially. In the first combination of organisations (A) and (B) both are basically bureaucratic, centralized and pyramidal. The opportunity for decentralised decision making and using creativity is minimum. The degree of work autonomy, process of goal setting, motivation, planning, monitoring, interaction-influence process are more or less same. Multiple job behaviour is absent.

In case of organisational combination (C) and (D) the non-significant 'Z' value indicates that both the organizations are perceived more or less similarly by the respondents. Both are open, democratic and a good deal of interaction is common. Motivation, leadership, communication, control etc. aim at helping the subordinates and achieving organisational objectives. As such perceptual difference is non-significant.

In rest of the combinations *i.e.*, AC, AD, BC and BD the difference in mean scores is statistically significant (at 5% confidence level) being highest (7.792) in (AD). The organisational cultures in these combinations are viewed significantly different.

Thus, the analysis of the above three tables shows that quality of organisational culture does significantly influence the level of commitment to work.

REFERENCES

1. Argyris, C. Personality and Organization, Harper and Row, New York, 1957.

   Integrating Individual and the Organisation, John Willey & Sons, New York, 1964.
2. Buchanon, B. "To Walk and extra mile"—The Whats, Whens and Whys of Organizational Commitment." The Progress of Management, Prentice Hall, Englewood Cliff, 1977.
3. Bachman, J. *et al.* "Bases of Supervisory Power: A Comparative Study in Five Organisational settings", in A. Tennenbaum (ed.) Control in Organisations, McGraw Hill, 1968.
4. Berrett, J.H. Individual Goals and Organizational Objectives—A Study of Integration Mechanism. Institute of Social Research, The University of Michigan, Michigan, 1970.
5. Etzioni, A. A Comparative Analysis of Complex Organisations, Free Press, 1961.
6. Ivancevich, J & Donnely, J. 'Leader Influence and Performance' Personnel Psychology 23, 1970.
7. Litwin, G. and Stringer, R. Motivation and Organizational Climate Cambridge, Mass, Harvard University Press, 1968.
8. Reynold, L.G. & Gregory, P. Wages, Productivity and Industrialization in Puerto Rico, Homewood, Illinios, Richard D. Irwin, 1965.
9. Singh P. Das G. and Mathew T. 'Organisational Culture and its impact on Managerial Remuneration' Decision, January, 1977.
10. Sharma, B.R. and Dayal, I. 'The Meaning of Work of Bank Employees: Implications for Supervisory Behaviour, Management and Labour Studies, Vol. I. No. 2, 1975.

APPENDIX I

Questionnaire

Please thick the answer. You need not sign or write your name anywhere.

PART I

Background Information

1. *Functional area to which you belong* :
   - (i) Personnnel
   - (ii) Finance and Accounts
   - (iii) Construction
   - (iv) Production
   - (v) Purchase and Stores
   - (vi) Marketing
   - (vii) General Admn.
   - (viii) Medical
2. *Experience in BSL* :
   - (i) Less than 5 years
   - (ii) Between 5 years to 10 years
   - (iii) More than 10 years.
3. *Education* :
   - (i) Post-graduate in Sc./Art./Mgt./Engg./Med./Humanities
   - (ii) Graduate in Sc./Art./Mgt./Engg./Med./Humanities
   - (iii) Intermediate
   - (vi) Matriculate

4. *Age* : (i) Upto 30 years
 (ii) Between 31 years to 40 years
 (iii) Between 41 years to 50 years
 (iv) Above 50 years.

5. *Marital Status* : (i) Single
 (ii) Married
 (iii) Widow
 (iv) Widower.

6. *Salaries (basic)* : (i) Less than Rs. 1000/- per month
 (ii) Between Rs. 1000 to Rs. 1500/- per month
 (iii) Between Rs. 1501 to Rs. 2000/- per month
 (iv) Above Rs. 2000/- per month.

7. *Family decision making* : (i) Head of the family
 (ii) Adults of the family
 When you were child who used to take decisions in your family? (iii) All members of the family.

PART II

Four hypothetical organisations are presented separately. Please read the descriptions carefully. Assume yourself as an employee of these organisations and your present positional hierarchy similar in all the four. Also please assume that these organisations are identical in respect of working conditions, technology, promotional plan, wages and salaries, product line, fringe benefits, scope of advancement, size of the firm, financial standing and none of them is likely to be wound up.

Read the statements and put your choice against the alternatives of the responses across all the organisations.

Answers are to be given on a five point scale with the alternatives—(1) to a very little extent, (2) to a little extent, (3) to some extent, (4) to a great extent and (5) to a very great extent.

ORGANISATION A

Dimensions	Profile of Organisational Characteristics
1. Leadership	: No confidence is shown in the subordinates by the superiors. Subordinates never feel like talking to supervisors about the jobs. Subordinates' ideas are seldom sought and used even if they are worth considering.
2. Motivation	: Fear, threat and punishment are predominantly applied for including motivation. The responsibility for setting goals, achieving the targets is mostly felt at the top and it is not diffused to the lower level of participants.
3. Communication	: Normally the direction of information-flow is downward. Downward communication is generally accepted with suspicion. Upward communication is often misleading. Superiors know very little about the problems faced by the subordinates.
4. Decision	: Formal decisions are mostly taken at the top. Top management is the original of the technical and professional data used in decision making. Subordinates are not at all involved in the decisions related to their work even. The decision making process rarely contribute anything to motivation and its in fact often weakens motivation.

5. *Interaction*	:	The amount of interaction is very little and always with fear and distrust. Cooperative team-work is absent. Superiors feel that subordinates are unable to influence the goals, methods and activity of the unit and deptt. Subordinates feel that they can influence only through unionisation.
6. *Goals*	:	Organisational goals are established and communicated as orders. Very strong covert resistance to goal is present in the organisation.
7. *Control*	:	Review and control functions are confined to top management. There is a strong informal grouping and eliques. Cost, productivity and other control data are used for policing and punishing subordinates.

Questions	Response Alternatives
1. To what extent the organisation described above is effective in getting you involved in meeting its needs and achieving its objectives?	(1) To a very little extent (2) To a little extent (3) To some extent (4) To a great extent (5) To a very great extent
2. To what extent the organisation is effective in meeting your needs and goals are an individual	(1) To a very little extent (2) To a little extent (3) To some extent (4) To a great extent (5) To a very great extent.

ORGANISATION B

Dimensions	Profile of Organisational Characteristics
1. *Leadership*	: Selective confidence is shown in subordinates. Subordinates do not feel comfortable in speaking about their jobs to their superiors. Sometimes subordinates ideas are sought and used if supervisors feel they are worth considering.
2. *Motivation*	: Primarily economic rewards are used in motivating employees. Sometimes punishment is also used as a tool for motivating people. Responsibility for achieving organisational goal is felt at the top and middle levels but is not diffused to the lower levels of management because they are not considered responsible.
3. *Communication*	: Some communication is aimed at achieving organisational objectives but largely not. The direction of the information flow is mostly downwards. Upward communication is normally censored. Superiors have some knowledge about the problems faced by the subordinates.
4. *Decision*	: Normally policy decisions are made at the top, but some delegation is made. The origin of technical and professional knowledge used in decisions making is from upper and middle levels. Subordinates are occasionally consulted in decisions relating to their work. Decision making process contributes relatively little to motivation.

5. *Interaction* : There is little interaction and usually with some condescension by superiors. Subordinates feel fear and take caution. Amount of cooperative teamwork is virtually nil. Superiors find virtually none of the subordinates capable of influencing organisational goals, methods, and activity. Subordinates feel that they can do so little except through unionisation.

6. *Goals* : Organisational goals and targets are communicated normally through orders, though some comments are invited at times. Moderately covert resistance is shown by subordinates.

7. *Control* : Review and control functions are relatively confined to the top management. Usually, there is an informal group resistance and opposing of policies. Cost, productivity and control data are used for reward and punishment.

Questions	Response Alternatives
1. To what extent the organisation described above is effective in getting you involved in meeting its needs and in achieving its objectives?	(1) To a very little extent (2) To a little extent (3) To some extent (4) To a great extent (5) To a very great extent.
2. To what extent the organisation is effective in meeting your needs and goals as and individual?	(1) To a very little extent (2) To a little extent (3) To some extent (4) To a great extent (5) To a very great extent.

ORGANISATION C

Dimensions	Profile of Organisatonal Characteristics
1. *Leadership*:	Substantial amount of confidence is shown by the superiors in the subordinates. Subordinates feel rather free in talking about their jobs to superiors.
2. *Motivation*:	Predominently rewards are used in motivating the subordinates though at times punishment is also applied as motivational tool. The responsibility for achieving the organisational goals is felt, though not well at all levels.
3. *Communication*:	Quite a bit of communication is aimed at achieving the organisational objectives. Information flows freely downwards and upwards in the organisation. Downward communication in accepted with caution normally. Upward communication may be satisfactorily accurate but it cannot be qualified further by stating that upward communication is of limited accuracy. Superiors know the problems faced by the subordinates moderately well.
4. *Decision*:	Broad policy decisions are made at the top and delegated down-ward for interpretation and execution. The technical and professional knowledge used in decision making are originated to a great extent throughout the organisation. All subordinates are generally consulted in decision making related to their work.

In a way decision making process makes some contribution to motivation.

5. *Interaction*: There is moderate amount of interaction with fair amount of confidence and trust. A moderate amount of cooperate team-work is present. Superiors feel that subordinates can influence goals, methods and activity of the units to a moderate degree. Subordinates feel that they can influence moderately directly and through unions.

6. *Goals*: Organisational goals are established afer discussion but it is communicated and implemented through orders. Some cover resistance is felt to organisational goals at times.

7. *Control*: Review and control functions are moderately delegated to lower levels. Sometimes the informal organisations resist the formal one. Cost, productivity and other control data are used for reward and for some selfguidance.

Questions	Response Alternatives
1. To what extent the organisation described above is effective in getting you involved inmeeting its needs and objectives?	(1) To a very little extent (2) To a little extent (3) To some extent (4) To a great extent (5) To a very great extent.
2. To what extent the organisation is effective in meeting your needs and goals as an individual?	(1) To a very little extent (2) To a little extent (3) To some extent (4) To a great extent (5) To a very great extent.

ORGANISATION D

Dimensions	Profile of Organisational Characteristics
1. *Leadership*:	Complete confidence is shown in subordinates. Subordinates feel free to talk to supervisors about their jobs. Their ideas are always sought and used if found worthy.
2. *Motivation*:	People are always motivated to perform by involvement and rewards based on goals set by the group. Responsibility for achieving the organisational goals are felt at all the levels of the organisation.
3. *Communication*:	A great deal of communication with both individuals and groups is aimed at achieving the organisational goals. Information flows down-wards, up-wards as well as sideways freely. Upward communication is always accurate. Supervisors know and understand problems faced by the subordinates very well.
4. *Decisions*:	All decisions including policy are formally made involving all the levels but in a well integrated manner. Technical and professional knowledge used in decision making are generated to a very great extent through the organisation. Subordinates are fully involved in decisions related to their work. Decision making process substantially contributes to motivation.
5. *Interaction*:	Interaction is extensive and friendly with high degree of confidence and trust. The amount of teamwork is very substantial through the organisation.

6. *Goals*: Except in emergencies organisational goals are established and implemented by group action. No covert resistance is present towards the goals thus established.

7. *Control*: Review and control functions are quite widely shared in the organisation. Informal and formal organisations have the same goals. Cost, productivity and other control data are used for self-guidance and group problem solving.

Questions	Response Alternatives
1. To what extent the organisation described above is effective in getting you involved in meetings its needs and achieving its objectives?	(1) To a very little extent (2) To a little extent (3) To some extent (4) To a great extent (5) To a very great extent.
2. To what extent the organisation meets your needs and goals as an individual?	(1) To a very little extent (2) To a little extent (3) To some extent (4) To a great extent (5) To a very great extent.

Now you have completed the questionnaire. THANK YOU

APPENDIX—II

Formulae for Measuring Commitment to Work

First take the lower of the scores on the two items and divide it by the higher of the two, then multiply this quotient by the mean of the two scores. The first operation provides a measure of how closely the two scores match *i.e.* it indicates the individual's and organisational needs are met adequately well or whether one set of needs is being met more adequately than the other. The second operation introduces a measure of average level of fulfilment of these two sets of needs. Reflected in the index score are both the general level of fulfilment and the degree of congruence in fulfilling the organizational objectives and the individual goals. When each set of needs is maximally fulfilled, the index score has its highest valued (*i.e.* $5 \div 5 \times 5 = 5.00$). When one of the needs is maximally fulfilled and the other minimally fulfilled, the index score has its lowest value (*i.e.* $1 \div 5 \times 3 = 0.60$). When both sets of needs are fulfilled equally but at a low level the index score remains near the lower end of the scale (*i.e.* $1 \div 1 \times 1 = 1.00$). Combining scores in this way makes the index a measure of commitment rather than merely an average of individual's satisfaction from and contribution to the organization. At the same time it assumes that the concept of commitment refers to a congruence in fulfilment of goals and objectives and a situation of equally fulfilled needs does not satisfy the definition of high commitment.

Source: Berrett, J.H.—Individual Goals and Organizational Objectives—A Study of Integration Mechanism, Social Research Instt., University of Michigan, 1970.

APPENDIX—III

Frequency Distribution of Commitment Scores across the Classified Organisations

Category	Possible scores	Organtsations			
		(A) Autocratic	(B) Benevolent Autocratic	(C) Consultative	(D) Democratic
		No. of Responses	No. of Responses	No. of Responses	No. of Responses
Low	0.60	15	12	5	8
	0.63	10	12	10	5
	0.67	10	11	8	3
	0.75	20	15	5	10
	1.00	15	16	10	5
	1.40	17	18	10	5
	1.50	11	12	12	10
Medium	1.67	9	10	8	8
	2.00	4	3	7	10
	2.40	2	2	10	7

High	2.63	3	3	8	10
	3.00	1	3	5	10
	3.60	1	1	12	9
	4.00	1	1	5	11
	5.00	1	1	5	9
Total		120	120	120	120

3

MANPOWER PLANNING—A PRIMER

PARTH SARATHI

Introduction

Manpower planning encompasses the activities relating to the planning; the acquisition, utilization, development and retention of human resources. This is essential for optimising labour cost, specifying recruitment needs, anticipating the manpower losses in order to smoothen the succession plan of the organisation.

The stages in the process are—Forecasting manpower supply, anticipating manpower losses, requirement forecasting after ensuring optimum utilization of existing manpower and taking steps to fulfil the shortages.

Manpower requirement forecasting is the most complex part of the exercise for which a number of techniques such as opinion survey, statistical methods, work study, Productivity measurement etc. may be used.

In this paper an effort has been made to present the whole gamut of Manpower planning in brief.

Manpower planning may be defined as "a strategy for the acquisition, utilization, improvement and retention of an Enterprise's human resources". It should ensure the availability of right number of men of the right quality (technical competence and other attributes) in right time, at right places, of course on right compensation.

Manpower is the key economic resource which is scarce and dynamic. Whatever may be the unemployment problem in the country, getting a right employee is always difficult. The optimum utilisation of human resources is not as easy as those of other resources. A very dedicated and highly skilled manpower may prove to be ineffective by erratic personnel policies. One wrong recruitment or promotion may erode the morale of thousands of workers. The personnel policies of the company are the indicators of the mental health of the organisation that play the pivotal role in attracting best talents to join the company which may not be possible otherwise even at a high salary bracket. Manpower planning has got an important position in all the progressive organisations, some of the reasons for this are outlined below:

(a) *Cost Optimisation*: to maintain a balance between the cost for skilled manpower and specialised machines etc.

(b) determination of the recruitment needs at specified levels.

(c) Anticipating the loss of manpower due to various reasons.

(d) Identifying the training needs at different levels to develop internal human resources.

(e) Rendering a basis for succession planning.

(f) Assigning future space and other facilities requirement.

(g) Planning incentives, formulating policies to increase the overall utilisation of human resource and to measure the effectiveness of such steps.

(h) Avoiding the incidence of Rush Recruitments as a result of "Vacuum".

Prerequisites

In the present era of rapidly changing political and economic activities, forecasting of any resource is difficult and Manpower is no exception. But for surviving in uncertainties, forecasting is the only way out. To have an accurate and reliable forecast the organisation should fulfil some necessary prerequisites as given below:

(i) Corporate Planning

Manpower planning cannot be effective if it is not integrated with other functions of long-term strategic planning. It should be oriented towards the fulfilment of the corporate objectives. It becomes more easy but essential in organisations practicing M.B.O.

(ii) Systematic Personnel Records

Personnel records provide the structural and basic data regarding the existing manpower such as Qualification, Trade, training, experience etc. A sound system will help a lot in carrying out statistical analysis for a reliable forecasting. The system should ensure and immediate updating and retrieval of the data.

(iii) Rational Personnel Policies

Manpower planning will not be of much use if the management does not believe in framing and effecting personnel policies. In the atmosphere of adhocism, the anticipation of future changes does not have any meaning and cases of large losses and intakes at irregular intervals shall be so many. Career and succession planning are the two major casualties in such situations.

Stages

The function of Manpower planning can be broadly divided into three stages:

(a) Manpower Supply Forecasting.

(b) Manpower demand forecasting.

(c) Manpower planning (proper),

Manpower Supply Forcasting

Sources of manpower supply are internal or/and external. For internal supply existing resource analysis and change analysis should be carried out as described below:

(*i*) *Current Labour Resource Analysis*

Proper analysis and evaluation of the current manpower is the first exercise. Important personnel data such as Name of employee' age, qualification, length of service training and other details should be compiled is a suitably designed format. This may be stored, department-wise or function-wise. In medium and big enterprises this data should be available on computers. It will enable to provide status of different categories of employees *i.e.*, whether on training likely promotions, retirement etc.

(*iii*) *Change Turnover Analysis*

This is necessary to reflect the changes in the manpower of different category. The changes or pattern of changes can be highlighted by graphs, charts and rations etc. The trend analysis may be a valuable guide for future. This analysis should be thoroughly carried out and effort should be made to take into consideration the company's policies regarding the changes in the manpower. Suitable ratios may be indirect to direct workers, sales or production per man, professional or technical to general manpower etc. Bar charts showing different categories on a time scale shall be more revealing. Turnover analysis will indicate magnitude of the likely losses in the manpower. The losses may be natural, voluntary and managerial or disciplinary and can be expressed as turnover (%) and stability ratio.

$$\text{Turnover ratio (\%)} = \frac{\text{No. of employee who left during the period}}{\text{Average No. of employees during the period}} \times 100$$

$$\text{And Stability ratio} = \frac{\text{No. of employees above 'X' yearsof service}}{\text{Total No. of employees employed last year}}$$

For different categories of employees, the rate of losses should be calculated separately. A 'survival pattern may be plotted to highlight the changes on losses. Tabular representation of the projection of agewise distribution over a number of future years will help to exhibit the age-groupwise strength during different periods. A retirement pattern over a number of years may also be exhibited in the same way.

(*iii*) *External Manpower Supply*

All the future labour requirements of a company can not be fulfilled by the internal sources therefore external recruitment becomes necessary. The supply of the external labour depends upon a number of factors some of which are—(a) unemployment level in the area, (b) competition from other organisations, (c) Residential or housing schemes, (d) transport andother facilities, (e) social and political situation, (f) welfare measures provided by the company (g) prospect of growth (h) prospect of growth and stability (i) output of trained/skilled/technical and managerial personnel (j) climate and proximity of other Industries etc. Some policy decisions like changes in working conditions such as working hours/holidays, overtime rules, working days, engagement of temporary or part time labour, age of superannuation etc. also affect the requirement and supply of manpower.

Manpower Demand Forecasting

As narrated in the para on prerequisities, the period of forecast should be suitably fixed. The company should clearly define the areas and objectives of business operations to be concentrated upon in the future years. The sales forecasting should be done and the estimation of the resources is to be carried out. The Manpower forecast is also to be made at this stage, based on the detailed objectives/targets/programmes etc. at each level. A successful corporate planning will make available the various basic informations regarding the specified objectives yearwise during the forecast period, companies organisation structure etc. which will be extremely helpful in a manipower demand forecast.

The methods of sales forecasting can be used for manpower demand forecasting also. No single method is self-sufficient, so far higher accuracy several methods can be used. Some of these methods have been summarised as below:

(*i*) *Opinion Survey*

The requirement of manpower in the forecast period is collected from each department/division starting from the direct worker level on the basis of the departments' objectives, plan etc. The discussions are held with the line executives. Carefully prepared questionnaires are also used. This method is widely used in small and medium sized organisations. It gives an opportunity to all key personnel to participate in the functions hence easy to sell.

(*ii*) *Statistical Methods*

There are two widely used methods—Time series method and Regression and Correlation methods briefly described as below:

Time Series Method

A trend line is determined by graphical plotting or moving average method or 'least square method'. This will give estimated manpower strength by being projected through the forecasting period. The forecasting unit may be either number of men or number of man-hours. The expected/anticipated changes in the country plan should be appropriately incorporated.

Correlation and Regression Method

Correlation indicates mutual dependence of two variables. It shows the relationship between two such variable in which with changes in the value of one variable, the value of the other also changes. This may be studied with the help of scatter diagram, correlation graph, coefficient of correlation (r) and correlation table. Correlation may be positive or negative—for perfect positive correlation r=1 and for perfect negative r=—1.

$r = \frac{\Sigma xy}{n\sigma x\sigma y}$ where x and y are the deviations from mean in two series.

n=no. of observations,

(*i.e* σx,σy) =Standard deviations of the two series.

If two lines are plotted on a graph, one of which shows the best possible values of y for a given value of x and the other *vice versa*' a study of correlation can be made from them. If there is a perfect correlation, they will coincide, the farther the lines are from each other, less is the correlation. If both x and y series are variables the 'lines of best fit' are known as the regression lines.

General equation is y=a+bx, 'b' being the regression coefficient. This equation gives the best possible value of y for given value of x and is called the regression equation of y on x. It is very helpful in forecasting the manpower requirement at the planned/estimated level of Sales, Production, Investment etc.

(iii) Work Study

Work study ensures the optimum utilisation of men, material and machines and determines the work-content. It is a very useful technique for assessing manpower requirement. Sales or out-turn during the planned period is forecasted which are translated in the Annual production plans and schedules. After establishing the work content by suitable technique and also specifying the resources to be applied, manpower required is determined. The steps can be enumerated as—(a) Finalising the products with quantities (b) operations to be carried out (c) Plants and equipment (d) operation times (e) manpower required categorywise (f) gap between available and required manpower.

It is a scientific technique and can be applied with confidence in all the organisations. Simultaneously this technique is used to find out the utilisation of the existing manpower also, which ultimately helps in determining the excess manpower required.

(iv) Productivity Measurement

This technique is very much close to work study. Instead of determining the time taken to carryout one unit of work, the output per unit of time (output per man hour *i.e.* the labour productivity) is determined. Though it looks simple, so many practical diffieulties are experienced in actualpractice. Changes in the product mix and difficulties is measuring output pose difficulties. The output may be measured in physical units but fluctuating prices will cause some problems. Thus the concept 'Value added' will help overcome this problem. 'Value added of here may be defined' as the value of the output in constant prices—the cost of intermediate goods and services consumed in production.

In the technique also sales forecasting is taken as the starting point. A productivity trend line (on previous years output) is then fitted. If smooth and consistent line is obtained, it may be taken up as a basis of forecasting. The probable changes should be clearly incorporated into by discussion with concerned executives. The manpower required for the projected output level of a year

$$= \frac{\text{Output for the forecast year}}{\text{Anticipated productivity rate}}$$

This method is also used with certain modifications in a good number of organisations. But as mentioned above, for the categories of manpower whose output is difficult to measure and for a frequently changing product mix, this technique is not suitable.

Manpower Planning (Proper)

As described, the forecasted manpower demand and manpower supply is determined. This exercise should be carried out every year during the span of forecasting. Before establishing the shortage of surplus manpower, it is essential to know the utilization of existing manpower at present and the desired utilization future. The optimum desired utilization after allowing provision for different allowances, leaves etc. comes around 85 per cent. If the utilisation is very low, efforts should be made to increase utilization by introducing incentive schemes, overtime or other suitable steps. If then the surplus or deficit manpower will be determined. A Table shown in Annexure illustrates with the help of a simple illustration.

The demand and supply figures should be highly helpful. Efforts should be made to bridge this gap by increasing the utilization and also by providing suitable training and job rotation, job enrichment etc. For still remaining gaps, external recruitments will become necessary. Different types of models designed as per the characteristics of the organisation are highly advantageous.

Hints for Success

Some of the important points for the success of manpower planning are:

(a) Support of the top management.

(b) Centralised approach on responsibilities, involvement, employees and Trade union.

(c) A long period of forecasting.

(d) Selection of appropriate techniques.

(e) Accurate and systematic personnel records.

(f) Forecast prepared for each category of skill not for the aggregate of the workers.

(g) A continuous revision of the techniques and results of forecasting.

Conclusion

This paper does not describe in detail the techniques of manpower planning. Effort has been made to present an overview to the whole gamut of the highly dynamic subject. No single technique is perfect in itself. A combination of techniques should be used keeping in view the nature and accuracy desired. A number of quantitative techniques such as Montecarlo Simulation etc. are being used these days in selective situations.

BIBLIOGRAPHY

1. "Company Manpower Planning"—Her Majesty's Stationary Office—LONDON.

2. "Manpower Planning and Workstudy"—Workstudy and Management Services, Sept., 1972.

3. Statistics theory and practice—By Sh. D.C. Sancheti and P.L. Kapoor Sultan Chand & Sons.

ANNEXURE

Manpower Recruitment Forecast for Turners

	1981	*1982*	*1983*	*1984*	*1985*	*Total*
Supply						
(a) Strength in the beginning of the year	450	490	535	555	570	—
(b) Likely to be inducted from Apprentices etc.	10	15	20	30	30	105
(c) Losses during the year-Superannuation	5	10	12	20	20	67
Deaths @ 2%	9	10	11	11	11	52
Voluntary resignation @ 2%	9	10	11	11	11	52
Discharge @ 1%	5	5	5	6	6	27
Transfers and Promotions @ 5%	23	25	27	28	29	132
Total	50	60	66	76	77	329
(d) Total existing strength at the year end (a+b+c)	410	445	489	509	523	—

Demand						
(i) Strength in the beginning of the year	450	490	535	555	570	—
(ii) Additional requirement for the year	40	45	20	15	25	145
(iii) Total strength at the year end (i+iii)	490	535	555	570	595	—
Additional Requirement during the year (iii—e)	80	90	66	61	72	369

4

ADMINISTRATIVE ASPECTS OF CENTRE-STATE RELATIONS

I

The distribution of legislative powers between the Union and the State Governments has already been discussed. The distribution of executive power among them is somewhat more complicated although it follows a similar pattern. We propose to study here the constitutional provisions regarding the distribution of executive powers and then have a look on the way this distribution has worked in actual practice.

II

SCHEME OF DISTRIBUTION

In general, the distribution of executive powers follows the scheme of distribution of legislative powers. It means that the executive power of a State is, in the main, Co-extensive with its legislative power. The executive power of the State thus extends only to its own territory and with respect to those subjects over which it has legislative competence (Article 162). Similarly, the Union has exclusive executive power over the following matters:

(i) The matters with respect to which the Parliament has exclusive power to make laws (*i.e.* matters in list-I of Schedule VII).

(ii) The exercise of its powers conferred by any treaty of agreement (Article 73).

Concurrent List

The above mentioned principle states that the Centre has executive jurisdiction over all matters included in List-I of Schedule VII and the State has executive jurisdiction over all the matters included in the List-II. The position regarding the concurrent list *i.e.* list-III is a little more complicated. The general principle is that regarding the matters included in the concurrent legislative list (List-III) the executive function shall ordinarily remain with the States, but subject to the provisions of the Constitution or of any law of the Parliament conferring such functions exclusively upon the Union. Under the Government of India Act 1935, the Centre had only the power to give directions to provincial executive to execute a central law relating to a concurrent subject. But this power of giving directions proved ineffective. Therefore, the Constitution provides that Union may, whenever it thinks fit, itself takes up administration of the Union laws relating to any concurrent subject.

In the result, the executive power relating to concurrent subject remains with the States, except in the following cases:

(i) Where a law of Parliament relating to such subject vests some executive function specifically in the Union. The examples of this type are to be seen in the Land Acquisition Act, 1894 and the Industrial Disputes Act, 1947. So far as these functions, specified in such Union law, are concerned, it is Union and not the State which shall have the executive power while the rest of the executive powers relating to this subject shall remain with the States.

(ii) Where the provisions of the Constitution itself vest some executive functions upon the Union, *e.g.*:

> The executive power to implement any treaty or international agreement belongs exclusively to the Union, whether the subject belongs to the Union, State or concurrent list. (Article 73(1) (b)).

(iii) The Union has the power to give directions to the State Governments as regards the exercise of their executive power in certain matters provided for in Articles 256, 257, 339, 350(A), 351 and 355 of the Constitution.

Emergencies

Besides the powers of the Union Government to give directions to the State Governments in normal circumstances, the Constitution also makes provisions for certain emergencies. Three kinds of situations have been envisaged which are mentioned below:

(i) A State of national emergency can be proclaimed under Article 352 of the Constitution. When such a proclamation is made, the power of the Union Government to give directions to State Governments extends to the giving of directions as to the manner in which the executive power of the States is to be exercised, relating to any matter (Article 353(a)). This brings State Government under the complete control of the Union without suspending its functioning.

(ii) When the President on the report of the Governor or otherwise is satisfied that the Government of the State cannot be carried out in accordance with the provisions of the Constitution, he may make a proclamation to this effect. When such a proclamation of the failure of Constitutional machinery in a State has been made, the President can assume to himself all or any of the executive powers of the State (Article 356). It may be recalled that during such a proclamation, the legislative powers of the State Legislature are also reserved for the Parliament. It means that the entire legislative and executive control of the State Government vests in the Union Government and the Parliament. This is in fact a complete assumption of the legislative and the executive functions of the State. Usually the Government of the State during such proclamation is carried out by the Governor acting on behalf of the President.

(iii) When the State Government is found unable to manage its financial affairs prudently, President may issue a proclamation of financial emergency in the State. On declaration of financial emergency, the President may issue the following directives to the State Government:

(a) To observe canons of financial property, as may be specified in the directions (Article 363(3)).

(b) To reduce the salaries and allowances of all or any class of persons serving in connection with the affairs of the Union or the State, including the Judges of Supreme Court and High Courts (Article 360(4)(b)).

(c) To require that all money Bills or other financial Bills should be reserved for the consideration of the President after they are passed by the legislature of the State (Article 360(4)).

III

DELEGATION BY CONSENT

To mitigate the rigidity which might arise from the Centre State division of administrative power, the Indian Constitution makes provision for inter-governmental delegation of administrative powers. This may happen either under an agreement between the Governments or by legislation. While the Centre can use both the methods to delegate administrative power to the State, the State can use only the first method to delegate administrative power to the Centre.

Delegation by the Centre with Consent of the States

Article 258(1) provides that the President may, with the consent of the State Government, entrust either conditionally or unconditionally, to the State or its officers, any function in relation to a matter to which the Centre's executive power extends. It is entirely for the Centre to determine whether the entrustment to be made to the state should be Conditional or Unconditional; and if conditional, what conditions are to be imposed on the State concerned. So while making delegation under Article 258(1), the Central Government reserves to itself powers to issue directions to the State Governments for the exercise of delegated power. It also reserves to itself a concurrent power to continue to exercise along with the State Governments, the functions being delegated to them. Delegation may be specific or general, to one State or many States, of any function whether within Union or the Concurrent list. This constitutional provision can be used to delegate Central functions to a State Government, when a statute makes no provision for the delegation of the powers of the Central Government to the States, but, even when a statute contains a provision authorising the Central Government to delegate its powers to a State, Article 258(1) can be invoked for the purpose instead of the statutory provision. Some examples of such delegation are indicated below:

(i) Functions of the Central Government under the Registration of Foreigners Rules 1959, the Foreigners Act, 1946 and Foreigners Order 1948 have been entrusted to the State Governments subject to two conditions:

(a) In exercising these functions, the State Governments are to comply with such general or special directions as the Centre may issue from time to time.

(b) Notwithstanding the entrustment, the Central Government may itself exercise in all these functions should it deem fit to do so in any case.

(ii) Under Section 7 of the Explosive Substances Act 1948, no Court can try any person for any offence without the consent of the Central Government. The Central Government has entrusted this function to State Government. Similarly, the Central Government, with the consent of the State Governments have entrusted their functions under clause 4 and 5 of Atomic Energy (Control of Production and Use) Order 1953 subject to the usual conditions of State Government complying with the Central directives and the Centre itself being able to exercise its functions when it feels like doing so.

Delegation by the Centre without Consent

According to Article 258(2) a law made by Parliament, even if it relates to a matter in the Union list may confer power and impose duties upon the State, its officers and authorities. For example under Central Sales Tax Act enacted by the Parliament under entry 92(A) List-I the task of assessment and collection of sales tax on interstate sales has been left with the States Sales Tax Authorities. Under MISA, the power of preventive detention has been conferred on all District Magistrates.

Whenever, the Central Government confers powers and imposes duties on the State Government, or its officers, the Centre has recoupe the States' expenses in respect of any extra costs of administrative incurred by the States in connection with those powers and duties. The Centre and the States may agree as to the sums payable in this connection, or in default of agreement, the amount may be determined by an arbitrator appointed by the Chief Justice of India. The payment to be made by the Centre to the States in this connection is entirely a matter between the two Governments and no third person can challenge the entrustment and the delegation of power and duties on the ground of absence of such payment.

Delegation by the State to the Centre

Under Article 258(A), a State Government may, with the consent of the Government of India, entrust either conditionally or unconditionally to the Central Government or its officers, functions in relation to any matter to which the executive power of the State extends. The article was inserted in the Constitution in 1956 at the corresponding provision to Article 258(1). The lack of the provision enabling the State to entrust its functions to Centre was found to be of practical consequence in connection with the execution of certain development works in the States. The High Court has ruled that the relationship arising by virtue of Article 258(A) between the Centre and the State Governments is not that of the Principal and the Agent.

IV

POWER TO CARRY ON TRADE

Article 298 has a bearing on the inter-relation of the Centre's executive power with that of State and *vice-verse*. Under this provision, the executive power of the Union (or of the State) extends to the carrying by it of any commercial or industrial activity (whether or not it is related to a matter within its legislative competence) and also to hold, acquire or dispose of property and make contracts for any purpose. This extends the executive power of the Centre and also of the State. However, it is subject to one condition. If an activity falls outside the legislative domain of the Government which carries it, then it would be subject to the law made by the other government having the necessary legislative power. It is the only case of its kind where the Central executive power has been made subject to the State legislative power. Article 298 enlarges the scope of the executive power of the Centre and the States by adding various matters in respect of which these Governments may exercise their executive power. The words "for any purpose" indicate that the executive power of the Centre and the

State to acquire, hold and dispose of property or make contracts is not limited by the division of the Centre State legislative powers. In this way, the width and the amplitude of the executive power of the Centre and the States has been extended. This means that executive power of the Centre (or the States) is apart from executive power granted under Article 73 (or Article 162). For example under this provision, a State Government has power to reserve the mining area for exploitation in the Public Sector even when it can not do so under Article 162, but this will be subject to the Central legislation.

V

CENTRE'S EXECUTIVE CONTROL OVER STATES

States not to Impede the Centre

The constitution places certain restrictions and obligations on the States in order to ensure that the Centre can exercise its powers unimpeded by their actions. Article 256 imposes a general obligation on the States to exercise their executive power as to ensure compliance with the laws made by the Parliament; and the executive power of the Centre extends to giving of such directions to the States as may appear to the Centre to be necessary for the purpose. Under Article 257(1), executive power of a State is to be exercised as not to impede or prejudice the Centre's executive power and the latter can give such directions to a State as may appear to be necessary for that purpose.

Centre's Powers to Issue Directions

Apart from Article 256 and 257(1) mentioned above, several other constitutional provisions authorise the Centre to issue directives to States in several matters falling under their purview. Thus, communication is a State subject but under Article 257(2), the Centre may give directions to State as to the construction and maintenance of means of communication declared in the direction to be of National or Military importance. This, however, does not restrict the power of the Parliament to declare highways or Waterways to the national; nor is the Centre's power restricted with respect to the national highways and waterways nor its power to construct and maintain means of communication as part of its functions with respect to naval military and airforce works. Article 257(3) empowers the Centre to give directions to a State as to measures to be taken for the protection of the Railways within the State.

Similarly, the Central Government has powers to issue directives to the States in matters pertaining to minorities. Article 339(2) entitles the Centre to give directions to a State as to the drawing up and execution of schemes specified in the direction to be essential for the welfare of scheduled tribes in the States. Under Article 305(A), a State is obliged to provide facilities for instruction in the mother-tongue at the primary stage of children belonging to a linguistic minority. President has been empowered to issue such directions to the State as he considers necessary.

Apart from the above constitutional provisions, several statutory provisions confer power on the Central Government to give directions to the States. For example, Section 23 of the Supply and Prices of Goods Act, 1950 empowers Central Government to give directions to any State Government as to the carrying into execution of any of the provisions of the Act or of any order or direction made therein. Similarly, under the Plantation Labour Act, 1951, the executive power is left with the States but Central Government has power under Section 41 to give directions to a State Government as to carrying out the provisions of the Act. Many more such examples can be quoted. Usually, whenever administrative power is delegated to a State under Central law, a reservation is made enabling the Centre to give directions to the States.

Consequences of Disobedience

These powers of the Central Government to issue directives to the State Governments are not mere hollow powers. The Central Government can take action in case the State Governments do not obey the directives. When a directive has been given under a statute delegating some functions of the Centre to a State, the Central Government can withdraw the delegation and resume the function itself. In case of persistent disobedience of constitutional directives, the Central Government can hold under Article 356 that it is a case of failure of constitutional machinery of the State. This empowers the President to take over the functions of the State Government under Article 356 of the Constitutions.

All India Services

Article 312 introduces an important feature into the Constitution namely that besides separate services for the Union and the States, the Centre can create certain services common to both. If the Rajya Sabha declares by resolution supported by not less than two-third of the members present and voting that it is necessary or expedient in the national interest to do so, Parliament may by law provide for the creation of one or more All India Services and regulate recruitment and conditions of services for them. At present, three All India Services are in existence, namely, Indian Administrative Service, Indian Police Service and Indian Forest Service.

These services give cohesion to the federal structure and help in achieving greater efficiency in the administration of the Union and the States. The members of these services get an opportunity of serving both at the Centre as well as in the states and are able to acquire national outlook as well as grass-root knowledge.

Some of the State Governments see All India Services as an affront to their autonomy. Only Central Government has powers to impose major penalties on the members of these services. The State Governments, therefore, feel that these services are outside their control. Since most of the members of these services are occupying very high positions in State

Governments, lack of control over them may prove a serious handicap. However, the State Governments have enough control over these services. They can impose minor penalties and regulate their transfers and postings. This gives them sufficient powers to manage these services well. At the same time, State Governments are able to get the services of the meritorious officers selected on the basis of All India Competitions. Moreover, having a common outlook, these services can provide for a better coordination between the Centre and the State Governments.

V

EMERGENCY PROVISIONS

We have already made a reference above to the provisions of the Constitution under which Central Government can assume emergency powers and fully control the executive functions of the State Governments. This may be done under Article 352 when a national emergency has been proclaimed due to war or external aggression or armed rebellion or under Article 356 of the Constitution when Constitutional machinery in the State has failed. In the first case, the State Governments continue to function but are subject to the direction and control of the Central Government in all matters. In the second case, the administration of the State itself is taken over by the Central Government. These two provisions have been a bone of contention between the Centre and the State Governments. The State Governments have always felt that it gives unlimited powers to the Central Government to control them. The problem did not arise in the initial years of the working of the Constitution as the same party was in power at the Centre as well as in the States. The power under Article 356 has caused great concern as it is exercised on the report of the Governor who is also appointed by the President and holds office during his pleasure. In the past many opposition Governments have claimed, not always without substance, that this power has been used by the Centre for partisan purposes. For that reason, the 44th Amendment of the Constitution provided many safeguards against the arbitrary exercise of powers under Articles 352 and 356 of the Constitution. Further, apprehension still continues specially because the use of Article 356 has been rather frequent. The provision has been used over 70 times since commencement of the Constitution. Apart from the provisions regarding distribution of finances between the Centre and the States, the emergency provisions (specially those under Article 356) have remained one of the most important issues in respect of Centre-State relations.

Central Enquiry into State Affairs

Another issue which has clouded the Centre-State relations is the question of Central enquiry into the State affairs. Question has been often asked does Article 355 allow some Central action other than that stipulated under Article 356. For example, can the Central Government legally constitute a commission of enquiry against a State Chief Minister on charges of corruption, nepotism and mis-use of power? Some legal experts argue that if the Central Government is competent to take over the administration of the State in furtherance of its constitutional obligation to ensure that the Government of the State is carried and in accordance with the provisions of the Constitution. There appears to be no convincing reason why it should not have the power to institute an enquiry to ascertain the facts about the allegations of nepotism, corruption and mis-use of power against the Chief Minister or other Ministers. Some others argue that Articles 355 and 356 do not envisage Central imposition of the standards of good Government, Central enquiry into the State affairs will, therefore, amount to interference in the affairs of the State Governments. The exercise of this power has given rise to much bitterness between the Centre and the States. The States have taken it as an attack on their autonomy.

VII

COORDINATION MECHANISMS

Though there is a division of functions between the Centre and the States in a federation, it would not be correct to assume that the various Governments act in watertight compartments. As many of the functions of the Central and the State Governments overlap and are of complementary nature, inevitably many types of relations arise amongst them and many instrumentalities to promote inter-governmental cooperation come into existence. The farmers of the Indian Constitution realised thut the Governments in a federation were arranged in hierarchically or vertically, but horizontally. No line of command runs from Centre to the States. Common policies among the various Governments can, therefore, be promoted not by dictation but by a process of discussion, agreement and compromise. Accordingly, the farmers of the Constitution incorporated in it, an infrasrructure to promote cooperation and minimise tension among the various Governments. Apart from the provisions in the Constitution, the Central and the State Governments have also devised a number of institutions to provide for smooth working relationship between the Governments. Some of the important arrangements in this regard are discussed here.

Inter-State Council

Article 263 provides that the President may by order appoint an Inter-State Council if it appears to him that public interest would be served by its establishment. The President may define an organisation, procedure and duties of the council. Generally, it may be charged with the duties of:

(a) Enquiring into and advising upon disputes which any have arisen between the States.

(b) Investigating and discussing subjects in which some or all of the States or the Union and one or more of the States have common interest.

(c) Making recommendation upon any subject and in particular recommendations for better coordination of policy and action with respect to that subject.

It appears from this that the council is envisaged to be an advisory body having no authority to give a binding decision.

Not much use has been made of Article 263 so far and only few bodies of minor importance have been created under it. The Central Council of Health, created by presidential order under Article 263 consists of Central Health Minister as Chairman and State Health Ministers as members. Similarly, a Central Council of Local Self Government has been created comprising the Union Minister as Chairman, and State Ministers for Local Self Governments as members. Both of these are advisory bodies. They advise on broad policy matters in which coordination between Centre and State Governments is necessary. Similarly, under Article 263, four more regional councils have been set up for making recommendations for better coordination of policy and action with respect to sales tax, a State subject.

Administrative Reforms Commission also suggested establishment of an Inter-State Council under Article 263 with a view to strengthen cooperation and evolution of common policies among the Centre and State Governments in many areas where the measures taken by these Governments from time to time are mutually interactive. The commission did not work out the details of the type of duties which such a council can discharge. It only made a general statement that the establishment of an Inter-State Council would be conducive to a better understanding. Some State Chief Ministers have also demanded setting up of such a council so that the federal problems may be discussed on a formal basis. Central Government has however, remained cool to the idea. Presumably it may have some mis-givings that the establishment of such a council might below up controversies on contentious issues rather than promote cooperation.

Zonal Councils

The States Reorganisation Act, 1956 provided for the setting up of 5 zonal Councils consisting of several States each:

Northern	Punjab, Haryana, Rajasthan and Jammu & Kashmir and the Union Territories of Delhi, Chandigarh and Himachal Pradesh.
Eastern	Bihar, West Bengal, Orissa, Assam, Nagaland, Manipur and Tripura.
Western	Gujarat and Maharashtra.
Central	Uttar Pradesh and Madhya Pradesh.
Southern	Andhra Pradesh, Tamil Nadu, Karnataka and Kerala.

The Zonal Council consists of a Union Minister to be nominated by Central Government and the Chief Minister and two other Ministers from each State to be nominated by the State Government. A zonal Council has a number of advisors to assist it namely, a person nominated by the Planning Commission, Chief Secretary to the Government of each of the States in the Zone. Development Commissioner or any other Senior Officer nominated by the Government of each State in the Zone. The Chief Secretaries of the states within the zone become the Secretary of the Council by rotation.

The Zonal Council discusses matters of common interest in the field of welfare and social planning, border disputes, inter-state transport etc. The idea is to promote inter-state cooperation and also coordination with the Centre ensured by the presence of Central Ministers. Zonal Council is an Advisory body and has no legislative or executive functions to perform.

Further, so far the councils do not have many spectacular achievements to their credit. Nevertheless, they have helped in developing some common approach to several regional problems. For example, the Eastern Zonal Council has agreed to form a common Reserve Police and set up a Standing Committee to review the implementation of minority safeguards.

Control Boards

India has a number of inter-state rivers and river valleys. The Constitution makers anticipated that with the execution of development of irrigation and power projects some inter-state disputes would arise regarding sharing of river waters. Article 262 empowers Parliament to provide by law for adjudication of any dispute or complaint with respect to the use, distribution or control of the waters of any inter-state river or river valley. Accordingly, the Inter-State Disputes Act, 1956 has been enacted to provide for adjudication of disputes relating to waters of inter-state rivers and river valleys among the concerned State Governments. Similarly, the River Boards Act, 1956 provides for the establishment of the River Boards for the regulation and development of inter-state rivers and river valleys. Water being a State subject, such Boards are appointed by the Central Government with the Consultation of the State Governments. The functions of the Boards are:

(a) To advise the Governments on any matter concerning the regulation or development of specified river or river valley.

(b) To resolve their conflicts.

(c) Prepare schemes for regulating or developing inter-state river or river valley.

(d) Allocation among the Governments of the cost of executing such schemes.

(e) To watch the progress of measures undertaken by the Government entrusted with the implementation.

(f) Any other matters.

Often, Control Boards are appointed on non-statutory basis by a resolution of the Centre or State Governments. At present there are 14 boards with varying compositions. These bodies have helped the States in resolving many of their problems. Although several disputes could still not be resolved and have to be referred for adjudication.

Other Statutory Bodies

Besides the coordination bodies mentioned above, there are several others like University Grants Commission, Damodar Valley Corporation, Drugs Consultative Committee etc. The detailed enumeration of such bodies is not necessary here. Suffice it to say that our federal system has evolved several bodies to ensure coordination.

VIII

CONSULTATION THROUGH CONFERENCES

Apart from the statutory and non-statutory bodies mentioned above, a net work of conferences and *ad hoc* councils has been brought into existence by the Central Government to act as an institutionalised channel for consultation among the States of a wide variety of subjects. These conferences take place at political, administrative and provisional levels. The National Development Council, the Chief Ministers, Conference and Conference of Ministers of different departments are examples of conference at the political level. They have been in existence for a quite some time and atleast two of them namely, the Chief Ministers' Conference and Food Ministers' Conference are even of pre-independence origin.

The conferences at the administrative level include, the Chief Secretaries' Conference and the Conferences of various functional secretaries. The conference of Inspector Generals of Police (now Director Generals) has acquired special significance in view of the deteriorating law and order situation in the country. Similarly, the Conference on Irrigation and Power attended by State Government Engineers and Consultants of river valley projects, the Conference of Vice-Chancellors etc., are the professional level conferences.

Again, detailed enumeration of such conferences is not necessary here. It would be enough to state that they have gone a long way in sorting out various policy matters among the Central Governments and the State Governments at political as well as administrative levels.

5

MANAGEMENT OF RURAL DEVELOPMENT PROGRAMMES AT THE DISTRICT LEVEL

K. SAIGAL

I

Introduction

The facts of poverty and age-old injustices in Indian society are well known. Dandekar and Rath have already given a concise and clear idea of the magnitude of the poverty in India[1]. It is now widely realised and accepted that the fruits of development have percolated to a small section of the people only and the absolute number of people below the poverty line is just as large as it was two decades ago. It is estimated that nearly two-fifths to one-half of the total population, *i.e.*, over 220 million people are living below the poverty line[2].

The emerging ethos of national development could be understood in terms of the basic premise of the Fifth Five Year Plan as elaborated in the foreword to the document:

> The participation of the people in the implementation of Plan programmes is vital. Why is it not possible to kindle

the interest of local people so that a new thrust is imparted to programmes such as the construction of rural roads, minor irrigation works, farm forestry and the like? If the people are convinced that the basic objective of the Plan is social justice they will be interested in programmes and will extend their cooperation. No plan can ignore the deep-seated urges of our people for greater equality. The reduction of disparities of all kinds—social, economic and regional—must always remain one of the central objectives of our developmental planning. The direction of our planning is to solve over a period of time the problems of the poor of all communities, especially tribals, harijans, backward communities and regions[3].

The two important basic elements of policy in the Fifth Plan are the direct line of attack on the problem of unemployment and mass poverty. Thus the primary task that has been set before the country is the amelioration of the condition of the people below the poverty line and the removal of age-old injustices in the society. The constraint in achieving this task is that results have to be achieved within the democratic framework. It follows from this that all the three wings of the government, *i.e.*, the legislature, the executive, and the judiciary, have to play a significant role in the achievement of the task.

In this paper we are concerned with the public services. It is estimated that over 10 million citizens of this country are employed in the public service[4]. It is thus a major segment of the population, which because of its education, technical and specialised knowledge, and administrative experience, is a force to reckon with. The question is: "Will this class of citizens direct its power for (a) self-development and interest, (b) the benefit of only the favoured stratum in society or (c) the amelioration of the economic and social conditions of the weaker and under-privileged sections of society?"

The vast mass of people living in abject poverty are in the rural areas. In general, this population is composed of agricultural labourers, small farmers, and rural artisans. In caste structure, most of the scheduled castes, scheduled tribes, backward classes and service castes would fall under the category of weaker sections. This is thus the main client population. For this population it is the district administration which is the government, and it is the district administration with which this population is vitally concerned.

Considering the emerging ethos of national development and the basic elements of national policy, the role and function of district administration in the solution of the two basic problems, *i.e.*, mass poverty and social equality needs to be determined. The image of the government depends upon the response the under-privileged poverty ridden mass of population get from the administration. The issues involved are:

To what extent has the district administration empathy for this class of citizens and is able to understand, its felt needs?

To what extent is the administration able to evolve adequate policy parameters and develop suitable programmes and projects?

To what extent is the administration capabla of withstanding the onslaught of vested interests?

To what extent is the administration able to create confidence in the weaker sections, help in improving their aspiration levels, strengthen their capacity and develop their courage to stand against the age-old injustices?

These are some of the issues that need to be sorted out and answered before one could say with confidence that the task set before the nation would be successfully achieved by the district administration.

II

Role and Functions of the Civil Service

In a democracy there are certain basic assumptions regarding the role and functions of the civil service. The foundation of democracy rests on the rule of law and equality before the law. The civil service thus functions within the area of authority determined by the law. The service funcions as the instrument of implementation of law, and in a sense, is "guardian" of the law. In a democracy since the sovereignty vests in the enfranchised people, the public services are meant to serve the people. Even though policy formulation is the responsibility of political executives, *i.e.*, ministers, it is the duty of the senior civil servants to advise the political executive by bringing out various ramifications of the policy. Once the policy decision is taken, the civil servants have a major role to play in taking executive decisions for operationalising the policy. Thus the services have to be reliable sources of facts and capable of objective analysis, constructive formulation of policy, and operational plans. It is also necessary that in both the process of policy formulation and programme implementation the civil servant tilts in favour of the weaker sections.

In a democracy it is also necessary that the administration deliver the goods without violating basic democratic principles. As Karve has observed, the civil services are specially selected, suitably organised, and statutorily protected to do the right things under the law in the best democratic manner. He warns us: "They are an elite, and if a democracy cannot rely on its administrative elite to carry out the rules of law in an appropriate democratic manner, the democracy will not receive continued acceptance by the electorate. It will wear out".[5]

All bureaucratic organisations are subject to well-known dysfunctions, such as impersonality, evasion of responsibility, evolution of methods and manners which create barriers between the people and the administration, assuming organisational conventions as the ultimate goals, and so on.[6]

If these weaknesses are due to structure and organisation of administration, and are inherent in any bureaucratic system, these could be removed, as is often suggested, by simple structural rearrangements, proper organisation of work or streamlining of the activities or by bringing in new management techniques and skills. An experienced administrator observes:

> A professionally efficient administration without having a great deal of emotion in it, is able to serve the people far better than an administration which is oozing with sentiments but is professionally incompetent...For example, in dealing with applications for loans you may be the most sympathetic human being, very courteous, very kind, full of fine sentiments, and yet if your work is not well organised, if you have not gone into the causes of delay in dealing with applications, you will certainly send the applicant back with a feeling that you are a good man and a courteous man, but he will not get his loan promptly. On the other hand, you may be a cold man. You may not be a man of very strong feelings or sentiments. But if you have gone into all the processes involved in dealing with a loan application, you have worked out a way of dealing with it quickly and correctly; you will give him far better satisfaction.

The above is, however, somewhat of a mechanistic approach. There is no doubt that high professional efficiency and expertise will give satisfaction to the people. The question is whether efficiency and expertise alone would be able to correct the existing distortions. It is often argued that for removal of age-old injustices and economic disparities high professional efficiency and expertise is a necessary condition though not the sufficient condition. The elite in the civil services participate at the policy making levels. Unless they are aware of the felt needs of the masses and have empathy for the masses, it would be difficult for them to give correct advice. Again, at the time of decision making, when priorities have to be decided and classes of individuals who would be covered by a broader decision have to be defined, they cannot be effective without having a deeper understanding of the emotional needs and psychological urges of the masses and a sense of commitment to their upliftment.

A factor of some importance in the district administration today is the emergence of panchayati raj institutions. One of the considerations, which has gone into the development of panchayati raj institutions, is the need felt by the political machinery to have control over the administrative machinery at various levels. However, it is well-known that between the modernising elite with all its sympathy with the urges and needs of the people and the masses, there exists an intermediate rural elite. This hard core of a traditional elite, which has a vested interest in the continuation of existing social and economic structures and processes by and large, controls various political, social and eeonomic institutions. What is the role and function of the district level functionaries such as the collector, district development officer, etc., in such an environment? Should they be guided by the interest of the local, lawfully elected political groups or should they be guided by the interests of the under-privileged, weaker sections, and by the goals and objectives as defined at the national level and which encompass the interests of the larger society?

The ethos of an administrative organisation is largely determined by the socio-political culture of the large society in which it operates. Such a statement should not, however, lead to the conclusion that the basic fault does not lie with the administrative machincry but is the outcome of the basic defects in the overall environment. For the administrative organisation which encompasses a fairly large section of the population cannot be a passive instrument and observor of the environment but should exert itself and contribute in changing the environment. But the fact that an administrative organisation is a part of the larger socio-political culture has to be kept in mind.

III

District Bureaucracy: Structure, Organisation and Culture

As already stated earlier, the vast mass of people living in abject poverty are to be found mainly in the rural areas. For this population it is the district collector who is, for all practical purposes, the government, and it is the district administration with which this population is vitally concerned.

The overall record of district administration in planning and execution of development programmes is not an enviable one. The many critical observations on the working of district administration in general, and about agricultural administration in particular, reveal that the symptoms of administrative deficiencies are many and varied, structural and organisational,[8] which manifest themselves in numerous forms, at different levels during the execution of programmes.[9] There are also other symptoms which draw attention mainly to be pathologies and dysfunctions of bureaucracy.[10] Also, by and large, the district administration has failed to develop the infrastructure for development, and to provide the necessary inputs to farmers even when huge funds are made available to it.[11]

To understand the reasons for such failures on the part of the district machinery it is necessary to examine the structure, organisation and culture of the district bureaucracy as well as its interaction with the political system at the district level given below.

In general, the collector and his staff, *viz.*, sub-divisional officers, deputy collectors and tahsildars going right down to patwaris are the corner stone of the district administration and one which the common man approaches for all his needs. The role of the collector has changed significantly after independence. However, he remains even today in the centre of the district administration. He is considered the chief representative of government in the district as well as the head of the revenue administration. His main function is to supervise and coordinate the work of sub-divisional officers, revenue officials and all other government departments in the district. He is also the district magistrate and has powers under the Criminal Procedure Code for maintenance of law and order, though consequent upon the separation of judiciary from the executive, the collector is relieved of most of the magisterial powers which he used to exercise prior to 1947. It is also the collector to whom the government turns in an emergency of any kind.

An important function of the district administration is the selection of villages for development programmes. It is seen that often the factors that are upper most in the minds of the block and district staff are easy accessibility and availability of facilities in the village. Also, selection of villages and of the beneficiaries is not made mainly on the basis of the potential for development, but on the basis of the existence of a developed area and the consequent facilities and amenities. The block staff is also generally interested in selecting those villages which are on the main roads where they can pay a quick comfortable visit by jeep or bus, and return home before night. Block staff also tends to be interested in those villages where there are rich influential persons who would take up new programmes without much persuasion and thus help the block staff to fulfil the pre-set targets without much effort. Such persons take up new programmes because they have the financial capacity and risk taking ability and know the benefits they would receive from them. In such a process the weaker sections and their needs obviously tend to get neglected.

Senior officers also do not discourage such a process of selection because it is convenient for them to supervise the work in easily accessible villages. Visitors and dignitaries can also be easily taken to such villages and shown the progress made. In short, the easily accessible and progressive villages attract the block staff and all the development schemes and consequently become more developed and progressive. Development programmes are rarely taken up in backward interior villages because of the fear of failure. In the process, the already backward villages in the interior areas remain neglected and tend to become even more backward.

District officials, especially subordinate staff, do not take kindly to innovations in the system and style of district administration. Even when some energetic, highly motivated official introduces some innovations in the administration such as new management techniques, it is not only appreciated but generally resented by the supporting staff and by other district level officers. Due to constant pressures the new techniques might get temporary acceptance. However, such acceptance is generally short-lived and no sooner the official leaves than the subordinate staff shelves the innovation. The reason is simple. The clerk, who is fundamental in the administration, does not like to change his way of working.

Notwithstanding the above discussed inadequacies in the district administration, in times of national emergencies, such as war, and natural calamities, such as drought, famine and floods, the same administrative machinery functions efficiently. In such crises, officers take quick decisions, achieve a high degree of coordination, provide relief to a large mass of people in the most difficult conditions, and solve many tricky problems on the spot with great courage and imagination. The reasons for high efficiency in such crisis situations are:

1. clear task definition before the organisation,
2. clear role definition and responsibility fixation,
3. delegation of authority commensurate with the task and responsibility,
4. wide discretionary powers,
5. a unified command,
6. flexible financial procedures,
7. close and constant supervision by higher officials and the polity.

IV

Summing up

We thus get a picture of a district administration which works with a high degree of efficiency and skill in times of national emergencies and natural calamities, but does not exhibit the same skills when dealing with socio-economic problems. The very fact that the administration functions effectively in some situations while not being able to do so in others raises pertinent questions about the socio-political environment especially the rural intermediate elite and the other vested interests in rural society. It has also shown that the administration can function efficiently if the necessary environment is created and proper direction and goals set for it. But while there are no doubt sound socio-political reasons for the inability of the district administration in carrying out the socio-economic objectives of the government, in this section the emphasis will be mainly on the manner in which the managerial ethos of the district administration could be altered so as to lead to the desired results.

It needs to be recognised at the outset that no management group can function effectively if the policy parameters are not efficiently specified. It has to be accepted that rural development efforts in a large part of the country have been inadequate to the multiple tasks of transforming agricultural production, providing an articulated infrastructure for the support of agriculture and other rural activities, and developing a system of rural social services. In agriculture, the strategy of depending on "progressive farmers" for increased productivity has secured some success. However, it has left behind millions of small farmers, tenants and landless farmers and their families. It has to be recognised that a strategy of working primarily with the most responsive and best endowed agriculturists is bound to yield diminishing returns. Rather than "build on the best", the policy must new rapidly shift to "build on the rest". The socio-political concomitants of this policy have also to be specified and relayed to the ground level.

In addition, a climate has to be created wherein innovative and incentive management can exist. To bring this about a self-induced change approach has to be fostered. Such an approach has to be based on three assumptions:

(a) it is relatively easier to introduce structural changes in organisations where the need for change is felt by the functionaries operating the system; in other words, structural changes should evolve out of the felt needs of the functionaries;

(b) structural changes should be in stages over a period of time to give the functionaries the time required for adjustment of role relations; and

(c) the administrative system being an organic whole, changes, at any level, would over a period of time, induce changes in the entire system.

Under this approach, the first step has to be the creation of an awareness of the need for change. This has to be followed by suitable changes in rules and procedures which, in turn, would ultimately crystalise in the form of structural changes. The awareness of the need for change can be created by introducing new administrative and management techniques like the setting up of control mechanisms, more efficient monitoring and control systems, etc., in the district administration. Once the functionaries try to adopt the new techniques, they are like to become acutely aware of the need for changes in the system, and therefore to exert pressure for suitable changes in the traditional procedures, and ultimately in the structure of the organisation. Since initially such pressures would generate slowly and involve small changes in limited areas of operation, the higher level functionaries are likely to react favourable to the demands for change as and when required. Efforts have also to be simultaneously made through suitable training programmes, to enable the higher level functionaries to appreciate the relevance of the new techniques. Structural changes will not bring results unless new tools and techniques are adopted at all levels of the organisation. To be effective these two processes must be synchronised.

The roles to be prescribed for the district administration within the manpower system and the programmes flowing from the new rural development strategies have also to be carefully defined. Within the clear task definition, proper role clarification and responsibility commensurate with the task has to be done within a system of flexible financial procedures and a unified command. By the very nature of the objective situation, the programmes of the different agencies and the roles performed by the personnel manning them cannot be static. The nature of rural development as a dynamic process further requires that roles and programmes be continually re-examined to determine whether they are the most relevant possible to the tasks at hand.

Besides, the administration has to be quick acting with empathy towards the needs, desires and aspirations of the masses. This means reorienting the attitudes of those manning the district administration at the different hierarchical levels. To enable this to be done there have to be the least possible hierarchical levels of authority so that the personnel feel involved in the decision making process and so get "committed" to the new goals and directions. Since the attitudes of the personnel manning the administration have to be significantly different from those permeating the law and other machinery, an in-depth study is necessary to determine whether such attitudes can coexist in one machinery or whether separate machineries need to be set up for the regulatory and non-regulatory functions.

In addition, it would be necessary to motivate the personnel manning the district administration so as to change their attitudes towards the rural areas and especially the rural poor. There is need for an extended programme which could both lead to a change in the attitudes of the personnel as well as give the most effective support to the new directions in rural development strategy. The programme and content of such training has to be planned in a manner so as to be instrumental to the success of the new strategies evolved in the rural development sphere. The training programme has also to be such as to inculcate the techniques of planning, control and evaluation in the district machinery.

The task set before the nation is a challenging one and the district administration would be required to play a key role in carrying it out in the rural development sphere. Unless the focus of attention shifts to this segment of the administration and adequate steps are taken to motivate, train and otherwise ensure the effective and efficient functioning of the district administration, the objectives of socio-economic development as elucidated in the Fifth Five Year Plan may prove difficult of achievement.

REFERENCES

1. V.M. Dandekar and N. Rath, Poverty in India, (Delhi Ford Foundation, 1971).
2. Government of India, Planning Commission, Approach to Fifth Five Year Plan, 1972, p. 1.
3. Government of India, Planning Commission, Fifth Five Year Plan, 1975.
4. Government of India, Ministry of Finance, Department of Economic Affairs, Pocket Book of Economic Information, 1971, p. 27.
5. D.G. Karve, Public Services in a Democracy, Indian Journal of Public Administration, Vol. 10, No. 1, January, March 1964, pp. 1-11 for a discussion on the supremacy of the Constitution and equality before the law in a democracy.
6. *Ibid.*, pp. 9-10.
7. L.P. Singh, New Horizons in Administrative Organisation and Behaviour (cyclostyled). Training Abstract-6, Training Division, Government of India, Ministry of Home Affairs, New Delhi, July 1970, p. 9.
8. These, in general, could be: "want of clarity or decision at policy-making level; wrong juxtaposition in which power is divorced from responsibility; because rules and regulations charging the officers and men are inept and illconceived; because at appropriate levels of reference a ready machinery for a decisive resolving of difference does not exist." Seminar 85, September, 1966, p. 13.
9. For such critical observations, see report of the Grow More Food Enquiry Committee, 1952, p. 42; Supplement to the Report of Grow More Food Enquiry Committee, 1952, p. 3; Evaluation of the 1958-59 Rabi Crop Campaign in Punjab, Rajasthan and U.P., Programme Evaluation Organisation, Planning Commission, Government of

India, 1960, pp. 7, 35, 65, 98, 99; Report on Seed Multiplication Schemes, Committee on Plan Projects, Planning Commission, 1961, pp. iii and 62; Study of the Multiplication and Distribution Programme for Improved Seed, Programme Evaluation Organisation, Planning Commission, Government of India, 1961, pp. 87-8, 111, 188-90; All India Rural Credit Survey, The General Report (Abridged Edition), Reserve Bank of India, 1955, pp, 82-85; Report of the Team for the Study of Community Projects and National Extension Service, Vol. I (Leader: Balwantrai G. Mehta), 1957, p. 5.

10. For example, according to Dube, "The major symptoms of the malady are failure to take decisions at the appropriate level, passing the buck, roping in others in decision-making, equivocal recommendations, anticipating what the boss wants, rationalisation of failures, underplaying the essentials and magnifying the grandiose covering the failure of small utopias with projection of larger utopias, and out-right sycophancy", S.C. Dube, "Bureaucracy and Economic Development" The Indian Journal of Public Administration, Vol. XII, No 3, July-September, 1966, p. 340.

11. D.K. Desai and Hari Prakash, Planning and Implementation of Financing Agriculture through Area Approach (cyclostyled), Indian Institute of Management, Ahmedabad, 1973; V.R. Gailkwad, "Execution of Agricultural Development Programmes and Administrative Deficiencies", Behavioural Sciences and Community Development, Vol. 3, No. 2, September, 1960, pp. 101-113.

6

PARTICIPATIVE MANAGEMENT

R. MALIK & OTHERS

Introduction

One of the greatest challenges thrown up by forces, unleashed by technological progress and the revolution of rising expectations is the harmonization of the objectives of organizational efficiency plus effectiveness and enrichment of the quality of work life. Unfortunately, the work organisation in most present day organisations falls far short of this ideal, the consequence of which is the rise of worker alienation and negative attitudes towards work and the organization. The symptoms of this malaise are turnover, sabotage, absenteeism and sharpening of conflict. The purpose of the present study is to examine—

(a) how far workers' alienation can be mitigated by the adoption of participative style of management;

(b) what can be the problems in the way of implementing participative management with special reference to the Indian situation.

Participative management involves participation by workers. Participation may be defined as an individual's mental and emotional involvement in a group situation that encourages him to contribute to group goals and to share responsibility for them. Another even more important aspect of participation is the participation by subordinates with their superiors in managerial decision-making process. Although the managerial subordinates are constantly participating in the production of goods and services and in the sharing of total revenue received by the enterprise the participation in management is much less frequent.

Our methodology would be to first examine the deficiency in the present work-system and then analyse the various means of ensuring participative management.

Features of Present Work Organisation

One of the most prevalent forms of work organisation is the bureaucratic form which characterizes most of the large private and public sector corporations, apart from the government. Some of the more prominent features of bureaucratic form have been identified by the German Sociologist. Max Weber, as follows:

(i) Specific spheres of competence legitimized as official duties. This is the principle of division of labour.
(ii) Hierarchical arrangement of officers.
(iii) Uniform rules for carrying out work.
(iv) Impersonality and objectivity.
(v) Selection of officials on the basis of competence only.

The logic that underlies such a system can be identified as follows:*

(i) The system can be rendered reliable by creating redundancy of human elements.

* "Participative Redesign of Work System" by Nitish R De in Management in Government edited by B.C. Mathur, K. Diesh, C. Sekharan.

(ii) Where the cost of human elements is low this redundancy principle leads to more layers of employees with unskilled labour at the base. Where the cost of human labour is high due to trade union or other environmental factors, it leads to more dependence on technological innovation as a labour saving device. This is compounded with a drive for exploitation of technology for standardized mass production for a consumption oriented national or global market.

(iii) Since the deviation from standards gets compounded (in an assembly line), there is need to lay down specific prescriptive content of job supported by stringent supervision based controls. Discretionary element in the work decreases as prescriptive element increases.

(iv) Control system is the key to operational efficiency so that the work system is designed in such a way that people are subjected to a decrease in variety of responsibility and their role is specific to a fragmented part of what could otherwise be an integrated people task system.

Though this system has led to spectacular achievements in the utilization of scientific knowledge and its conversion to technology, its unintended and unanticipated consequence has been worker alienation which has already been referred to.

Factors Causing the Malfunctioning of Present-day Organizations

An organization is, in fact, a socio-technical system. It is essential to take an integrative view of technology or the work process and the social or human aspect. The two are interdependent elements. It is necessary to redesign jobs and work environments to suit the human personality along with taking advantage of technological progress for organizational ends. The present-day work organization, as referred to above, neglects the socio-psychological dimension and concentrates on the economic and technological aspects.

In terms of Leavitt's model, an organization is a pattern of tasks, techniques, structure and people. Change in any one of the four elements trigger off significant changes in the others.

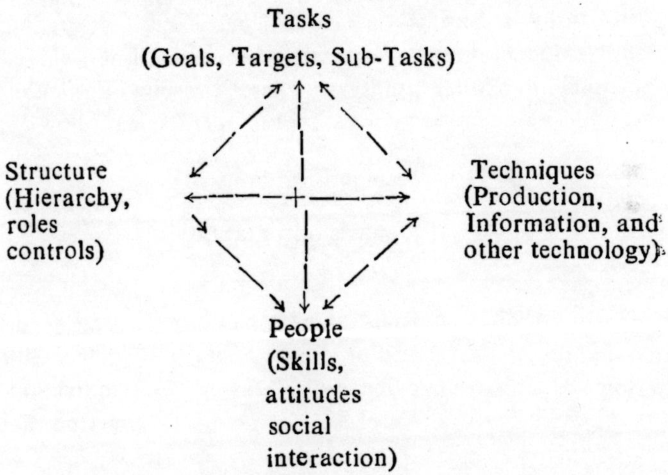

The bureaucratic organization neglects the interaction of "people dimension" with others. It is based on defining structure according to the task and technology.

The organization is also an open system.

Inputs	Throughout	Outputs
1. Environmental conditions	Organizational Transformations	Goods Services
2. Societal norms	Subsystems	Manpower
3. Human resources	Functions	Strategies to
4. Material resources.		influence environment

———Feedback———

A negative feedback from the environment should trigger off changes in the tasks, technology, structure and people and acting as a corrective, it should ultimately bring the organizational outputs in tune with the client and environmental needs.

This, however, does not happen in a bureaucracy for reasons put forth by Robert K. Merton. This is because organization members generalize a response from situations where it is appropiate to similar situations where it results in unanticipated and undesirable consequences.* This operates as follows:

Demand for Control
↓
Emphasis on reliability
↓

↓		↓
Defensibility of individual action	Rigidity of behaviour and organizational defence of status	Felt need for defensibility of individual action
	↓	↑
	Amount of difficulty with clients	←—

The demand for control made on the organizations by the top hierarchy takes the form of emphasis on reliability of behaviour within the organization. This leads to reduction in amount of personalized relationships, increased internalisation of rules of the organization by participants, use of categorization as a decision making technique (which incidently leads to a decrease in amount of search for alternatives). It further leads to defensibility of individual action in that simple categories are rigorously applied to individual cases without regard for personal features which can only be challenged at higher levels. The unanticipated consequences are rigidity of behaviour and difficulty with clients of the organization reducing client satisfaction. Client dissatisfaction itself reinforces rigidity as well as felt needs for the defensibility of individual action.

2. R.K. Merton (1940) "Bureaucratic Structure and Personality" Social Forces No. 18, pp. 560-68, as interpreted in Organisation Theory ed. by D.S. Pugh, pp. 31-35.

Thus the present form of work organisation fails to achieve:

(i) One of the two major objectives of organization *i.e.*, quality of work life.

(ii) It fails even in achieving organizational efficiency and effectiveness.

(iii) It fails especially in rigid bureaucratic forms in responding to rapidly changing environment and to it's clients.

Methods of Achieving Participation in Management

Methods of achieving participation are actually clusters of practices in management which focus on some specific area or objective of participation. These methods may be employed in an organisation singly or simultaneously depending upon the situation. In practice different situations arising from environmental variations and cross-cultural distinctions would call for different forms of participative mechanisms. The fact that participation is sought at different levels of organisational hierarchy would also necessitate differences of mechanism. We have broadly classified the various participative mechanisms under two categories—Work Related, and Interest Related.

Work Related Mechanisms

Work related participative methods are mainly concerned with the work itself and aim at improvement in it through participation. Some widely used participative methods under this category have been discussed below:

Consultative Management—As the name implies, it involves frequent consultations betweem the managers, and the workers. Final decisions are arrived at after a process of consultation in which workers are encouraged to think about problems and give suggestions for improvement. The initiative for this type of participation in decision making comes from the management itself and as such managers should be open minded and receptive to the ideas coming from below. The response of workers depends mainly upon managerial attitude and the fact that they are in a position to make constructive work-related suggestions.

Consultative management has certain benefits which make it readily acceptable to free market economies. It does not lead to disturbing changes in the organisation affecting the authority—responsibility relationships. Moreover, the management remains free to take the final decision independent of suggestions coming from below.

Consultative style of management is very popular in Japan where it has certain special characteristics. Japanese style of Management is basically consultative because the managers usually try to ensure workers' acceptance of a policy before it is finally decided and implemented. As a result managerial policies find wide acceptance and are quickly implemented. The concept of life-long employment of the worker in an organisation and the managerial tradition of looking after employees' extra-work life further strengthen their identification with the organisation and motivation for organisational goals.

Work Committees or Production Committees—The committees are groups of workers and managers organised primarily to consider job problems and suggest improvements at the shopfloor level. The usual modus operandi of these committees is that the management, being a part of the group, asks the some to recommend action before taking a final decision. The group makes its recommendation after a process of discussion, that is group dynamics, in which concerned managers also participate. The result of such participative decision making is that the decisions finally arrived at have a wider acceptance. Moreover, since these committees are usually concerned with job problems, participation leads to greater involvement, motivation and productivity.

Work committees can be of various types: labour management committee, work-improvement task force, safety committee etc., depending on the objective of committee formation. Participation through work-committees is popular and has been applied successfully in different socio-industrial environments as well as in unionised and non-unionised organisation. But for successful adoption as participative technique these committees require continuous and genuine support from higher levels of management. The workers too should be in a situation conducive to constructive participation in group dynamics.

Work Redesign—Work redesign or improvement is a way of ensuring self-satisfaction, involvement and motivation of the worker through modification of job structure. This is done in such a way that they have some power to plan and make decisions about their work and modify it. These modifications can include job enlargement job enrichment, etc. Work Redesign increases variety in the job content and individual workers perform a complete task instead of a repetitive activity. The workers are allowed greater, responsibility and flexibility in organising their work environment. The power to plan and make decisions about the work gives him a sense of power sharing with the management. The feeling of self-importance in turn leads to a closer identification with the organisation and considerably reduces alienation. Finally, in terms of Herzberg's analysis, Work Redesign builds in what may be called motivators in the job content such as responsibility, opportunity for advancement and recognition. It would therefore appeal to workers' desire for more challenging and meaningful work.

Work Redesign as a technique of participation was successfully employed in an experiment by the Indian P&T Department; (refer of Case Studies in this Report).

Quality Circles—The word 'quality' here is a misnomer in the sense that quality circles are actually mechanisms meant to improve inter and intra-departmental coordination in an organisation. Their basic goal is to involve more and more persons in decision making so that decisions have a greater acceptance and inter-departmental frictions are reduced.

Quality circles as a form of participative technique origin from some horizontal level or different levels of organisation. They may also belong to different departments. For example, a Production Manager forms a Production Committee comprising himself, a foreman who is trusted, a Quality Control Manager and the Maintenance Manager for cooperative decision making and better implementation of the same.

Quality circles as a form of participative technique originated in Japan, Now-a-days they are also gaining acceptance in other countries.

Management by Objectives—MBO as a management technique has in-built possibility of participation. Fundamental to the MBO process is the mutual setting of objeetives between each position holder and his supervisor/and use of these objectives as standards for performance evaluation. The process of setting objectives begins at the top level of organisational hierarchy and goes down to the shop floor level. Since the objective setting is a two-way process in which both managers and employees prrticipate at various levels, it may even result in modification of the overall target set at the top.

Participation through MBO technique increases acceptance of objectives as well as motivation and involvement on the part of workers.

Interest Related Mechanisms

Interest Related participative methods aim at ensuring workers' participation in management and decision making with a view to protect tne employees' group interests. These are often state-mandated and may involve change in traditional authority responsibility relationship in an organisation. Some major forms of participation under this category are discussed below:

Democratic Management: Under this type of participation major organisational decisions are referred to workers' groups, which through a process of discussion arrive at a decision and refer it back to the management for implementation. In its most democratic form it operates on the principle of consensus or "one man—one vote" concept. Since managerial decisions are arrived at on the basis of majority vote such a form of participation is possible only when either the management voluntarily relinquishes control or is forced to do so.

Although democratic management offers the possibility of making fuller use of group ideas, it does not-fit in hierarchical task oriented organisational frame work. It leads to a high rank-and-file morale but may fail in promoting identification with the organisation and motivation for its goals. As a result while the workers are able to look after their group interest, the long term interests of the organisation as a whole may be ignored. To make democratic participation operative in a task oriented organisation, it is necessary to provide for managerial discretion which can be exercised when group decisions are found inconsistent with organisational goals. Decisions are still taken by the majority but they become subject to managerial approval.

The concept of Democratic Management is not easy to implement. It would require a completely different socio-industrial climate, structural changes and a new set of attitudes for its successful adoption.

Participation through Collective Bargaining: The concept of collective bargaining gives both the management and workers a right to lay down certain rules concerning latter's employment conditions, wages etc. on the basis of collective agreements. These agreements are normally binding on both the parties with the force of law. This approach to workers' participation in decision making is based on the concept of balance of power. Both the parties bargain to get maximum advantage out of the other party.

Participation through collective bargaining is primarily interest related and may be harmful to the efficiency of the organisation. Threats and counter-threats of strikes and lock-outs play a part in the bargaining process seriously affecting the organisational efficiency.

Participation through Ownership of Enterprise by Workers: Though simple ownership of the enterprize by the workers does not ensure participation on its own, it may provide a useful background for developing the same. Workers even when they own shares have mainly operative functions different from managerial ones. But if a suitable participative mechanism is provided they are likely to participate constructively because of greater involvement and motivation which they have as owners of the organisation.

Joint Management Councils and Committees: These are joint bodies comprising the representatives of the management and workers. Their functions may range from decision-making on some issue to merely advising the management as consultative bodies. In Britain and India, the JMCs are the commonly used forms of workers' participation in management. Their role is largely advisory and consultative, with decision-making being left to the top management. Since they lack the power to enforce binding decisions, they have proved ineffective in ensuring participation.

Industrial Democracy: Industrial democracy is a term coined for describing state-mandated workers' participation at various levels of organisation, especially with regard to those decisions which affect their group interest. Depending upon the legal mandate it may be applied at lower levels of management through the formation of staff or workers' councils and at the top level through appointment of workers' representative on the Board of Directors.

Staff or workers' councils are exclusive bodies of workers' elected representative. There may be one council for the entire organisation or a hierarchy of councils from shop floor to the Staff Board. Workers' councils have different functions in the management of an enterprize, ranging from eliciting information on management's intentions to full share in decision-making. For instance, in West Germany and Yugoslavia these councils have wide decision making powers concerning the group interests of the workers. Sometimes, workers' councils give rise to conflicts especially with trade unions which feel threatened on account of their growing decision-making powers concerning the workers. It has been found that workers' councils are more effective in protecting and promoting working class interests within an organisation.

Appointment of workers' representatives on the Board of Directors makes for workers' participation in decision-making at the very top. The Board of Directors is usually concerned mainly with profits, and other interests like those of labour are secondary to it. As a member the workers' representative, too, is expected to contribute to this goal. But in practice he acts as a negotiator for workers' interest with other members, for the profit motive is secondary to him. Despite this limitation, the workers' representative can play a useful role which is relevant to the overall and long term interests of the organisation. He can serve as a control mechanism and influence the managerial policies concerning workers. To agreat extent the success of this participation will depend upon the caliber of the representative appointed.

Cases Studies

The experiment of participative management in India might be illustrated with the help of four case-studies *viz.*, those of TISCO, BHEL, Post-Office, and Tavistock.

Participative Management at TISCO

The Tata Iron and Steel Company (TISCO) at Jamshedpur is the poineer in establishing participative management in India. Although close association of employees with management at TISCO began as early as 1919, it was only in 1957, after several years of the study of the subject and discussion with the recognized union that the TISCO at Jamshedpur set up a three-tier machinery of consultation consisting of a Departmental Council, Joint Works Council and Joint Consultative Council. The purpose of joint consultation was to promote increased productivity, provide a better understanding to the employees of their role and importance and to satisfy the urge for self-expression. It was also intended to maintain orderly and cordial relations between the company and the union so as to promote the interests of the employees.

For each department, there is a joint Departmental Council consisting of anything between four and ten representatives of management and equal number of workers' representatives. The terms of the members is two years. The Joint Departmental Councils are to study operational results and production problems, improve productivity and discipline and seek to encourage suggestions. Improvement of working conditions also fall within their purview.

The Joint Works Council, the second tier of the system, was to review every month the working of the Departmental Councils and a few other joint committees which the Tatas had already set up such as Suggestion Box Committee, Safety Committee, etc.

The Joint Consultative Council of management advises on all matters concerning the working of the industry in the field of production as also with regard to economic and financial matters which are placed before it by the management. The Chairman of Joint Consultative Council is usually a director.

The TISCO concern sought to remove practical difficulties like lack of skill on the part of managerial personnel to conduct a council meeting and their tendency to speak English by introducing a "Running a Meeting Course" so that management and Unions' representatives can effectively utilize this facility.

The TISCO experiment is regarded as the most successful and sustained experiment in participative management and is working fairly satisfactorily. From 1957 to the middle of 1972, for which the data are available, the Joint Departmental Councils have discussed a total of 14,104 suggestions of which 70.3 per cent have been implemented. These suggestions have covered a wide range of topics and issues *i.e.* 47 per cent of the suggestions deal with various aspect of safety, about 15 per cent with welfare, 1 per cent with discipline and 18 per cent with miscellaneous subjects. Its successful operation is also borne out from the fact that in 1969, while a politically motivated strike paralysed TELCO and other engineering industries in Jamshedpur, it did not affect the TISCO employees. Even the Works Committees which have not been very successful elsewhere have functioned well at TISCO. This changed environment has also increased the production.

The key to success at TISCO lies in careful planning, existance of only one recognized union and responsiveness of management to the problems of the employees.

Case Study of BHEL (Hardwar)

One of the most important cases of participative management is that of Heavy Electrical Equipment Plant located at Hardwar which is one of the four production units of Bharat Heavy Electrical Limited (BHEL). Previously the units of BHEL had a poor record of capacity utilization and were losing heavily. This made the top management anxious to reorganize the work system for ensuring operational efficiency.

The BHEL unit at Hardwar is a large public sector unit, employing over 9000 employees. The experiment began in May 1975 and was inspired by the experiments of production units from Norway, Sweden and Italy, as they were discussed in a "Equality of Working Life Workshop" held in 1974.

The participative behaviour on the part of the workers was encouraged by work-redesigning, improving job relations, promotions on merit, respect for ability and quality of work done rather than status. There was also a system to promote evolution of ideas from the shop-floor to the middle level of management and further to the top management. The general feeling was one of psychological satisfaction and identification of the worker with the organization.

The concrete steps taken included:—

(a) The introduction of the work module system according to which a worker handling one type of activity could devote part of his time to learn other activities. The multi-skilled learning process was planned in such a way that it did not affect the tempo of work adversly, while imparting multiple-skills to the working. By providing multiple-skills, the organization provided an incentive for the workers to stay on as these skills could best be utilized in BHEL, thereby reducing employee turn over.

(b) An attempt was made to provide that type of theoretical knowledge to the workers which would be helpful to them in acquiring proficiency in certain skills.

(c) Members of the task force were free to rotate among themselves. Internal norms for maintaining discipline, including granting of leave, giving time off to the colleagues and dealing with the problem of absenteeism were evolved by the group and were accepted by the supervisor.

(d) The supervisors were released from routine supervision jobs and their services were utilized in liaison work with other departments and in handling grievance problems.

(e) The experimental groups were encouraged to have discussions in seminars which were specially organized to share their experiences on new forms of work system with managers, workers and trade unions.

The initial results were quite satisfactory. The experiment led to the improvement in production. Both the task groups between February 1976 and March 1977 completed their target production ahead of time and took up new jobs which brought about the credibility about the experiments amongst the more sceptical of managers. There was a great deal of enthusiasm on the part of participants. The task groups met frequently, displayed the weekly production progress on notice boards and tried to solve the problems of maintenance and delay mutually. For some time, the top management support aided the successful functioning of the experiment.

Problems arose when those workers who were not covered by the experiment resented the discretion granted to the task group of deciding their leave matters, internal discipline etc. They were aided by the union leaders who anticipated in the success of the experiment an erosion of their base and a reduction in their power in the organization as bargaining agents for the workers. They, therefore, vehemently put forward demands for extending such benefits to all workers. Sinee the experiment could not be extended to all workers within such a short time and without adequate training, the experiment itself was called off.

Participative Management Experiment in Post-Office

As part of the training and applied research activity, a study was undertaken of the work flow and work environment in all the post-offices in Shimla. As a result, a project to streamline the work was launched at the Chaura Maidan Post-Office which had 43 employees, which included two union leaders.

A diagnostic study of the post office revealed certain problems such as inadequate work space in the post-office, no physical facility at the counters for the customers to fill in forms and inadequate lighting. An attempt was made to rectify these difficulties whereby more space was created functional furniture was brought in and a recreation room was set apart for the employees. On the spot action was generally taken.

While this process was going on, a socio-technical analysis of the work system was under taken which revealed the following tasks of the post-office:

(a) *Mail delivery activities*

(b) *Counter Service* activities (Saving bank function, booking of money orders, registration of letters, parcels, etc., selling of postage stamps)

(c) *Cable and telephone activities*

(d) *Control functions*: Supervisory activities, maintenance of records and flow of correspondence with other offices.

It was found that these activities were organized in the usual fragmented manner. After this diagnostic study, a series of meetings were held with the employees in order to develop better work systems, which could relieve them of undue pressure of work, provide better service to the customers, and to overcome avoidable delays thereby saving their time and energy.

An integrated delivery group was created whose membership included posting postmen, delivery postmen and the clerks concerned with maintenance of reeords of accountable items. The group decided to have one employee for doing liasion work with the sub-postmaster. The internal allocation of tasks devolved on the group itself. The work lay-out was redesigned to facilitate group-work. While there were initial difficulties in developing group norms, gradually the system got stabilized with the result that sorting and delivery time for the mail was cut down by about three quarters of an hour per shift.

The counter system was also redesigned whereby multiple counters were introduced. Under this system, all counter activities could be conducted at each counter except for the savings bank activities.

Encouraged by these results, similar projects were initiated in Delhi. In July 1977, Janpath Post Office initiated the project and four of the counters were converted into multiple counters. In this post-office, savings bank account counter also took up the registration of broadcasting licence work unlike what was operating in the Post Office at Simla. The new system had increased the co-ordination work of the postmaster at the end of the work day as he was now required to consolidate statements of daily activities carried out simultaneously at several counters. At the same time, he felt that some of the new work pressures were reduced as temporary absence of the counter-clerk from the work spot was no longer a serious problem because they could close one counter while other counters were active.

Some of the salient features of the initiation strategy can now be pin-pointed:

(a) There was a persistent feeling that in the postal system, being part of the government bureaucracy, the initiation of any change process was difficult within the rigid framework of government rules, and regulatlons. The low key manner in which the three experiments were started at Simla without giving publicity provided the initial validation to the change agents who primarily came from the senior cadres of the postal services.

(b) Whereas in Simla, under a more controlled environment, a total system of work restructure could be attempted with success, the same could not be done in Delhi. Here the environmental forces such as the presence of senior officers as well as the key trade union leaders in the vicinity could not be ignored. The legitimacy of the multiple counter system having been established at Simla, it was possible to generate a feeling of cautious experimentation among the senior officers in Delhi. The counter-reorganization system also did not cause much difficulty to the union leaders, and that is why in Delhi, the initiation process started with counter reorganization rather than reorganization of the mail handling group.

(c) Comparing the Delhi experience with that of Shimla, it had been discovered that in smaller post-offices like those at Simla, a small number of employees could respond to the participative opportunities faster and with positive interest. In Delhi, while the post-offices employ larger numbers of employees, there was a culture of impersonality. As such, much more time was required to initiate changes.

(d) In a two year period (1975-77) it had been established that in a government bureaucracy, like the postal system, a number of projects could be initiated with a reasonable degree of success because of the strategy that had been adopted in developing a net work of change agents. They were drawn from amongst the ranks of social scientists, committed postal service officials, trade union leaders etc.

(e) The case also revealed that there were systematic linkages somewhat more salient to a government system where initiation of work redesign projects would confront certain difficulties. Status and rank are two significant items perhaps because other forms of extrinsic reward, including merit-based promotion, have limited applicability. Sorting postmen enjoy a different pay-scale which is higher than that of delivery postmen. They are also usually senior in length of service. This generates status consciousness amongst them and they see a threat to their status if they have to work in a work group with inter-changability of work role. Moreover, different post-offices are earmarked for post masters of different grades and seniority and a post master having succeeded in the operation of this experiment in one post office can't be transferred to another, as his rank might not permit it.

Tavistock Experiment

Gautam Sarabhai, the Chairman, Ahmedabad Chemical and Calico Printing Co. Ltd., approached the Tavistock School for conducting this experiment in his company and Dr. Rice, a pro-consultant, visited India in this respect in 1953. The Tavistock School combined a knowledge of therapy with the knowledge of the social psychology and sociology of organization. The first operational step was to gain acceptance from the component sub-systems of the organisation and then to study the system as a whole and they were constantly aware of the relation of one sub-system to the other.

At the Cailco Mills, the major problem being faced was that the introduction of expensive automatic looms from Japan had not increased productivity—neither the quantity not the quality of cloth woven was higher than what was achieved by the old semi-automatic looms. Dr. Rice discovered that the social system of the workers had been broken down by the new technical change. There was a confused pattern of inter-relation and a tendency for each group to blame other groups for poor performance.

Dr. Rice, therefore, worked out an approach for organisational changes. This reorganisation permitted the organisation of large and small integrated work groups. Instead of 29 workers with different job roles being in charge of 224 looms, he proposed that a group of workers would be responsible for all jobs related to a group of looms, and members of the group should be prepared to do each other's work with an overall group leader.

The elements of the idea were proposed to the lower level supervision, who in turn, proposed them to the workers. The workers accepted the plan and organized the experimental groups following the new pattern. They formed 4 groups of 7 men each, four in the weaving sub-group, and three in the gatting and the maintenance sub-groups. Productivity increased and the basic change in traditional working relations was accepted. The experiment was gradually increased to the entire weaving shed and had its impact on the other sheds where the traditional looms were being operated. There was an intensive scheme of earning above 85 per cent capacity utilisation, and so the worker's earning went up. A third shift, hitherto regarded as impracticable in the Ahmedabad climate, could also be introduced. While the cost of the organizational experimental shed was 12 per cent higher than that of the other shed, as the workers were earning more, the damages were 50 per cent less and the out-put was 25 per cent higher.

The experiment was later given up due to internal reasons but its achievements rcmained remarkable. Firstly, the changes were introduced when there was much resistance against the introduction of labour saving methods, but the change was maintained in spite of the hostile atmosphere. The workers volunteered to participate in the experiment, and the conclusion was that, despite the great difference between the industrial climate of Gujarat and that of the west, the industrial workers in Gujarat reacted in the same way as workers in Western Society in similar circumstances. The Calico Mills experiment proved also the 'Hawthorne effect' which describes how an especially chosen experimental group shows heightened production. The experiment also illustrates the power of participation to win acceptance of technical change in an organization. It also showed that cooperation between the technical and social systems within an organization is possible when (a) a task is so organized that those engaged in it can experience the completion of a whole task, (b) a task is so organized that so far as possible those engaged upon it can control their activities, (c) related tasks should be so organized that those performing them can have satisfactory relationships. The effect, however, petered out after a few years, probably due to lack of Management Commitment.

Legal Framework of Participative Management and Scope Its Implementation in Government

Participative management as a concept, was thought about as a partial solution to the industrial relations problem and also as a means to foster the ideals of industrial democracy. This was couched as an objective in the draft of Second Five-Year Plan and later in the Industrial Policy Resolution of 1956 which suggested Joint Management Councils. Its fundamental importance was emphasized by enshrining it in the Directive Principles of State Policy in the words: "The State shall take steps by suitable legislation or in any other way to secure the participation of workers in the management of undertakings, establishments, or other organizations engaged in any industry:" (Art. 43-A).

The legal framework for participation of workers in management was provided in Section 3 of the Indian Defence Act 1942. Briefly it states in the sub-clauses 1 and 2 that there shall be a "Works Committee" in any industrial establishment of 100 or more workmen. And the Works Committee shall try to farther amity and good relations among the employer and workmen.

There is no elaboratc laying down in legal terms the exact mechanisms of such participation, as is evident from the above. The government thought it fit to let the participative management grow in various establishments in its own way, from within and not to impose it from above. The study group on the participative management in 1957, constituting top industrial relations managers, bureaucrats and labour leaders voiced much the same opinion in its report.

Before examining the possibilities of its application in the Government departments, one can make a few preliminary observations:

(i) that the dysfunctionalities in the old Weberian model of democracy *i.e.*, the hierarchical arrangement of officers and top-down communication be taken care of and a bottom up approach to both decision-making and communications be adopted;

(ii) that as in the case of workers' participation in industry, no specific legislation can be made covering all the departments because of difference in the internal and external environment of different organizations. Therefore, it is wiser that participation in governmental organizations also be allowed to be evolved on its own from within. Perhaps, it would be of far more suitable variety and more permanent.

(iii) Conceptually, it would mean an expansion of the original applications of worker's participation in management from industries to the participation of employees in governmental and often non-industrial settings. For example, district administration, Secretariat etc. But it still leaves out the question of participation of workers in the unorganized sector.

We could in dealing with the possibilities of adopting the "Participative management" concept in the government, deal it at essentially three levels, *viz.*, at the level of district, at the level of the Secretariat and at the level of specific departments like P and T and Defence.

Taking it up at the district level, the most significant experiment in this regard is the Ahmednagar experiment. In the Ahmednagar district of Maharashtra, the DM. Shri Anil Lakhina had introduced reforms which at the time of implementing them created much more conducive atmosphere for the participation of the lower levels in the management of the district. It had a three-fold objective of (a) regulation of public-clerk contact; (b) accessibility of documents both to the staff and the public; and (c) improve working conditions and creation of an environment of efficiency.

For realising the first objective, two steps were taken, *viz.*, categorisation of visitors as per their needs and designing the office to fit the task sequence. Also a "token system" like in the Banks was introduced to answer public grievances and enquiries. This ensured that immediate attention was given to the public problems.

For the second task of hand, pamphlets regarding various procedures and formalities of public interests were issued in simple language so that everybody clearly knew what they had to do and the public knew what they wanted. Also the filing system was modernised with the introduction of the "six-bundle system". The record room was rearranged as per the principles laid down by the "Anderson Breving".

The working conditions were vastly improved by providing the staff with new tables, cleaner surroundings proper lighting arrangements, tiffin-rooms, toilet facilities etc. Besides, the concept of training was introduced to up-date the knowledge of the lower-level functionaries. Also a change in their job-content, provided them the "intrinsic motivation".

At the level of the Secretariat, these reforms can be introduced like in the Ahmednagar experiment. Besides, one can take a cue from the marketing set-up of SAIL. As it happens, each section in the Central Marketing Organisation of SAIL sends a number of representatives on the basis of strength to an electoral college which ultimately elects the office-bearers of the union. Each representative of the section takes active interest in the day-to-day affairs of the section and often has an effective say.

And at the level of the implementations of participative management in specific departments we can take two examples *viz.*, the P and T experiment and the Desk Officer system in the Defence Department.

The officer oriented system or the Desk Officer system is one in which the initial consideration of a proposal is at the hands of an officer rather than of the office *i.e.*, clerks and assistants. The diarist in the section puts up a paper to the officer concerned. The latter issues appropriate direction and the reference clerk/steno who is attached to him puts up the relevant file to him, after docketing and referencing. The first-noting in respect of the paper is, as a rule, done by the officer himself, and in case the paper is such as can be disposed of at his level, he, dictates the reply. The cases, final disposal of which is not within his competence, are to be put up to the appropriate officer.

The general findings of this experiment are:

(i) The cases under the officer oriented pattern were dealt with more expeditiously than under the conventional one. Saving in time was to the tune of 100 per cent.

(ii) A paper took less time to reach the officer.

(iii) The pay-bill of the organization went higher than under the conventional system.

It must be clearly borne in mind that the officer oriented pattern is suitable to handle work which is non-routine in character.

The officer oriented system in itself does not enhance participative management, to the extent that subordinate staff no longer make a first noting, their participation is further reduced. But to the extent that the Section Officer now disposes of most of the letters himself there is an increase in his responsibility and he is gromed to take up higher roles in the organisation, thereby increasing his participation. But necessarily, a line has to be drawn, as to which level in the government will take the decisions.

The third kind of setting *i.e.* government departments, has been covered in other parts of the report. The BHEL and the Post Office experiments, illustrate the scope of its application, the consequences and the limitations. The only difference that set apart a Public Sector Undertaking (PSU) from a private industrial unit for this purpose is that in PSUs managerial commitment is also a function of the political commitment in that the ministries in reality do exercise considerable influence over operational policies of these enterprises.

Problems Involved in Implementation

Our objective in this chapter would be to probe the factors that may cause the failure of participative management and also to examine in what conditions it would be most successful. The various factors which could be considered are our social milieu, the nature of technology, the relative stability of the environment, management commitment, etc.

The imbibing of democratic values in the essential prerequisite of participative management, because participative management in essence is the participation by all levels of the organisation in decision-making, which is the exact reverse of hierarchy and authority. Our country has a short tradition of democracy and an attitudinal change in terms of acquiring democratic values has not really taken place. Peoples' attitudes by and large are still fashioned in the feudal mould. The concept of hierarchy, status orientation and position based authority are still the dominant elements of our cultural milieu. An example of this influence of culture hindering the success of participative management is the implementation of the work redesign experiment at the Delhi Hauz Khas Post Office mentioned earlier in report. Work redesign, as it happened in this case, may often involve the formation of whole task groups instead of fragmented activity being assigned to a single worker. This would result in an inter-changeability of roles among group members, thereby denying the existance of status differentials. For such a restructuring of work to come about, certain group members who were holding higher positions in the hierarchy and therefore the advantage from this status differential may have to sacrifice their superior status. Given our cultural milieu this will be quite tough to achieve.

Even though culture is a hinderance to the implementation of participative management, in certain sectors of organised industry this influence may not be strong. In fact, the nature of the environment and the level of technology are important factors in determining the success of participation. In high technology areas with rapidly changing environments and unstable markets, participative management ends to be much more successful as the top management itself is of sure of what is the best decision which it can impose authoritatively on the organisation members. An example is the Silicon Valley of United States which is inhabited by electronics firms. These firms have to rely greatly on a team oriented style of functioning and expert advise so that solid support of organisation members is available to the measurement to weather crises.

Top management support is an essential pre-requisite for the success of participative management. Although participation narrows the domain of a manager's power and is thereby resented by some managers, its long term positive impact must be realised. A failure on the part of the top management to lend whole hearted support to participation, as happened when the post office experiment was transplanted in Delhi, may seriously undermine the positive consequences of participation. Apart from top management support, it is essential that the prior acceptance of all those who are going to be affected by the introduction of participative management be ensured. The results of participation may not be immediate and spectacular. So patience is required in any programme for its implementation.

Another major hinderance to implementation of programmes of participative management is the dynamics of union politics. Union leaders often feel that their role as bargaining agents of the workers is being undermined and their power reduced, hence they often oppose such programmes in their own vested interest as had happened with the BHEL experiment.

In conclusion it may be stated that there is considerable scope for the implementation of participative management in all areas of governmental activity, though certain conditions are necessary for its success. Regarding the rationale for participation, considering our ideological commitment, to democracy, participative management may be considered as an end in itself, being the extension of the ideology of democracy to the sphere of social relations in a work sctting or organisation. At the same time it is essential to recognize that participative management does not in any way climinate the clash of interests between the workers and the management, which is fundamental and economic. It can only act as a palliative and since it does not really eliminate the basic clash of interests it can affect worker alienation only in a limited way.

BIBLIOGRAPHY

1. Alexander, KC—Participative Management, The Indian Experience, New Delhi, Shri Ram Centre for Industrial Relations and Human Resources, 1972.
2. Virmani, BR—Workers' Participation in Management, Delhi, The MaCmillan Company of India Ltd., 1978.
3. Boone, LC & Kurtz David L—Principles of Management, New York, Random House, Inc., 1981.
4. Carroll Jr, Paine, F and Miner JB—The Management Process, Cases and Readings, New York, The MaCmillan Com., 1973.
5. Chatterjee, NN—Management of Personnel in Indian Enterprises Calcutta Allred Book Agency, 1978.
6. Coates Ken—Can the Workers Run Industry, Great Britain, Chaucher Press Ltd., 1968.
7. Davis, Keith—Human Behaviour At Work, Organizational Behaviour, New Delhi, Tata McGraw Hill Publishing Co. Ltd., 1981.
8. De Nitish R—New Forms of Work, Organization in India—Submitted to Conditions of Work and Life Branch, International Labour Office, Geneva (n-d).
9. Deep Samuel, Human—Relations in Management, London, Glexcoe Publishing Co., Inc.—K-78.
10. Huneryager SG and Heckman IL—Human Relations in Management Ohis, South Western Publishing Company, 1967.
11. Koontz, H & O'Donnell Cyril—Management: A Book of Readings, New York, McGraw Bill Co., 1964.

12. Kosman, AK—Organizational Behaviour, Prentice Hall, 1971.

13. Margulies N and Raia, AP—Organizational Development: Values, Process, and Technology—New York, McGraw Hill, Inc. 1972.

14. Mathur, BC, Diesh K, Sekharan—Management in Government, New Delhi, Publications Division, 1979.

15. Pugh, DS—Organization Theory, New York, Penguin Books Ltd., 1971.

16. Sargent Howard, Fishbowl Management—A Participative Approach to Systematic Management, New York, John Wiley & Sons, 1978.

17. Sharma KC, Singh Harinder and Diesh K—Participative Design of the Work System, New Delhi, Human Resources Development Unit, Deptt. of Personnel & Admn. Reforms Min. of HA, 1978.

18. Sheth, NR—The Joint Management Council: Problems And Prospect New Delhi, Sri Ram Centre for Industrial Relations and Human Resources 1972.

19. Tanic, Zivan—Workers Participation in Management, N Delhi, Sri Ram Centre For Industrial Relations, 1969.

20. Thakur, CP, and Sethi KC—Industrial Democracy, Some Issues & Experiences, New Delhi, Sri Ram Centre for Industrial Relations and Human Resources, 1973.

Report of the Study Group on Worker Participation in Management, Delhi. Albion Press, 1957.

7

HUMANISATION OF WORK THROUGH UNION—MANAGEMENT COOPERATION

J.S. JOSEPH

Development of collaborative action between union and management with the specific purpose of humanising work without jeopardising their bargaining relationship is a neglected area of a action research. Only through a participative endeavour many aspects of prevailing working conditions could be changed for the better. This paper focuses on certain essential principles that should govern the cooperative relationship between the members of the management and the union. The need for an assessment of the existing quality of working life is emphasised. This is for having objective data on problems relating to working conditions and also perceptual data relating to similarities and differences among the members in the conception of the problem, goals and priorities and methods of improvement. Feed back of these findings coupled with experience based training workshops to help them learn "participative action" skills are also proposed as essential practical steps for building collaborative efforts.

The recent concern about improvement of working conditions or making work more human, a call of the

International Labour Organisation for improving the Quality of Working Life entails two related notions. First, it is a reiteration of the goals of job satisfaction, job security, job involvement and control, productivity, safety and health of people at work. Second, there is a re-emphasis of the need to have a systematic, rather than a piecemeal approach to achieve these goals.[1] While the total well-being of people at work at all levels should be the concern, the need for taking action to make work more human is seen differently by different interest groups. These expectations of outcomes could be grouped as work-related outcome such as job satisfaction, productivity, job involvement on the one hand and personal/social-related outcomes such as safety and health, personal development, security and general well-being of the people on the other. These two sets of expectations are based on conflicting needs, beliefs and value systems of, for example, workers or union leaders, employers or management, work science specialists and policy makers or Government. It is not denied that there may be some degree of overlap of concern between the interest groups.[2] However, the contention of this paper is that the realisation of the goal of humanisation of work will lag behind as before, unless the inevitable conflicts are resolved at the organisational level where actual changes should take place for betterment. Full participation of employers and workers and their organisations is an essential instrument for formulating goals and priorities for improving working conditions and environment[3]. A deliberate attempt in this regard at the unit level is a propitious step towards bringing about the required changes in the organisation for the total well-being of the people concerned, Psycho-social constraints and occupational hazards should be as much serious a concern of union and management as work compensation. While a culture of bargaining relationships prevails, is cooperation between union and management for the specific purpose of improving working conditions likely to coexist? In the absence of well thought out experiments in this regard, no definite answer can be given. However, experience gained so far with various schemes of workers' participation as well as findings of various studies and action research programmes in organisational development in our country and elsewhere suggest certain principles and steps for developing cooperation between union and management in humanising work.

The purpose of this paper is two fold:

(a) it is designed as the initial stage of launching field experiments in the area of improving working conditions and

(b) it is intended to be of some help to managers and union leaders as well as work science specialists in interpreting problems that they may encounter in their collaborative endeavour of changing the working conditions.

Launching Cooperative Projects on Humanisation of Work

Humanisation of work through cooperative endeavour between union and management calls for decisions and actions in a wider sphere of concern than what they are usually engaged in their bargaining relationship. As such, a reorientation of their relationship to achieve the goal humanisation of work is warranted. Past experience indicate that this reorientation will not automatically follow just because of constitutional or legal provisions. Industrial policy resolutions or executive orders at the national or even at the enterprise level regarding employees' participation in management. These measures may be useful to the extent of germinating a positive value concerning participation or cooperation and to make far reaching demands and nothing more.[4] What is required is to have a process of open communications within the organisation with a view to institutionalise and legitimise the concept of union-management cooperation in the area of humanisation of work. This involves detailed discussions among organization members on the concept and goals of humanisation of work and on cooperation as a means to achieve the objective and on how to go about it. Here, it is pertinent to note that what needs to be emphasised is that the goal of humanisation of work should be considered as an end in itself and cooperation or participation as the means of instrument to achieve it. Otherwise, the concept of workers' participation or union management cooperation would be viewed as a goal in itself leading to plurality of objectives and interpretations and the objective of humanisation of work would very likely recede to the background. If a workers' participation scheme is functioning in an organisation, humanisation of work as a special project should be initiated through that form. In other cases such a project shouid be launched within an organisation as a cooperative endeavour between union and management. In specific terms, launching of a project on humanisation of work as a cooperative endeavour between union and management involves the following[5]:

1. Establishment of a top level joint union-management committee to provide organisation-wide focus, sanction, support and viable commitment from the highest levels of union and management.
2. Developing by the said committee a document of agreement that establishes the structure of such committee and clauses to safeguard the interests of both union and management.
3. Identifying by the committee the broad goals and where pilot projects will be carried out and if necessary appointing humanisation of work committees at the work place or shop floor levels.
4. Developing by the committee its own goals and directions and appoint a third party consultant team to work with it for a specified period of time.

Launching of the project on humanisation of work in an organisation as noted above with union-management cooperation may take considerable time and energy, because getting a project underway using consensus decision-making process remains a slow and complex process. Much of the start up activity involves dealing separately with union and management leaders by a third party consultant prior to any joint discussions and once begun, joint discussions frequently continue for several months before a project is actually launched.

The process of discussions should be facilitated by conducting tailor-made training and development programmes for the members of the committee on group work, conflict management, group process analysis and feed back. This will be dealt with towards the end of this paper.

Past experience on the working of workers' participation in management indicates that the following principles should be borne in mind while developing cooperation between union and management in the area of humanisation of work. Flouting these principles has lead to the demise of cooperation between union and management in the past.

The Principle of Ensuring Freedom to Cooperate or Assert

Union and Management by tradition are conflicting interest groups and as such it is unreasonable to expect spontaneous cooperation on an all-encompassing area like humanisation of work. Quite often the sectorial interests come in class with what is objectively required to be done in order to humanise in a particular context and time. That is why a cooperative problem solving approach is warranted. If that is so, binding them together from without into a participative structure or framework alone may not lead to coopration between the two. If the parties do not feel a sense of freedom to withdraw their cooperation, and feel free to assert to get their interests protected, it is observed that the two groups feel insecure and take a competitive, avoidance or accommodative strategy rather than compromising or collaborative strategy in conflict resolution. Binding the two interest groups as an irrevocable alliance is a negation of the principle of responsible choice and freedom of intent on which the concept of coopration rests as an expression of free will, and because of which it has relevance. Given the prevailing socio-economic and political elimate in the country, where a capital controlled managerial srstem prevails, it is essential to leave the union unbound to the system, and make it feel free to cooperate with the management or assert itself to improve the work environment and make management accountable to this process.

Principle of Accepting Conflicts and Their Management

When an attempt is made to develop union-management cooperation one obvious outcome would be inter-intra conflicts among union and management leaders regarding their new roles, priorities, objectives and means. It may be noted that organisations require functional conflicts if they are to survive. But such conflicts are quite often considered as undesirable phenomena and as such ignored or suppressed. If the principle of conflicts and their management is accepted as inevitable, the other side of the conflict management coin-conflict stimulation should not be ignored.[6] Because, in the process of cooperative functioning between management and union in the area of humanisation of work, there may be situations in which conflict levels may be too low which could be a symptom indicating complacency or "group think" towards the task they are engaged in. Acceptance and management of role conflicts became all the more important just because union and management is moving from a bargaining relationship which should exist in traditional areas of confrontation to a cooperative stance which naturally leads to coflict generating changes in the quality and content of relationship between them. Non-acceptance and mismanagement of role conflicts among union and management members have retarded the growth of cooperative endeavour in many organisations.

Principle of Unity Regarding Objectives, Direction and Degree of Cooperation

As humanisation of work involves effective management of change, one of the important principles of management, namely, the managerial objectives and directions should be the same for all concerned—in this case for union and management leaders who are entrusted with a task—cannot be over emphasised. It is more easily said than done. Even if the purpose of cooperation between union and management is specified as humanisation of work union and management leaders have been found working at cross purposes, resulting in confusion and disappointments. In the past, divorce of interest-related issues, from work-related issues, as dictated under workers' participation scheme has caused a lot of problems in most of the organisations. Under cooperative projects of humanising work, the idea is to develop cooperation between union and management on areas other than the traditional bargainable issues in a particular industry and/or organisation. Then, the question arises which areas are considered as bargainable and which are those to be dealt under cooperative endeavour and who will decide about it? Past experience indicates that unless these issues, as a deliberate exercise, are taken by union and management leaders for satisfactory solution, unity of purpose and objective in their collaborative endeavour to effect the required changes in the working environment will not be attained. Coupled with the problem of deeiding about the area of cooperation on a consensus basis, is that of degree of cooperation that union and management leaders expect and are prepared to have on those areas between them. The question arises as to whether a particular area or issue, say, fixation of Production targets or change in job methods or a particular personnel policy would be dealt with through a joint decision making or information sharing or consultative processes or through assertion by the management and/or union. Reaching concensus regarding the scope of cooperation in terms of area and the manner in which they take decisions at a particular point of time should be a matter of concern to the union and management leaders for developing meaningful cooperation between them.

Principle of Third Party Intervention

Special efforts and strategies have to be evolved to form the joint committee on Humanisation of work projects specially because the forces working against cooperation between union and management are very many. Multiplicity of unions, the traditional adversory relationship between union and management, their conflicting goals, fear of loosing power and control over the other in the event of cooperation are a few to mention. How will be the committee constituted? Are the members nominated or elected? How many members should be from management and union and the like are some of the basic questions which require unbiased consideration. As these forces and problems are complex in nature, the services of a third party consulting team which is well versed in principles of group dynamics and organisational behaviour would be advantageous to sort out the issues and to identify the facilitating forces for cooperation by following a participative action research model of enquiry and action. The initial step by such a consulting team would be to have a series of discussions with union and management leaders separately prior to any joint discussions. Once the joint discussions are in the offing, the consultants have to ensure that principles enumerated above are followed by the managements, unions and the concerned members as a basis for developing cooperation and by working through and with the committee members. After a few initial meetings of the joint committee, the members are likely to clarify the rôle and scope of the committee on humanisation of work projects, and to realise the need for consensus decision. At the same time they tend to experience the need—(a) to identify the areas where improvement should take place for humanisation of work and to explore the ways and means of achieving it and (b) to improve their social and joint decision making skills. This searching and grouping behaviour of the committee members constitutes a critical stage in the development of a joint committee into a responsible forum for launching specific projects of improving working conditions in the organisation. To enable them to take consensus decisions on areas of mutual interest, two vital steps would be found necessary.

Assessment of and Feed Back on Working conditions

At this critical stage of committee's life as a joint decision making body on humanisation of work, the members begin to realise that the more subjective the reasons for a particular decision is at the union or management level, the greaterwould be the inclination on their part to hide both the decision and the information on which it is based. They also begin to appreciate the notion that action programmes and related decisions should be based on the evaluation of existing aspects of working conditions such as level of temperature, noise, vibration, energy expenditure, physical effort, mental stress and the like. While sophisticated instruments and methods are availabe to assess the physical conditions of work, such data obtained through work science specialists, even after having done the assessment with the support of the committee, may not always serve a very useful purpose. What is required to have is a simple but reliable and valid system of studying all the critical jobs simultaneously in terms of physical and psycho-social conditions of work in such a way that the relative stress levels of the jobs in respect of these conditions could be assessed by a representative task force of the people concerned. The task force members after having obtained adequate knowledge and skill through a short training should be able to assess the working conditions as noted above which will find more acceptance among the concerned people than otherwise. While such a method of assessment has not yet been developed in our country, an attempt by the experts in the areas concerned to assess working conditions through an action research strategy[7] will help the members to own the findings and decisions on action plans that are required for improving the existing quality of working life.

Sharing these hard data alone by the members of the joint committee may not help them to arrive at decisions about priorities of action. What they have to share in addition to hard data is the so called "soft data" relating to their frame of reference, opinions, feelings, perceptions and priorities and the like. In short, the following assessment package have been found useful for facilitating problem solution both at the group process level and task level.[8]

1. Hard data on physical working conditions.
2. Soft data which are subjective and relating to:
   (a) Management leaders' and union leaders' differential perception of importance relating to areas under humanisation of work in their organisation.

(b) their attitude towards cooperation.

(c) their mutual perception of abilities and willingness to participate on work related and interest related issues.

(d) evaluative assessment of the process of discussion at their meetings for joint decision making.

Training Workshop

The second step to make the joint committee function as a cohesive and effective decision making body is that of conducting tailor made training programmes on social skills, conflict resolution, team work and cooperation for the benefit of its members. The soft data noted above will form the subject of their study and deliberations to increase their awareness about the human problems in small group working and joint decision making. A training workshop model which was found useful to achieve these learning objectives may be seen in the Figure. This model lays emphasis on feed back of "soft data" as well as group process evaluation "to shock the actors in a system into a reappraisal of their commonsense view of their own situation"[9] and help them to develop social skills required for effectiveness in cooperative working relationship.

In the process of discussions by the members of the joint committee on aspects relating to their own perception (soft data) and working conditions, relevant skills required for decision making could be brought out. Thus, instead of having a teacher-taught learning model, the knowledge, the skill and attitude which are required for effective functioning of the cooperative forum could be learnt by its members during the workshop, through discussions, role plays, exercises and feedback process as an experience based learning exercise.

Conclusion

Improvement of working conditions or humanisation of work even in the organised sector has not kept pace with the knowledge and technology of work sciences which are presently

An Experiential Learning Model for Facilitating Humanisation of Work

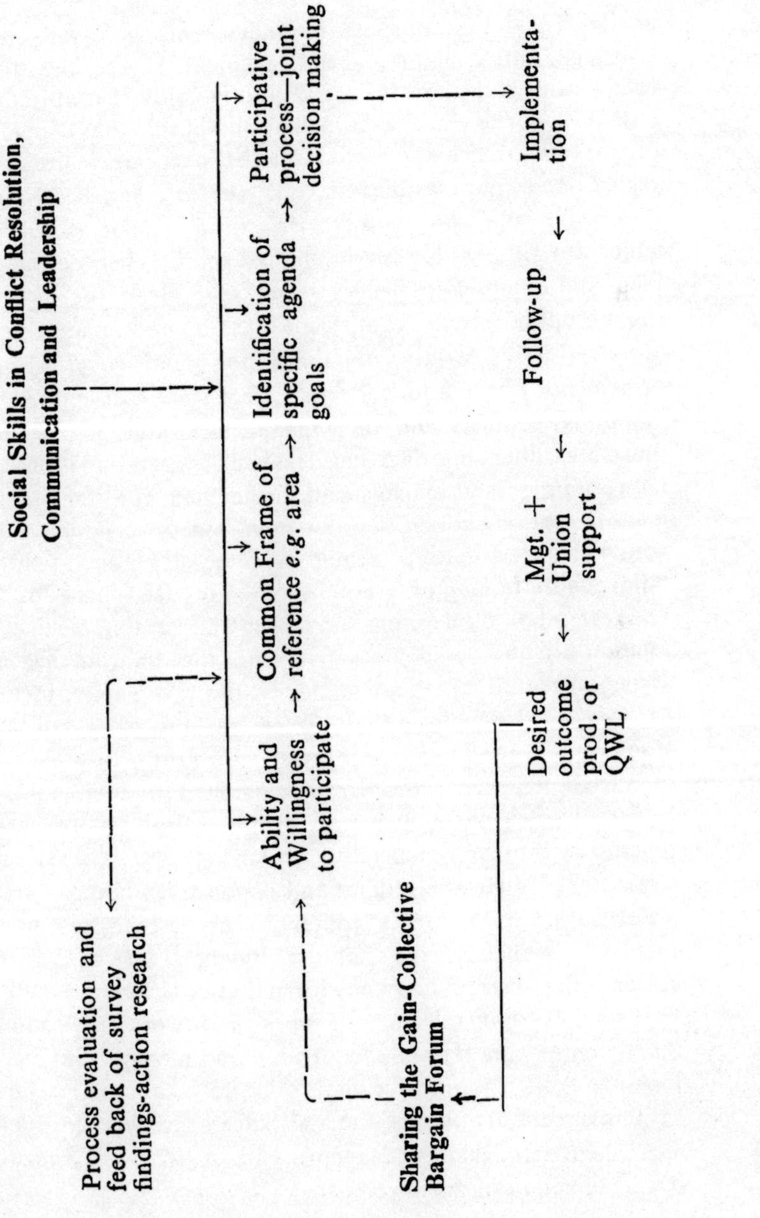

available for that purpose in India. This gap will remain unbridged unless union and management at the organisation level came together to work jointly with the objective of humanising the work environment and decide that cooperation of workers' participation would be the means or instrument to realise it. Major hurdles in this venture has been lack of knowledge and skill and proper attitude among all concerned which are required for developing cooperation between management and union. Experiences show that given the prevailing socio-economic and democratic system and climate in the country, a cooperative relationship which is governed by the principle of freedom to cooperate or assert, the principle of accepting conflicts and their management and the principle of unity regarding objectives and degree of cooperation is necessary between union and management in the long run for improvement of working conditions and environment as a joint endeavour. This relationship should also be strengthened through tailor-made training programmes based on feed back of hard and soft data on working conditions and existing participative relationship and by integrating it with the total management system. Because of the complexity of the dynamics involved, experiences also indicate that engaging a third party consulting team who is well versed in *inter-intra* group dynamics and organisational behaviour by the joint union-management leaders to help them overcome the initial problems of working together will prove beneficial in the long run. It is needless to stress that systematic studies and action research programmes are necessary in the Indian context to understand the process involved in making the full use by the people concerned of research findings and new knowledge that are being accumulated in the area of humanisation of work and work environment. Such attempts are far and few. Union and management at the local or unit level are the vital forces to take initiative jointly in this direction, and seek the assistance of work scientists and technologists in their endeavour. This paper is intended to stimulate action in this direction

NOTES AND REFERENCES

1. Ursula Engelen—Kefer: Humanisation of work in the Federal Republic of Germany—A labour oriental approach, International Labour Review, Vol. 113, No. 2, March-April, 1976.

2. See Ishwar Dayal: "Pre-requisite of Workers' Involvement in work organisation" in Readings in Management, Edited by Joshi, N.C. and Kesary, V.G. Allahabad, Wheeler; 1980, p. 166.

3. Givry, Jean de: The ILO and the quality of Working Life. A new international programme: PIACT, International Labour Review? Vol. 117, No. 3 May-June, 1978.

4. Bertil Gardell: Production Techniques and working conditions, Current Sweden, Stockhelm, Swedish Institute, August, 1980, p. 16.

5. Based on Edward E. Lawler III and Lee Ozley "Willing Union Management Cooperation on Quality of Worklife Projects" Management Review, AMACOM, March 1979.

6. Stephen P. Robbins: Conflict "Management and Conflict Resolution are not synonymous Terms", California Management Review, Vol. XXI, No. 2, 1978.

7. The term includes not only an approach but also strategies having client, research and consultant roles as discussed by Keith E. Thurby in Planned change in Bureaucratic organisations. International Studies of Management and Organisation, International Arts and Sciences Press, New York, Fall 1971.

8. J.S. Joseph: A Study on Making Workers' Participation Effective—Developmental factors from within and A Training Workshop Design. Industrial Psychology Division, C.L.I., Bombay 1977.

9. Keith E. Thurley: *Ibid.*

8

GOVERNMENT—PUBLIC ENTERPRISES RELATIONS IN INDIA: SOME ASPECTS

R.R. IYER

I

Public enterprises have taken two main forms in India: they are either statutory corporations set up by Acts of Parliament or companies registered under the Indian Companies Act. Only a few public enterprises fall into the first category; most are of the second kind. Soon after it, emergence as a free country, India decided on an important role for the public sector in the planned development of the country. At a later stage, it became the declared policy of the Government that the public sector should occupy the "commanding heights" of the economy. This called for the establishment, over a period of time, of a large number of industrial and commercial enterprises in the public sector covering a wide range of activities. It was in this context that at an early stage the device of establishing such enterprises as companies under the Indian Companies Act was adopted. This device has facilitated the establishment of numerous industrial and commercial enterprises in the public sector without making them departmental units within the Government. Though some differences arise from the two alternative forms mentioned, namely statutory corporations and government companies, the differences in terms of the relationship with the Government are not very significant.

The mode of financing of public enterprises has been determined by the organizational form which they have taken: government investment is in the form of share-capital and long-term loans. In other words, the Government plays the role of entrepreneur-cum-investor as well as that of a development banker to public enterprises. For their working capital requirements, public enterprises are ideally expected to depend on their bankers, though there are cases in which finance to cover working capital needs or cash deficits is provided by the Government, or bank finance is facilitated through government guarantees. Each public enterprise is under the "administrative control" of a Ministry in the Government of India, which is responsible for the enterprise and is answerable to Parliament for its performance. Further, as the agency responsible for the planned development and regulation of certain sectors of the economy, the Ministry would be interested in and concerned with the public enterprises in those sectors as units in the industry as a whole. Many of the concerns of the Ministry are shared by or form part of those of the Ministry of Finance and the Planning Commission. There is also the Bureau of Public Enterprises which undertakes a coordinated overview of the performance and problems of the public sector and brings out periodical reports on these.

These varying stands in the relationship between the Government and public enterprises, namely, the Government as owner, the Government as planner, investor and development banker, the Government as regulator, the Government as the Executive answerable to Parliament for the public enterprise: all these are seflected in a network of formal and informal controls and institutional arrangements. The Articles of Association of public enterprises usually provide for certain kinds of governmental approvals; for instance, for approval to the capital budget and for the sanctioning of capital expenditure proposals beyond certain financial limits. There is also usually a provision for the issue of directives by the Government, though this is rarely invoked. Even without a provision in the Articles of Association, the capital budget and the major investment proposals of public enterprises are bound to come to the Government because they are incorporated in the overall national Plan and substantial investments of government funds are usually involved. The governmental planning and budgeting processes thus become instrumentalities of control over public enterprises. The third instrumentality is through the exercise of the Government's powers for the constitution of the Board of Directors and for the appointment of the Chief Executive as well as the full-time 'functional' Directors. Thus the public enterprise has to go to the Govenment for its top-level appointments, for the approval and funding its capital budget, for the appraisal and approval of its major projects, and in a sense even for its long-term corporate planning as this is integrally related to the Five Year Plan formulation. Where there is a system of administered pricing, the public sector enterprise has to go to the Government for pricing decisions as well.

In relation to the public enterprises, the Ministry also plays a role which is not easily subsumed undcr either its role as owner or its role as regulator: there is yet another role which might be called a 'managerial' role. There are periodical performance reviews covering production and financial performance costs, profitability, sales, inventories, the progress of projects, and so on. This kind of monitoring and reviewing cannot be described as a shareholder's function; nor is it merely a means of ensuring public accountability: it is the kind of function that a holding company might perform *vis-a-vis* its subsidiaries. That is why it is in the nature of a 'managerial' function. As regards the aspect of public accountability, the instrumentalities here are Parliament Quesiions, the Budget Debate, audit by the Comptroller and Auditor General of India and reviews by Parliamentary Committees.

That was a broad overview of the kind of relationship that prevails between the Government and public enterprises in this country. When we lock back upon the manner in which this has evolved, it is possible to describe this as a process of reluctant venture, or of 'one step forward, two steps back'. Initially it was felt that certain activities and functions could not be readily performed by governmental organizations and that something akin to business concerns was necessary. The Industrial Policy Resolution of 1956 recognised the need to provide freedom of management to public enterprises and to ensure that they were run on business lines. However, there has also been a tendency over the years to curtail that freedom of management. On the one hand, there is the recognition that business operations are not best conducted through government departments, and that a separate entity needs to be established which can function on businesslike lines; the usually tacit but sometimes explicit intention is to keep such organizations at an arm's length from the Government and to grant them freedom of management for businesslike functioning. On the other hand, the importance of the purposes in view and the consequences of the operations of a public enterprise for the economy in general and the government budget in particular, mean a continuing governmental interest and involvement in the functioning of the enterprise; and the Governments finds itself unable to accept the logic of the organizational form it has given to the enterprise and let the managers manage. Soon after a public enterprise is established and distanced from the Government, a reverse process sets in, of reducing that distance and trying to bring the enterprise more and more within the ambit of governmental influence and overseeing. This has been particularly marked in India.

II

The relationship between the Government and public enterprises is a subject on which there has been a considerable amount of discussion and debate. Issues have been variously formulated as "autonomy vs. accountability", civil service culture vs. industrial culture", and so on. Unfortunately, there are conflicting criticisms and prescriptions, and it is usually possible to match each one by its opposite. For instance, some public enterprises have been criticised for making losses and others have been criticised for making excessive profits; public enterprises have been criticised for being bureaucratic, inflexible and slow of response to changing situations, and also for being too free and easy, ignoring procedures, and not documenting their decisions properly.

A discussion of such matters often runs into difficulties because of a lack of fundamental clarity in regard to the issues involved and the tendency to accept too readily certain general statements without a rigorous examination. One such proposition is that public enterprises are "public" institutions, established to serve "public policies and purposes"; that they must therefore be under constant surveillance and control by the parent Ministries and other governmental agencies; and that in the circumstances an "arm's-length" relationship is not really feasible. The argument seems superficially plausible, but a closer examination will show the hidden fallacies. Public enterprises are of course "public" institutions; but they are also enterprises. That public enterprises have both a "public" dimension and an "enterprise" dimension is now a commonplace; indeed, it seems almost trite. Unfortunately, though the distinction itself is often repeated, it does not seem to enter into and influence the thinking of people on this subject as much as one would expect it to. In other words, the distinction is perhaps not so very trite, and could bear reiteration. To state the obvious, then: public enterprises are often set up as separate entities outside the normal government system precisely because they are expected to function in a manner unfamiliar to Government departments; this logic cannot be negated by any sophistries of argument. If freedom of management cannot be granted and if an 'arm's-length' relationship between enterprises and the Government is not feasible, and if there is bound to be constant governmental involvement, intervention and interference in the operations of public enterprises, then the "enterprise dimension" disappears altogether, and the raison d'etre for the establishment of a public enterprise (as distinguished from running the operations departmentally) gets undermined.

A second proposition often put forward as axiomatic is that public enterprises must realize that the demand for autonomy must be moderated by considerations of accountability. That sounds very reasonable. We frequently hear references to the need for a balance between autonomy and accountability. However, a little reflection will indicate the unsoundness of assuming that there is a conflict between autonomy and accountability, that these pull in opposite directions, and that a balance needs to be found between the two. A better understanding of the matter would be facilitated by a different metaphor, namely, that autonomy and accountability are the obverse and reverse of the same coin. That may sound paradoxical, but is not really so. Autonomy is not an end in itself; not only writers on management but even the managers themselves urge the grant of autonomy to the Management, not for its own sake but for the purpose of enabling them to achieve the assigned tasks. Autonomy then has a purpose in view; and that purpose is what the manager has to be accountable for. Autonomy thus implies accountability, which in turn is accountability for something, whether it be the results which were expected to be achieved or even the means and processes adopted towards the achievement of those results. Clearly, this is an ex-post facto concept: a manager has to act before he can be held accountable for his actions. Clearly also, he can be held accountable only for his own actions and not someone else's. When managerial autonomy in public enterprises is abridged by the Government, accountability gets simultaneously abridged. Autonomy is thus a prerequisite for accountability. To sum up this point, autonomy is purposeless and unacceptable without accountability, but accountability is meaningless without autonomy. In this understanding there is no conflict between the two: the two terms go together. The real antonym of "autonomy" is not "accountability" but "control".

III

Among the numerous links and mechanisms which bring Government and enterprises closer together and narrow the arm's-length distance which was the original objective of establishing enterprises qua enterprises, one is via governmental officials nominated to the Boards of Directors of enterprises. There have been two views in regard to this matter. One is that the concept of an arm's-length relationship means that there should be no government officials on the public enterprise Boards, which should be constituted entirely of (a) full-time Directors with responsibility for certain functions and (b) others (part-time Directors) with industrial, technological, professional or other relevant experience, drawn from appropriate sources outside the Government. The other is that given the multiplicity of objectives cast on the public enterprises and the importance of many of these from the point of view of governmental policies, the nomination of government officials to the Board of Directors of public enterprises provides a very useful link between public enterprise managements and Government; and further, that given the complexities of modern industry and business, it is very desirable and nseful for Government officials with responsibility for dealing with such matters at their desks in Government to have first-hand knowledge and experience of the actual problems, needs and requirements of industry and commerce, which can be obtained only through participation in Board meetings.

This is a complex and difficult question. While official directorships can be a very useful link, if properly used, the case for removing this link can be argued. We need not go into this here beyond noting that if it is necessary and desirable for some Government officials to function as Directors on the Boards of public enterprises, they must clearly understand that they are functioning partly as members of the top corporate management of the enterprise; that their watchdog function should not be over-emphasized to the extent of creating an adversory relationship between them and the other Directors; that their role should be primarily one of facilitating and not hindering the proceedings of the Board: and lastly, that they should as far as possible avoid the paradox of taking one position on the Board and another at their desk in the Government. It would in fact be in the fitness of things for Government itself to spell out these matters in a clear charter for their official nominees on the Boards of Directors of public enterprises.

IV

Let us turn now to the question of coordination. The need for coordination among or in relation to public enterprises can arise at different levels and for different purposes, but this paper will deal with only two of these issues.

The first is the question of coordination among a number of public enterprises in the same industry or engaged in the same line of activity. This is a much-discussed subject. For instance, if there were a number of steel plants in the public sector and each was a separate corporate entity, there could be need for some coordination in regard to raw materials and transportation partly to even out the supplies of scarce materials and partly to avoid unnecessary cross movements. Under some circumstances marketing might also to be a coordinated effort. Production planning with reference to market demand and the marketing strategy might also involve interplant coordination. Pricing policy is another matter in respect of which coordination might become necessary. In fact, when there is a cluster of public enterprises in any particular sector of the economy some degree of sectoral coordination might be called for. One method of securing this, which has been tried out in different countries, is the establishment of sectoral corporations with individual companies as their subsidiaries. The usefulness of sectoral corporations or holding companies, their effectiveness as a pattern of management for public enterprises, and the extent to which they can take over the sectoral coordination responsibilities of the Ministry concerned, are large questions which cannot be gone into here.

The second is the question of coordination at the governmental level in relation to public enterprises as a whole. Is there a case for a central coordinating machinery to monitor public enterprises, articulate the Government's relationship and policies towards public enterprises as a whole and in general function as a "focal point" in the Government-public-enterprise relationship? The subject was debated at considerable length at a Round Table on the theme of "Focal Point" which was held under the auspices of the International Centre for Public Enterprises and some other international organizations at Ljubljana, Yugoslavia in July 1984. There seemed to be general agreement regarding the need for some central coordinating agency in Government in relation to the totality of public enterprises. Considering the number and diversity of public enterprises and the magnitude of the public investment in them, an agency of some kind is certainly needed for performing certain coordinating and facilitating functions: providing for a transfer experience from one public enterprise to another, acting as a clearing house of ideas; assisting the Government in the formulation of policies applicable to public enterprises as a whole; interpreting the Government to the public enterprises and *vice versa*; and functioning as a storehouse of information. However, the stress here should be on coordination and facilitation and not on control.

V

One important strand in the relationship between the Government and public enterprise is audit by the supreme audit institution. Broadly speaking the pattern in India is that of a primary audit carried out by the statutory auditors of the Company or Corporation (*i.e.*, the auditors appointed in terms of the Companies Act or in terms of the provisions of the statute establishing the Corporation), followed by a supplementary or super-imposed audit by the Comptroller and Auditor General of India. The supplementary audit by the C & AG involves both a check of the adequacy of the audit done by the commercial auditors and a supplementary of that audit by way of test-checks on the accounts and transactions. The results of the C & AG's audit of a public enterprise are communicated in three forms:

(a) comments on the accounts which have to be placed before the Annual General Meeting along with the accounts and the primary auditor's report;

(b) comments on individual transactions or cases which appear as paragraphs in what is known as the C & AG's Commercial Audit Report; and

(c) a comprehensive review of selected schemes, activities or operations of a particular enterprise, or indeed of an enterprise as a whole.

There have been differences of views regarding the scope and style of the C & AG's audit of public enterprises in India. It has been argued that the audit control in this country bears down too heavily on public enterprise managements, particularly has they have to go through two audits and have the accounts considered twice by the Board of Directors, and then place the accounts and audit reports before the Annual General Meeting before the final date stipulated under Company Law; and that the C & AG's Organization should leave the normal cycle of accounting and audit to the Chartered Accountants (as in the case of private sector companies) and confine itself to overall reviews and appraisals. However, such views have not prevailed, and the arrangements for the audit of public enterprises in India continue on the lines already indicated.

Another issue to be considered in this context is that where the supreme audit institution in a country undertakes the audit of the operations of public enterprises, the action and decisions of the managers tend to come under *ex post facto* scrutiny. That is in the very nature of the audit function. Nevertheless, it is a function which needs to be performed with great circumspection. There can be some question as to whether this *ex post facto* scrutiny should be confined to the overall results achieved with reference to the assigned tasks, or should also go into the soundness of individual actions and decisions. Even assuming that isolated actions and decisions, contracts, purchases, and so on should come under audit review, the question still remains as to what would constitute the legitimate kind of audit comment. If the audit comment consists in pointing out that a particular decision or action was taken without a full consideration of all the relevant facts, or that it was based on wrong assumptions or incomplete or inaccurate data, or that it was manifestly absurd or perverse, then that would be a fair comment against which the management cannot reasonably complain. On the other hand, if there is evidence of a proper process of consideration before a decision or action was taken, and the audit comment questions the soundness of the decision or implies that a better decision was possible, then that would amount to the expression of opinion or the wisdom of hindsight or the substitution of the auditor's judgement for that of the manager. This could have the effect of undermining the confidence of the executive and the manager and making him unwilling to assume responsibility and take action or decisions on a future occasion. When this happens, audit which ought to be an *ex posr facto* activity virtually becomes an *ex ante* control.

This is true also of what in India is referred to as the 'vigilance' machinery. This is yet another *ex post facto* control which has the potential of having an *ex ante* influence on managerial action. The need for a machinery to look into cases of alleged impropriety, misconduct or corrupt practices is evident; what is difficult is to ensure that this machinery does not operate in such a way as to have an intimidating effect on managerial decision-making or executive action.

VI

It may not be inappropriate to make a passing reference at this stage to the question of judicial review. There have been a few cases in which there have been observations of the courts regarding the nature of public enterprises and their relationship to the Government. In brief, these amount to treating a public enterprise as an extension or arm of the State. One consequence of such a view will be that procedures and modalities of the functioning of public enterprises should be similar to those of the Government. If this process is carried far enough, it will tend to emphasise the 'public' dimension of public enterprises to the detriment or indeed the negation of the 'enterprise' dimension, and will eventually obliterate the distinction between

Government departments and public enterprises. A second consequence of such a view is that whereas an aggrieved employee or disgruntled contractor can go to courts against the management of a private sector company only on the basis of the terms of the appointment order or the contract, he can go to the courts against the managements of public enterprises in the same way as against the State, that is, on the basis of the Articles of the Constitution and the provisions for writs. If these trends are carried to their logical conclusion, the device of a government company or corporation, as a mechanism for enabling a style of functioning akin to business rather than Government, would have failed; and the position will be that the Government can function only through government departments and in accordance with the modalities, procedures and styles appropriate to the government machinery. This may not be the position today, but there is a distinct possibility of such a situation developing in this country. It needs to be examined whether a legal view to the effect that government companies and corporations are no different from government departments and should function exactly like these is prevalent in any other country. This is a very important matter which deserves study by the Ministries concerned with public enterprises, the Bureau of Public Enterprises, the Law Ministry and management institutions.

VII

Let us now pass on to yet another strand in the Government-enterprise relationship, namely, monitoring. Considering the important objectives and purposes for which public enterprises are set up, and the magnitude of public funds invested in them, the need for governmental monitoring can be taken for granted; what we need to consider would be questions such as what should be monitored, what kind of information system is needed for this purpose, who should do the monitoring, what should be the periodicity of and institutional arrangements for monitoring and what the monitoring should lead to.

Unfortunately, there is often far too much information of diverse kinds, not all of it useful, flowing into different Ministries and agencies in the Government from public enterprises. Under such circumstances, there are two dangers. One is that the enormous inflow of information into the Government disappears into files and cabinets and that it is not studied, much less responded to. This is not a monitoring system at all; it is merely a waste of stationery, office space and managerial time. The mere fact that reports and returns of all kinds are flowing into the Government does not mean that a monitoring system exists.

The other danger is that the over-abundant information that comes in is subjected to bureaucratic scrutiny, questions are raised and correspondence started leading to further demands on managerial time; and that far too many meetings are held for the ostensible purpose of monitoring public enterprises and sectoral developments but in effect providing the Ministries and other agencies in Government with an occasion to get involved in the details of the day-to-day administration and operations of the enterprise, asking questions about matters which ought to be entirely within the sphere of the top management of the enterprise. This goes far beyond the needs of any monitoring. The manager's time tends to get taken up more and more with the preparation and submission of numerous reports and returns and attending meetings in the Ministries; and he has less and less time for his managerial responsibilities proper. The Government on the other hand gets more and more involved in the affairs of the enterprise and virtually tends to run it. We would do well to keep in mind the salutary principle that the Government must monitor and not seek to manage public enterprises.

It is necessary to remember in this context that any well-managed public enterprise must have an internal monitoring system. Monitoring has to be done at various levels for various purposes. To the extent that there is a good monitoring system within an organization, which serves the purposes of the top management of the enterprise, that system should have in it elements which ought to be able to meet the requirements of governmental monitoring, without a fresh expenditure of executive time and energies on data collection or tabulation. However, monitoring by the top management is bound to be far more detailed and managerial than monitoring by the Government. This distinction ought to be kept in mind, and in laying down an information system for monitoring Governments should not expect the same degree and depth of information as is made available to the Board of Directors.

VIII

Finally, we come to the question of the evaluation of the performance of public enterprises, which is an important aspect of the government-enterprise relationship. In India, we have been toying with different ideas in this regard from time to time. At one time there was an attempt to introduce the concept of a targeted rate of return, a system which the British have tried. Under this system a rate of return is prescribed or laid down, having regard to various factors that are likely to have an effect on performance, and then the public enterprise is judged by its ability to achieve that prescribed or targeted rate of return. It may not be entirely easy for us to adopt this method for the reason that it assumes a degree of autonomy on the part of public enterprises, which is not available in this country. If we are going to prescribe a rate of return to a public enterprise, we should prescribe nothing else, we should leave the enterprise free to take appropriate managerial decisions and function freely in a businesslike manner without interference or intervention and hold it accountable for only one thing, namely, the achievement of the prescribed rate of return. That is not the kind of relationship which prevails in this country between the Government and public enterprises. Besides, under the conditions prevailing in this country a purely financial yardstick is not an adequate measure of performance. We shall probably have to adopt a number of physical indicators of performance such as production, capacity utilization, consumption efficiencies. and so on. It may be added that production by itself may not be an adequate measure of performance either, if it means merely the accumulation of large unsold stocks.

Sometime in 1980 the Bureau of Public Enterprises held a workshop at Ahmedabad which was attended by some Secretaries to Government and Chief Executives of public enterprises, to consider the question of evolving a performance criteria model for public enterprises. After a consideration of the proceedings of the workshop in consultation with the Ministries, the Bureau issued in due course a document entitled 'A Performance Criteria Model for Public Enterprises', which attempts to lay down some agreed targets, both financial and physical, with reference to which performance will eventually be assessed. While the effort was commendable, it cannot be said that this document represents a significant advance in the effort to evolve a new model for performance evaluation.

Currently an attempt is being made to adopt a modified version of the French system of a performance contract or agreement between the Government and public enterprises in certain sectors. It must be noted that what this system involves is really the definition of the entire relationship between the Government and public enterprises and not primarily a question of performance evaluation. Under this system agreements are entered into by which the public enterprise binds itself to a whole range of performance targets and the Government in turn binds itself to do its bit in the form of compensation for non-commercial obligations, investment authorizations, subsidization at the agreed level (where this is envisaged as part of the agreement), and what is more important than anything else, non-intervention except as indicated in the agreement. The interesting element here is that the Government recognizes that its own actions and omissions have an important impact on the performance of public enterprises, and so the system is not merely one of the Government laying down goals and targets to be achieved by the public enterprise managements, but rather one of a mutual agreement between the Government and an enterprise with each undertaking certain responsibilities and obligations. We shall have to see how the experiment works in India.

The evaluation of the performance of public enterprises is a subject which is currently engaging a good deal of attention internationally. The Public Enterprise Management Unit of the World Bank is deeply interested in this question; so also is the International Centre for Public Enterprises in Developing Countries at Ljubljana, Yugoslavia. Any discussion of this subject tend to go into questions of methodology, techniques, criteria, indicators, and so on. The problem of performance evaluation in relation to public enterprises in developing countries is generally perceived as a methodological problem demanding technical solutions. But the essential problem with the evaluation of the performance of public enterprises is not so much a methodological or technical one, as one of getting the public enterprises managements and the national Government to agree on what needs to be evaluated, facilitate an objective evaluation, make the necessary data and information freely available, face the hard issues involved and not shy away from them or take refuge in detensive justification or *ex post facto* excuses and rationalisations, and lastly accept the findings that emerge from the evaluation exercise and undertake the necessary consequential actions. Further, it is necessary to provide a tool which can be used by administrators in the Government and public enterprise managers, with a modicum of technical or expert assistance; taking care to see that the technical content of the evaluation exercise does not become so predominant or complex or sophisticated as to be only intelligible to and usable by high-order specialists (mathematicians, econometrists or computer scientists). The evaluation of the performance of public enterprises is a practical managerial activity to be performed by the top management of the enterprise itself and by the senior administrators in the Ministries concerned with public enterprises; it has to be performed effectively; and it has to be intelligible to the legislature and to the general public.

The difficulty is that in most cases there is no clear charter for a public enterprise, setting out the objectives behind its establishment and the goals and tasks assigned to it by governmental agencies or adopted by the management, which can be taken as the basis for an evaluation of performance. It will be very useful if the Government, when deciding on the establishment of a new public enterprise or approving a major investment decision on a new project or scheme proposed by an existing enterprise, could provide the new enterprise or projects or programmes with a charter setting out clearly and comprehensively the aims, objectives and expections. With reference to such a primary charter from the Government, the top management of each public enterprise should in turn be expected to adopt a corporate statement of goals and aims. If it could be ensured that such documents invariably exist at least in the future the task of evaluation will become enormously simpler.

Meanwhile, the first stage of an evaluation exercise has to be the construction of a statement or checklist of objectives, goals, aims and expectations—a kind of presumed charter for the enterprise. This should not be unduly difficult. In each case there would be a range of objectives, primary, secondary, tertiary, and so on, on the part of the Government, the management and other agencies concerned, and a variety of expectations on the part of diverse groups. Through a study of documents and through discussions with the persons and agencies concerned it should be possible to compile fairly quickly a brief checklist of the important objectives, goals, aims and expectations with reference to which an evaluation will be attempted. The effort should be to concentrate on essentials and to keep the checklist reasonably short. Having built up a presumed charter for an enterprise on these lines, the process of evaluation should consist in turning each one of the explicit or implicit goals, aims and expectations into a question which need to be answered with reference to the relevant facts. There will have to be, broadly speaking, an evaluation of (a) financial performance, (b) physical performance, (c) economic performance and (d) performance with reference to non-financial, non-economic goals and objectives, that is, the so-called "social objectives". The different parts of the evaluation exercise could finally be brought together in an overall evaluation report.

IX

What has been attempted in this paper is to indicate briefly in outline certain aspects and focts of the relationship between the Government and public enterprises and the issues that have come up for consideration, particularly in the Indian context. In the process, an effort has been made to clear up some misconceptions and indicate the right approaches and institutional arrangements in respect of matters such as control, monitoring, coordination and evaluation. The paper will conclude by placing before the reader for their consideration a paradigm of a healthy relationship between the Government and public enterprises. As the writer sees it, it will be a relationship in which the Government is clear about what it wants from a public enterprise and makes it clear to the enterprise; selects the managers carefully and lets them manage subject to an eventual answerability for their actions; monitors the functioning of the enterprise but does not seek to manage it; insists on accountability but appreciates that there is no adverse relationship between accountability and autonomy and that the one requires the other; endeavours to ensure that the coordinating machinery, if one is established, does not become one more regulatory bureaucracy; institutes arrangements for a periodical professional evaluation of the performance of the enterprise with reference to the aims and objectives behind its establishment, the corporate goals and tasks, and the (reasonable) expectations of various governmental and other bodies and groups which have an interest in the operations of the enterprise; and is willing to accept the findings emerging out of an objective evaluation and take the appropriate actions. It is perhaps naive and unrealistic to expect to find actual instances of such a relationship but it is only by postulating a sound relationship that we can hope to get even halfway towards it.

9

TRANSACTIONAL ANALYSIS AND CONSCIENTIZATION

P. BHATTACHARYA AND S.K. SEN

The Social Situation

In India, as in all under-developed and developing nations, the social situation can be seen in terms of two polarised groups; the Oppressors and the Oppressed. What makes the existential predicament of the Oppressed all the more inevitable in this country is the heavy cultural scripting with the weight of several millenia behind it. Assuming the Bernean Cultural Script model as an axiom, we seek to apply it to the Indian situation. In T.A. theory, the P1 in C2—the electrode, or the Pig Parent—plays a dominant role in determining the script-decision early in life. In cultural terms, this can be exemplified in India by the Gajendramoksha myth and the Avatarhood belief which appear to obssess the Scheduled Castes, Tribes and other backward and depressed classes, extending upwards to include the bourgeoisie.

The Myth and the Belief

Long long ago in a dense forest lived a huge white elephant with four gleaming tusks. This elephant was an ardent devotee of Lord Vishnu, the Preserver, and he used to worship his God with lotus offerings plucked from a lake in the forest. In this lake dwelt a massive marsh crocodile who detested the elephant. One day when the elephant had stepped in a little too far into the lake to pluck a lotus, the crocodile clamped his jaws around his leg and began to drag him into the deepest recesses of the waters. Finding that struggle were of no avail; the elephant prayed fervently to Vishnu, who appeared and slew the crocodile to liberate his devotee. By Vishnu's grace, the elephant was restored to his original form as a king who had been turned into an elephant by the curse of a sage.

The Belief is summed up in two slokas from the Gita, IV. 7-8:

> When Dharma fades and adharma flourishes, I lose myself forth into birth. To deliver the good, to destroy the wicked. To establish Dharma. I am born from age to age.

Taken together, the belief modifies the myth into a pattern of passivity which could be described as Waiting for Godot: the Oppressed, unlike the elephant, do not even struggle because they "know" it is ineffectual, and wait for the descent on the Avatara, which does not take place in their lifetime.

The situation has been succinctly projected by Seymour Lipset in Political Man (New York, 1960, p. 66): "The poorer a country and the lower the absolute standard of living of the lower classes, the greater the pressure on the upper strata to treat the lower as vulgar, innately inferior, a lower caste beyond the pale of human society . . . . the upper strata in such a situation tend to regard political rights for the lower strata, particularly the right to share power, as essentially absurd and immoral."

The Oppressed Script

Paulo Freire who formulated the concept of Conscientization described the Oppressed as typically a Massified Society, *i.e.*, a people manipulated by the elite, using Oppression or assistencialism (policies for the symptoms not the roots of social ills), into an unthinking, manageable agglomeration with the centres of economic and political decisions located outside the Oppressed society, Erich Fromn, in Escape from Freedom (New York, 1956, p. 4) adds another aspect to this picture when he writes that Man is not free to act because he is unaware of his needs, thoughts and feelings because; "He conforms to anonymous authorities and adopts a self which is not his. The more he does this, the more powerless he feels, the more is he forced to conform......modern man is overcome by a profound feeling of powerlessness which makes him gaze toward approaching catastrophes as though he were paralyzed."

In T.A. terms massification implies:

1. Exclusion of the Adult Ego State. The Massified Society is incapable of formulating autonomous projects to solve its problems, but constantly looks up to the elite for solutions transplanted from outside which, inevitably, fail.

2. Missing Parent Ego State (cf. Francis Jayapathy, Tasi Darshan 1.6, p. 229) *i,e.*, the Oppressed keep turning to the Oppressor for all their Parental strokes. Their typical behaviour is limited to the Complaint Child ego state (fig. 9.1).

3. Symbiosis between the Parent Ego State of the Oppressor and the Child Ego State of the Oppressed (fig. 9.2). On a second-order level, the symbolic relationship is between the Critical Parent of the Oppressor and the Complaint Child of the Oppressed. In terms of the Myth and the Belief, this can be described as the Gajendra-Vishnu and devotee-Avatara relationship: the one does not exist without the other, and together they make a whole.

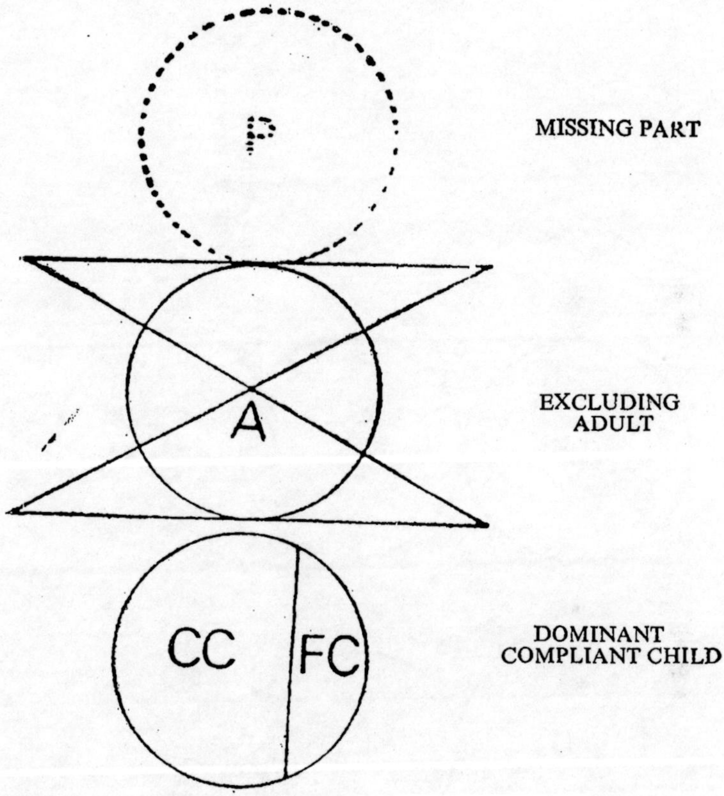

Fig. 9.1

4. A strong contamination of the Adult Ego State of the Oppressed by the P1 in the Child Ego State, *i.e.*, by the Electrode or the Pig Parent, where the Myth is looked in (fig. 9.3).

5. Passive behaviour of all four types is a consequence:
   (a) Doing nothing: the "culture of silence" among the Oppressed;
   (b) Over-adaptation: resulting from the symboitic relationship stressing the Complaint Child Ego state in the Oppressed;

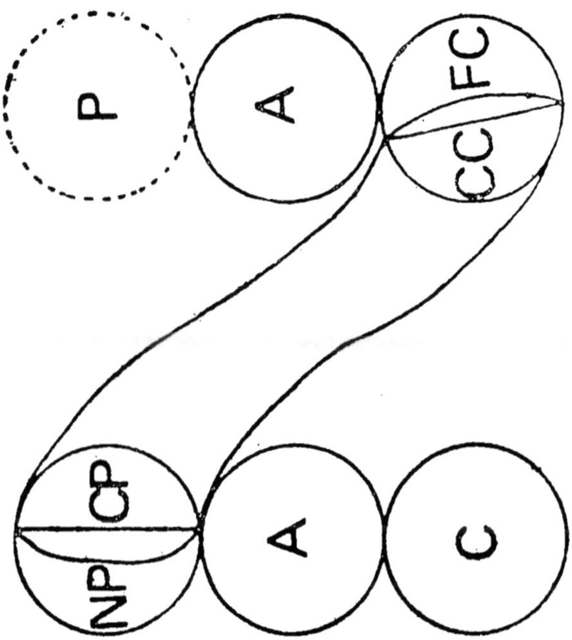
P
A
CC
FC
NP
CP
A
C

Fig. 9.2

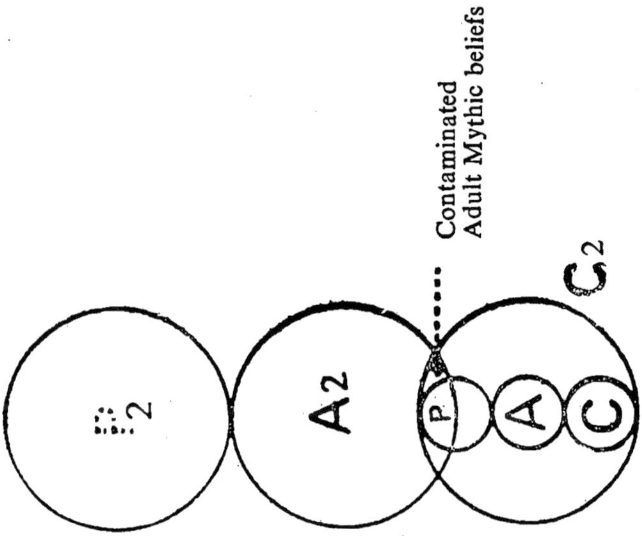
P2
A2
Contaminated
Adult Mythic beliefs
P
A
C
C2

Fig. 9.3

(c) Agitation, seen in fits of weeping;

(d) Violence: abuse of the family and of the self (alcoholism).

6. The Oppressed also give away their power in four ways:

   (a) The Gene theory, *i.e.*, "we are born this way, stupid and powerless".

   (b) The Karma theory, *i.e.*, "we suffer now because of our sins in an earlier birth".

   (c) Deprived theory, *i.e.*, "We are illiterate, hence we are stupid".

   (d) Impossible dream theory, *i.e.*, the Gajendra-moksha myth and the belief in an Avatara who will rescue them as Messiah.

Discounting plays a major role in denying themselves the power to break free. Firstly, they are unaware of their oppressed situation. Secondly. if aware the significance of it escapes them hence they put no energy into solving it. Thirdly, change possibilities are denied even if the significance of the situation is realised, *i.e.*, the problem is seen as insoluble. Finally, even if the possibility of change is admitted, they discount their personal abilities and keep waiting for someone else to initiative and carry out the change for them. In this the Myth and Belief act as negative reinforcement. The not o.k. Complaint Child, the contaminated AC (Adult contaminated by C Pl in C2) and the Missing Parent supplied by the not-o.k. CP of the Oppressor complete the vicious triple bind.

The script of the Oppressed assumes greater complexity and poses a veritable Gordian knot because of a deep-seated duality within their innermost being, which is the root cause of their unending suffering. To put it in a couple of phrases, the Oppressed believe that to exist, *i.e.* To BE is possible only if one accepts the Oppressor and, at most, imitates him. Hence, TO BE is TO BE LIKE THE OPPRESSOR. Paulo Freire explains this in Pedagogy of the Oppressed (Pengi, p. 24-25):

"They discover that without freedom they cannot exist authentically. Yet although they desire authentic existence, they fear it. They are at one and the same time themselves and the Oppressor whose consciousness they have internalized. The conflict lies in the choice between being wholly themselves or being divided; between ejecting the oppressor within or not ejecting him; between human solidarity or alienation; between following pre-scriptions or having choices; between being spectators or actors; between acting or having the illusion of acting through the action of the oppressors; between speaking out or being silent, castrated in their power to create and recreate, in their power to transform the world. This is the tragic dilemma of the oppressed."

In T.A. terms, this deep-seated problem is a 2nd degree and 3rd degree impasse. The 2nd degree impasse is between the P1 and the A1 in the Child Ego State of the Oppressed (fig. 9.4). The injunction from the Pig Parent is "You die if you don't obey" and the early life decision for survival is from A1 "O.K., I'll obey, but ......" The 3rd degree impasse is between the Free Child and the Complaint Child within the Child Ego State of the Oppressed (fig. 9.5). The Free Child wants freedom because this is natural to it, while the complaint Child is scared of it because of the Pig Parent injunction (the Myth) and the Surrogate Parent of the Oppressor (the Belief). This double psychological bind is virtually paralysing.

The Oppressor Script

Driven by an over-powering craving to dominate his environment, the key to understanding the Oppressor's script is to realise that, as Paulo Freire writes (p. 34-35, Pedagogy), "For them to be is to have and to be of the 'having' class . . . . The oppressors cannot perceive that if having is a condition of being, it is a necessary condition for all men . . . . the humanization of the 'others', of the people, appears as subversion, not as the pursuit of full humanity . . .. They cannot see that, in the egoistic pursuit of having as a possessing class, they suffocate in their own possessions and no longer are; they merely have . . . . Humanity is a "thing", and they possess it as an exclusive right, as inherited property . . . . If others do not have more, it is because they are incompetent and lazy, and worst of all is their unjustifiable ingratitude towards the 'generous gestures' of the dominant class. Precisely because they are 'ungrateful' and 'envious', the oppressed are regarded as potential enemies who must be watched . . . . hence the necessity for constant control. And the more the oppressors control the oppressed, the more they change them into apparently inanimate 'things' . . . . (which) unquestionably corresponds with a tendency to sadism."

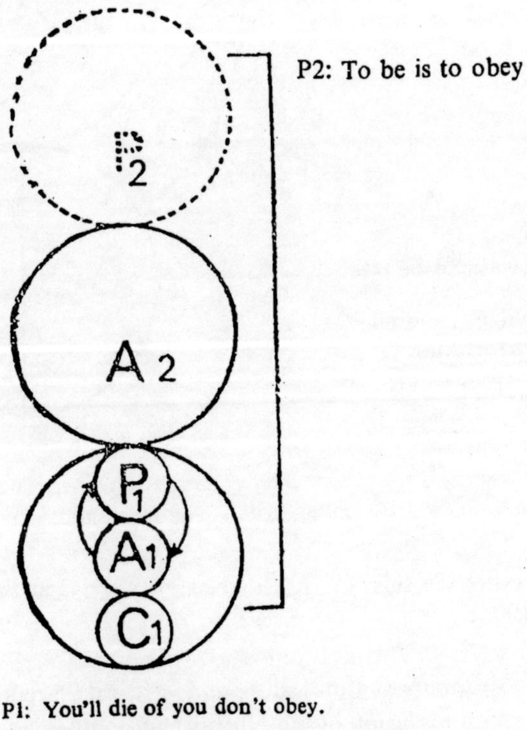

Fig. 9.4. 2nd degree Impasse

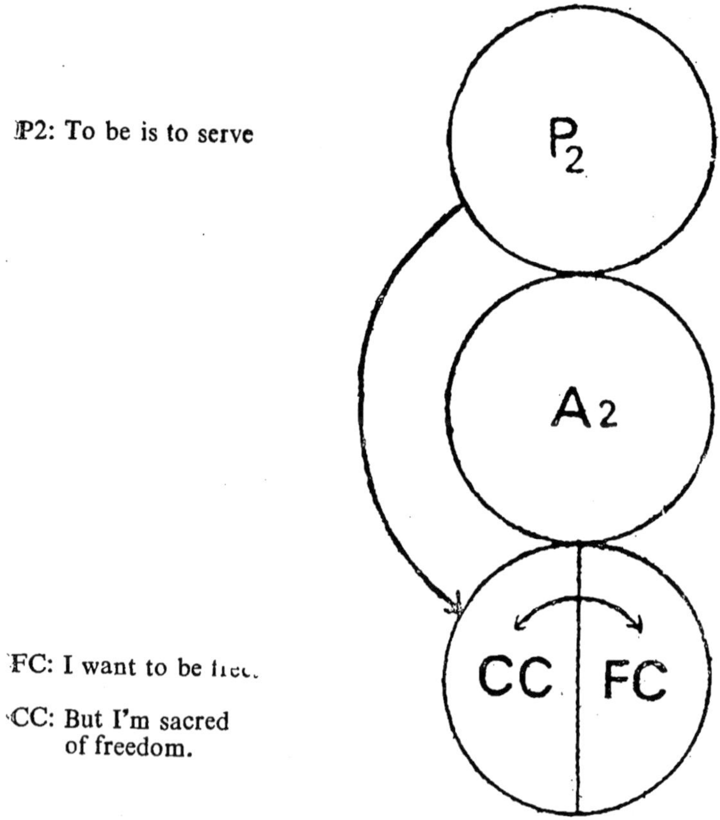

Fig. 9.5. 3rd degree Impasse

Interpreting this in T.A. terms, we arrive at the following conclusions:

(1) A dominant Controlling and Critical Parent Ego State with exclusion of the Nurturing Parent.

(2) A strong contamination of the Adult by the CP and the Not-o.k. AC.

(3) Exclusion of the Natural Child.

(4) Contamination of the A1 in the C2 by the P1 or AC so that the Oppressor instinctively manipulates the Oppressed by a show of false generosity and 'assistencialism' when he finds authoritarianism not paying adequate dividends (figure 9.6).

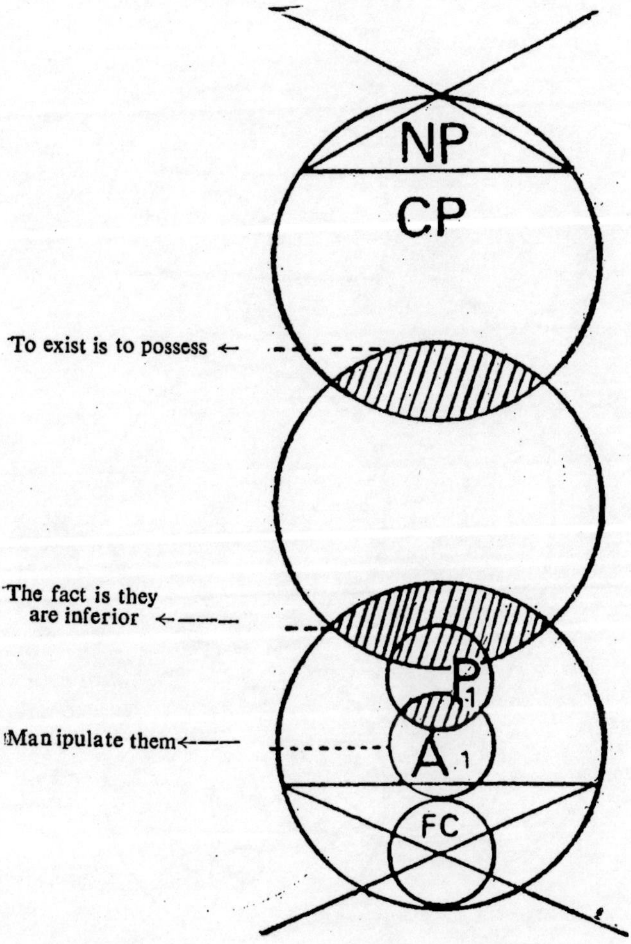

Fig. 9.6

(5) An impasse between the inherited Pl in P2 of the Oppressor, which believes that to exist is to possess, and that enjoyment is possible only through domination, and the Cl in C2, which complies with this but does not enjoy dominating (figure 9.7).

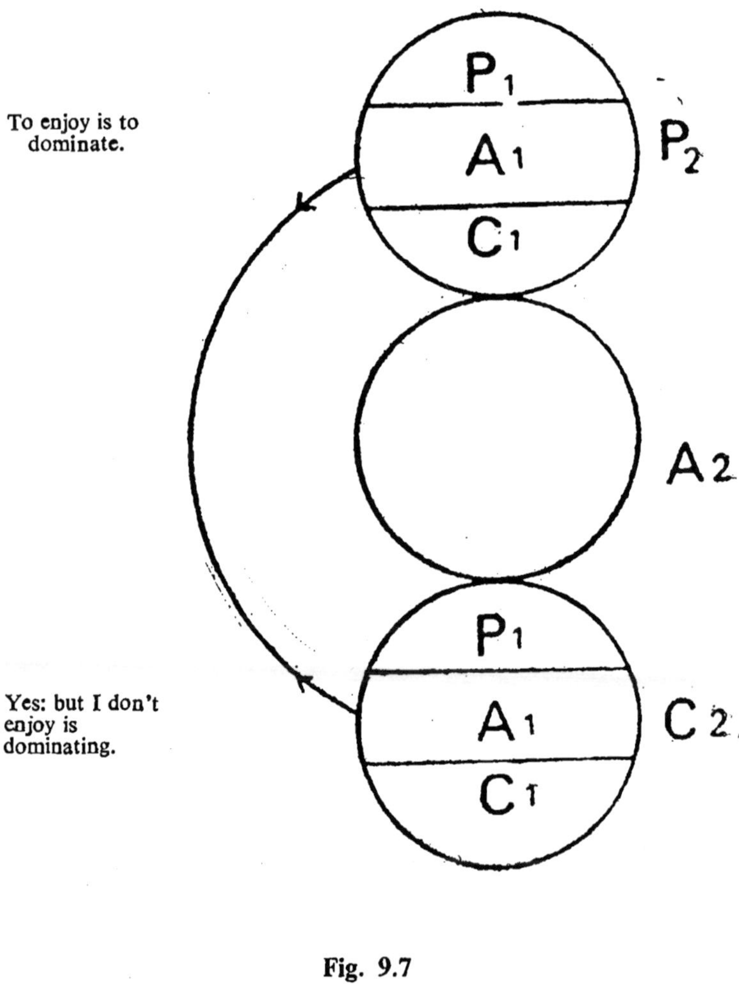

Fig. 9.7

(6) There is also a triple contamination with all three ego-states intermeshing (fig. 9.8). The PA (Adult contaminated by Parent) area is the source of the belief that any attempt by the Oppressed to share power or assert their rights is "absured and immoral" (*vide* Seymour Lipset *op. cit*). The PC area (Parent and child intermeshing) gives rise to the self-righteous anger, "How dare they?" The AC (Adult contaminated by Child) leads to decisions to either destroy the oppressed (to teach them a lesson) or to manipulate them by playing on religious beliefs and myths. That is why they emerge as patrons of religious festivals, builders of temples, worshippers of gurus. Thus they deliberately activate the cultural script introjected into the Oppressed's script, an operation made all the more simple because of their Missing Parent syndrome.

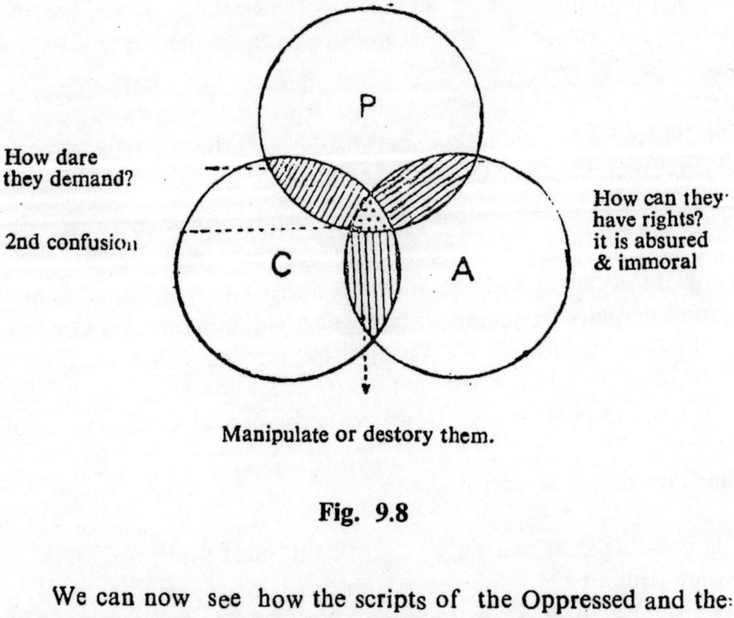

Fig. 9.8

We can now see how the scripts of the Oppressed and the Oppressor interlock to create a virtually insoluble tangle.

Interlocking Scripts

The resultant interlocking of the scripts has been described by Freire as the semi-intransitivity of consciousness on part of the Oppressed, characterised by an interest only in biological needs and a tendency to magical explanations of reality, and the naive-transitivity of consciousness on part of the Oppressors who reject the common man, practice polemics instead of dialogue, refuse to investigate reality and prefer fanciful explanations. The script diagram (fig. 9.9) shows the interlocking.

Looking at this interlocking script we can understand why it is that the oppressed persons indulge in necrophilic behaviour *i.e.* the destruction life, whether their own (alcoholism or opium addiction) or of their fellow-oppressed (abuse of wife and children). Their existential predicament is that of every man is an island, every family a republic. That is why when atrocities are committed on one of their own brethern, they look the other way and withdraw. Two of the most revealing statements of peasants recorded by Freire deserve to be studied in this light (*vide* p. 40 of Pedagogy):

> "There is no difference between us and the animals except that they are freer than we are."
>
> "The peasant is a dependant. He can't say what he wants. Before he discovers his dependence, he suffers. He lets off steam at home, where he shouts at his children, beats them and despairs. He complaints about his wife and thinks everything is dreadful. He doesn't let off steam with the boss because he thinks the boss is a superior being. Lots of times, the peasant gives vent to his sorrows by drinking."

The Government Script

This Gordian knot can only be cut by a third force. An intervention without the Oppressor-Oppressed invironment is called for. In India, by the very nature of the Welfare State and the Directive Principles of State Policy which make up its Etiquette (in Bernean terms), the Government is almost inevitably pushed into the Rescuer Trap of the Drama Triangle. Centuries of colonial domination and the structure of the Constitution foster an explicit belief that the people are incapable of identifying their needs, critically analysing their problems and evolving solutions. Like the Gajendra the people are seen as Victims to be Rescued by the all-powerful Government—Vishnu. This reinforces the Oppressed script from yet another angle, encouraging a virtual paralysis in the face of crisis. However, as the Character sabotages the Etiquette (of. Pearl Drego, Tasi Darshan, 1.6. p. 241) by turning the Technicalities of rules into red-tape, fostering corruption, the Government switches from the Rescuer to the Persecutor position. In between, when its externally imposed solutions inevitably fail to uplift the downtrodden, Government switches to the Victim position, seeing the depressed classes as Persecutors in "refusing to cooperate" in their own development. From here either Government adopts a rigid anti-Rescue stance (Steiner, Scripts People Live p. 359) refusing to respond at all to these "undeserving, stupid" people, or manipulates the people's dependence to benefit individuals. In both cases, the Persecutor role is obvious (Fig. 9.9). The Oppressors shift to the Manager role via Spectator of the whole drama.

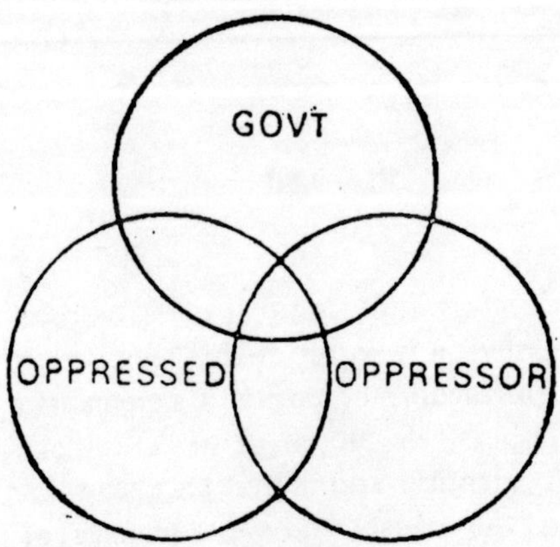

Fig. 9.9

With Government intervention and the work of Voluntary Organisations, there is some stirring among the Oppressed. To this the Oppressor's respond in two ways. Either there in an authoritarian backlash, seen in the attacks on Harijan chaupals, rape, burning of huts, murder etc. Or assistencialism is adopted and armies of so-called social workers are let loose along with religious leaders in order to restore "peace" and "order" at the expense of law. Figures 9.10 and 9.11 show this in T.A. terms.

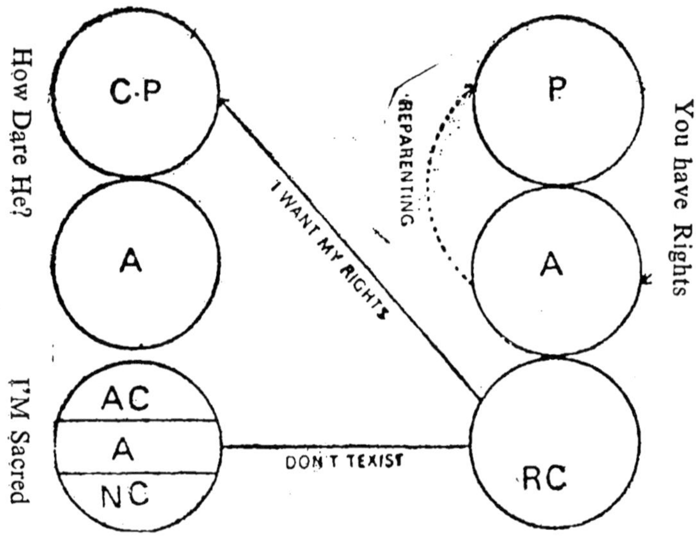

Fig. 9.10

Conscientization

Paulo Freire suggested a way out of this impossible situation. Calling it "Conscientizacao," he posited its elements as awakening of the consciousness, development of a critical awareness of a person's own identity and situation, reawakening of the capacity to analyse the causes and consequences of one's own situation and acting logically and reflectively to transform that reality (the process of Praxis).

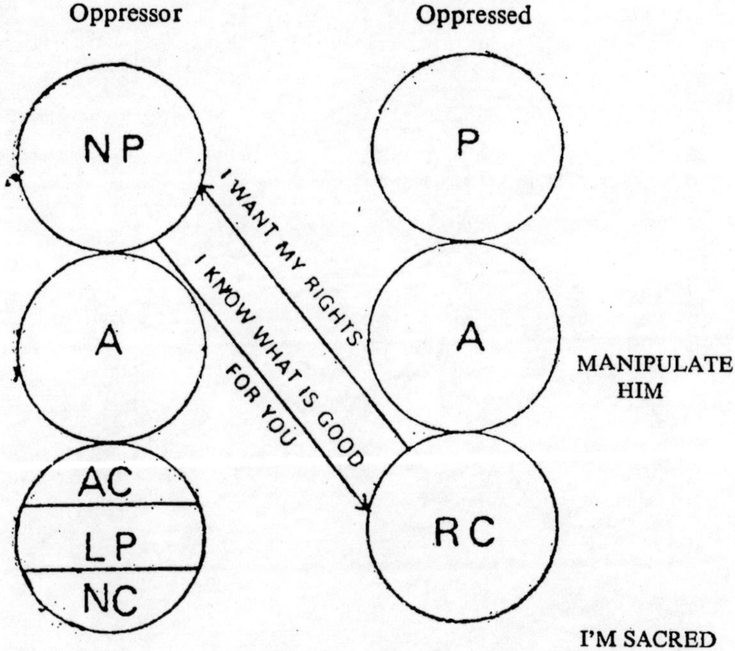

Fig. 9.11

Reducing this to T.A. terms, this basically requires decontamination of the Adult Ego State and developing it into the Integrated Adult, which filters P and C material through A (Born to Win, p. 270) (Fig. 9.12) to design a personal ethical code after re-examining the existing value system. This also leads to breaking of the symboitic relationship and the impasses. By extrojecting deliberately the Oppressor's personality and taking back their own power, the oppressed can break free.

For Government, a decontaminated Adult Ego State implies avoidance of the Rescuer Trap, and making interventions in the social process in order to facilitate the breaking free of the oppressed along lines of action evoled by them through reflection (Praxis). This means facilitating the development of a critical attitude to the world which predisposes the oppressed to re-evaluate reality constantly, analyse the findings and adopt

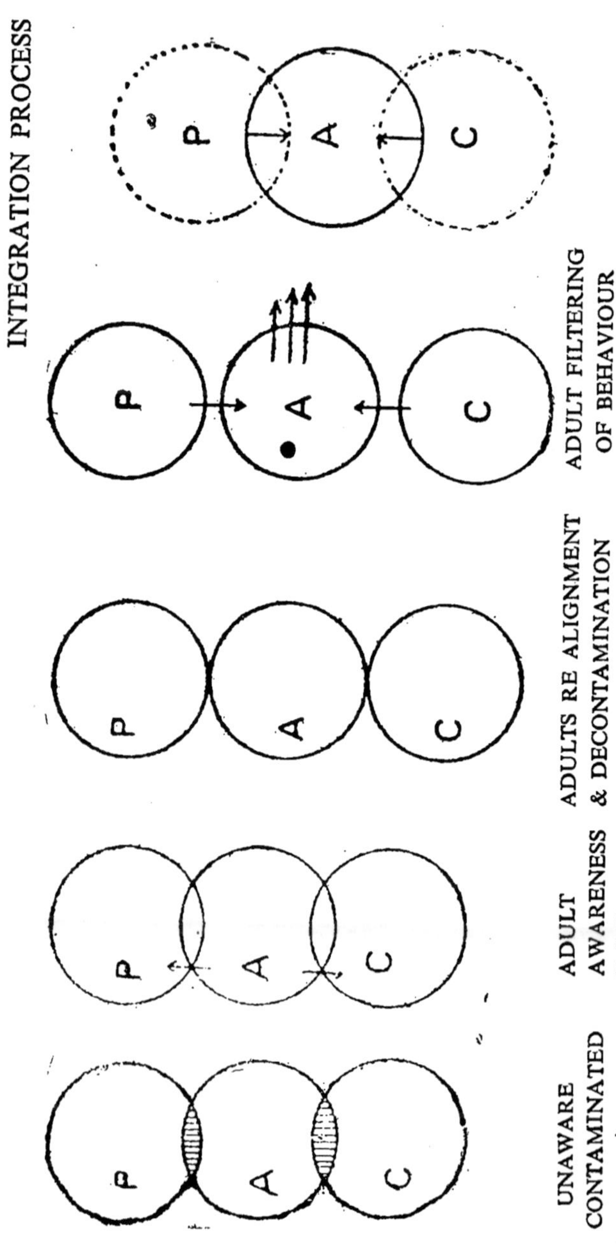
INTEGRATION PROCESS
P
A
C
UNAWARE CONTAMINATED A
ADULT AWARENESS P & C
ADULTS RE ALIGNMENT & DECONTAMINATION
ADULT FILTERING OF BEHAVIOUR

Fig. 9.12

scientific methods to solve their problems and transform the reality around them.

An example of the self-evolution of such a breaking free is Halku Patel of Patalkot, is a breathtaking geological phenomenon in the North of Chindwara District, Madhya Pradesh. Here about 14 villages (Government is not yet sure of the figure) lie hidden in dense forests 1200 feet below the surrounding hills in a gorgelike depression. Government decided to develop this area by building a road and planting bamboo plantations. When Halku Patel, the headman of one of the villages, met the engineer who had come the lay the road, he bluntly told to push off. Halku's logic was simple. No official would bother to check if he certified that a road had been duly constructed. So, the money would be better utilised if half was given to his village in cash and he would not ask what happened to the rest. Further, a road meant the coming of traders, moneylenders and the like implying long term exploitation of the tribals there. Again when the Forest Department decided to have bamboo plantations there for the economic upliftment of the tribals, the signboards were uprooted and the plantations spoilt. Halku pointed out that a forest plantation meant forest guards, which implied a daily "tool" of chicken, country, liquor (mahua) and occasionally a woman from the community. He felt that his people were quite happy as they were and did not need the benefits of such development.

Naturally, Government, which came as a Rescuer, felt atrociously Victimised and shifted to the Persecutor stance stating that Halku was a rogue diverting all development funds to this own pockets, an obscurantist, authoritarian, feudal tribal Patel. But Halku continues imperturbable as ever, autonomous, spontaneous and assertive.

But Halku's existential situation is precisely what is not meant by 'Conscientizacao'. His view of the world does not make for the transition from the intransitive consciousness to the transitive consciousness whereby the oppressed becomes the subject and not the object of his environment. Halku cannot transform the reality around him through praxis because his is essentially a withdrawal reaction to the attempt of the Welfare State to bring him into the mainstream of development.

While, therefore, the oppressed has to be conscientized it is equally imperative that the agent of this change, namely the bureaucrat, should go through this pedagogic experience first. The oft repeated complaint of lack of commitment on part of the world's largest bureaucracy—numbering nearly 7½ million—is basically an insight into the nexus between the Oppressor and the Bureaucrat and the latter's fixed attitude of "handing-down" change instead of working-through to change with the oppressed.

Freire had enumerated the successive stages through which Conscientization moves. These can be related effectively to the TA process, as in the chart below:

Conscientaizacao	*Transactional Analysis*
1. Codify Reality and apprehend it a whole	Photographic Audlt.
2. Split up the totality descriptively	Combining Adult.
3. With the rest of the community reintegrate the whole reality	Combining Adult.
4. Critically analyse what the codification represents and the reality it expresses	Combining Adult.
5. Perceive the contradictions in the reality	Integrated Adult (filtering out P and C) beliefs and adaptation.
6. Identify own needs	do
7. Praxis to change the reality to fulfil the needs through community effort	Awareness, Spontaneity, Intimacy Autonomy.

Essentially, from a relationship which is vertical and one-down (between Bureaucrat as change-agent and Oppressed as the Object) emerging out of a matrix which is non-empathetic, loveless, arrogant, hopeless, distrustful and a critical lasedon the life position "I'm o.k. You're not o.k." and "I'm not o.k.—You're o.k.", it is an evolution of a mutual "I'm o.k.—You're o.k." life position emerging out of a matrix which is empathetic loving, humble, hopeful, trusting and 'critical' (in the Freirean sense), based upon a relationship which is horizontal and between equals, adopting the methodology not of communique and antidialogue but of communication and dialogue. The liberation is not imposed on those below from the top, but takes place insideout. And in such a situation, the Bureaucrat is as much a Subject of the historical situation as the Oppresed. Together they work out their own salvation in a joint effort as two poles in a joint quest.

10

EDUCATION AND HUMAN RESOURCE DEVELOPMENT

S. SUROLIA

Education as an accredited tool of social mobility and national development is in existence since time immemorial. All societies, excepting some primitive ones, accept it as an effective mode of human resource development. It helps in obtaining potential personnel in varied walks of life for achieving numerous social, political, administrative and technological goals. Being an important sub-system of the community system, the educational system stands organically interwoven with the existing-socio-politico-administrative realities of a given society at a given point of time. As a sociological phenomenon it has spatio-temporal connotations. Its concept and variety vary from society to society. Education, therefore, is a relative concept.

Educational patterns, in a particular society, are normally based on its social, administrative and developmental needs. In the past, when the societies were not diffracted, highly specialized personnel to execute various functions were usually not required. But, in recent time, owing to advancements in the field of science and technology, rapid increase in urbanization and industrialization, and because of and ever increasing complex bureaucratic set up, it has become all the more imperative that various levels of education and its vocational relevance are worked out in a systematic and meaningful manner.

Education: Conceptualized

Education is a process of learning. The scope of learning is far and wide. It has varied dimensions, tones and connotations. Learning in one sense is a mode of acquiring knowledge by studying facts about a particular field in an organized and systematic manner for acquiring skills and developing requisite attitudes. It can also be understood as a modification of human behaviour through varied interactions with social environment. Education, thus, is an efficient instrument for cultivating mind, feelings and manners. With particular reference to human societies, education covers within its ambit all those disciplines which endeavour to enlighten understanding. It can successfully correct temper, cultivate tastes, form manners and habits. In a narrower sense, education is a sort of training pursued to secure any or all the goals of human activities.[1] Some educationists confine the scope of education to mere induction of maturing individuals into life and culture relating to his group. Others restrict its use to the conscious and purposeful control of learning by more experienced members of the society. Still others limit its scope to specified work of certain special agencies such as tutor and school, which presumably are devoted exclusively to the two fold task of teaching and learning.[2]

Anatomy and Morphology of Education: An Indian Perspective

Post-independence educational system in India has passed through many stages of growth and expansion. The literacy rate of 15 per cent at the time of Independence has increased to 40 per cent. About 87 per cent children in the age group of 6-11 as compared to 33 per cent 1951, are going to schools today. The number of schools, colleges and universities have multiplied considerably to give growth thrusts to the education system. Expenditure on education has also increased. As against Rs. 153 crore in the first five year plan the target allocation of the sixth five year plan on education has been Rs. 1.955 crore. Emerging key points[3] of the post-independence era also prove that education in India is an on going reality.

According to the provisions of the Indian constitution, education is the subject of 'concurrent list.' But it is the responsibility of State to look after educational needs of the citizenary and set academic goals and standards in their respective states. The Centre makes the policy, coordinates various educational facilities, determines standards of higher, scientific and technical education, promotes Hindi, regional languages and opens up cducational avenues for the weaker sections of the society. The Centre also runs seven universities and about 300 central schools all over the country.

A few levels of education in India with minor modifications and deviations are the primary, middle and secondary school levels. At the higher levels there are university and technical institutes. Lack of absolute uniformity at different levels and in policy execution has made educational system in India a heterodox and kaleidoscopic reality. The organizational heterogeneity with functional overlap is visible throughout the system of education. The education commission's formula of 10+2 is expected to bring about a substantive evenness and uniformity in the Indian education system.

On an average, eighty per cent students who join academic institutions and prosecute their studies up to primary middle or further standards intend to join public services. The econometric and sociometric over-tones of education in India are, therefore, public service oriented. In this respect all levels of education naturally become vocationally meaningful. Since thereis no system of eliminating the human potential at various stages, the backlog keeps piling up and the enormous rush at the higher levels create mammoth problems, namely, students indiscipline, unemployment and uneven academic standards. In the present contexts, therefore, attempts should be made to critically evaluate the existing levels of education in India with a view to obtaining maximum cost benefit outputs of educational endeavours. The existing loopholes in the various academic levels should also be examined to suggest remedial measures for making education at different stages vocationally more meaningful and cost effective to avoid rush at higher levels by providing timely break up of students with lower academic qualifications to fit in varied jobs. Such endeavours must see that human resources are best utilized, and further wastage is avoided in the national interest.

Pre-primary Level: A Neglected Grassroot Academic Socialization

Pre-primary level of schooling in India is neither identified properly nor recognised appropriately. In wider national interests and narrower parental and infancy interests this level should be introduced as an integral and continuous part of Indian education system. The pre-primary schools must be run more on the principles of 'home keeping' where children from one to five years of age are provided with all opportunities in homely environment and affectionate surroundings, exposing them to situations of internalization of roles, self identification and assimilation of personality. A scheme of this education, introduced and implemented in positive and correct perspectives, will provide strong foundation for building up a new, meaningful and goal-oriented education system.

Pre-primary Level: A Social Indispensibility

A society, that does not give requisite importance, to its infants runs risk of self destruction. Like young saplings, infants require utmost care, nursing and nourishment for their physical, mental and emotional health and growth. Amidst a joint family, a child in the past had enough social interactions to simulate varied roles and see the roles being enacted to socialize himself through internalization of those roles. With the disintegration of joint family system coupled wlth economic and professional constraints of parents, a child today is quite aloof, alone and alienated. He is also deprived of siblings and peer groups of joint families. The anomie has also confiscated his neighbour peer group.

Economic and professional constraints, shortage of time and space, social anomie, environmental pollution, familial alienation and such other factors have imprisoned small children to the tiny, unhealthy and congested home precints subjecting them to negligence and harshness of enervated parents. A well planned scheme of pre-primary home schools in these conditions will be a sigh of relief for the in-service couples. These schools in healthy, open and natural surroundings will provide adequate growth thrusts to infants. Their dormant potentials when harnessed will convert them into useful citizens of future India. These hypotheses have been proved by the empirical investigation conducted by the author to verify the validity and utility of the pre-primary schooling concept in the Indian conditions.

Empirical Realities: A Tested Investigation

A field survey was conducted by the author to examine utility and acceptability of infant home schools at pre-primary level in the Indian society. Twenty serving couples, ten non-serving women and ten enlightend citizens including administrators, academicians, doctors and businessmen were interviewed. Almost all respondents accepted the utility of these home schools. The in-service respondents felt that introduction of such toddler schools will relieve them of their present tensions. These respondents admitted that they would feel happy in putting their infants to healthy, hygienic and responsible government-run home schools for toddlers. The non-serving women respondents also realised that after three years the children could be sent to a school like one providing them with entertainment, playing facilities and socializing situations. The other respondents also accepted the utility of these institutions. Some respondents doubted the success of this idea. They had the apprehension that it was a very sensitive and delicate programme and required utmost sincerity, and commitment for its fruitful and successful implementation. Five of the serving women respondents who were already using the facilities of privately run toddler institutes said that government-run schools being situated in open and spacious premises would provide better service and care to infants.

Pre-primary Toddler Schools: The Feasibility

Pre-primary toddler schools in India are needed and demanded in the narrower interests of the needy families and in the wider interests of the community for national development. The establishment of these schools will not be costly as compared to their cost effectiveness. Two or three teachers, a few nurses and auxiliary staff with playing equipments and a moderately constructed school in a plot of two thousand yards will be able to cater to the needs of a hundred toddlers. Since these schools will be semi-academic institutions it will not be improper to charge a fee of Rs. 59 for one toddler. This is the minimum fee being charged by the private toddler institutions. The recurring and non-recurring expenditures of these schools probably will not exceed their income. The idea being somewhat radical may have some snags at initial stages of its implementation. But in the right, earnest with service orientation, in the hands of capable and empathetic staff, these institutions in course of time, may fill the prevailing emotional gap and parent-child lag in the serving and non-serving Indian families.

Much of confusion and corruption have been allowed to gather around this infant movement of education, because of the lack of control, direction and guidance from the government and experts. Consequently, a mushroom growth of private toddler institutions in tiny, congested and unhygienic surroundings managed by low paid, untrained and selfish people have explored the avenues of profit making at the cost of infant exploitation. The government and academic elite should realize the urgency of appointing a high powered child care committee to look into both, finer and vital, aspects of child care and development at the pre-primary stage so that the existing policy of *laissez faire* in the field of child development is abandoned and parental harassment and child exploitation are stopped. The movement of pre-primary schooling of infants must be appreciated as a social work. It has vital importance in channelizing the national human potentials for evolving a healthy socialist pattern of society. It is the call of the age that the child education be released from its morass for occupying an appropriate place for the development of human personality in the emerging cultural and national perspectives.

The new approach of infant development in contemporary context should, therefore, concentrate on vital child necessities. The early socialization, mental growth and overall development of children should be the guiding principles. These objectives may be achieved by nourshing children on variegated socio-cultural, psychological and academic experiences. In informal and natural surroundings, toddler with sympathetic and psychological treatment by trained and affectionate adults will grow and develop nicely. The social realities, academic necessities, parental constraints and empirical field findings, establish beyond doubt that the pre-primary infant care has suffered from criminal neglect in India. In the national, parental and infancy interests this neglected grass-root stage of academic socialization should be given top priority because of its feasibility, relevance and indispensibility for the growth and care of infants. Moreover, this scheme will also provide a sound basis to primary education in India.

Primary Education: An Amorphous Academic Level

Under Article 45 of the Indian Constitution, free and compulsory education is mandatory for all children upto the age of fourteen years. Consequently, all states have provided for free primary education for children in the age group of 6-11 years.[6]

Primary education in India has a dual role. It is a measurement for the national literacy rate as well as a vocational base to the lowest positions in public and private employment like that of a peon. Normally, registration at the primary level begins at the age of five. Composition of primary education is from class first to class fifth. The syllabi of these classes are elementary in nature and include teaching of simple arithmetic, drawing, craft and subjects of general interest. The methodology of teaching is confined to traditional class room situations. Attempts are not made to develop the receptive, perceptive or experimental faculties of children. Psychological endeavours, through educational games and modern techniques, are also not made to develop requisite learning skills in primary school children.

Primary education has suffered with academic apathy as well as governmental neglect. Post-independence endeavours to shape and modify this level have failed in restructuring the system and reorienting the student psychology. Primary education, as a natural sequal of events has relapsed either to stagnated and unproductive or ultra modern or ambitious contexts. Owing to academic lacunae the primary schooling has not been able to germinate powerful seedling for post-primary levels. Consequently, a costant fall in the educational standards is visible throughout the country.

In order to provide vigour and vitality, strength and relevance to the Indian education system, the syllabi, objectives, structures and functions of primary education should be re-examined in the contemporary socio-economic and academic perspectives. A country like India on march to progress, prosperity and technological development has to raise its educational standards through improved quality of literacy and new orientations to its varied academic levels.

It is in the fitness of things that the primary level be made an exclusive yardstick of literacy by devoiding it of its existing vocational relevance. This will improve the rate and quality of literacy. Various professional anamolies and administrative inconsistencies, existing at present, will also be resolved.

The duration of primary education and number of its classes should also be increased. Instead of keeping it confined to fifth standard it should go upto the sixth standard. In addition to the existing subjects, the syllabi should concentrate on inculcation of human values, patriotism and ethical norms in young citizens. The existing void of moral values, patriotism and disintegration of child personality will then be replaced with a new set of values. The early schooling should invariably be utilised for converting the young ones into good citizens of India. In order to achieve these objectives the prevalent pattern of teaching and course contents should be re-evaluated and redrafted to provide equilibrium and balance to academic needs and other requirements of personality development and character building.

Vocational relevance of primary education has made it inconsistent to literacy standards and has generated varied administrative anamolies leading to misutilization of man power. On an average a person passes class fifth at the age of ten years. The minimum age requirement to join government service is eighteen. A primary pass person desiring a job must wait for eight years to obtain the age eligibility. A person in such circumstances is left with the option of prosecuting his studies further or working somewhere or idle away his time. In case he continues his studies, he may pass matriculation or even graduation. He then becomes eligible for other jobs. If he fails to get an employment commensurate with his qualification, he tries to secure a job of the lower category. This is a case of misutilization of man power and under employment. If after passing his primary level examination he does nothing the man power of the country is wasted.

These academic anamolies and inconsistencies causing wastage of manpower and misutilization of human potentials were unearthed during a survey conducted by the author to test some of the hypotheses formulated in connection with this study.

Twenty-five class IV employees and twenty-five constables of armed police were examined to work out their academic standards, age of joining service and their activity during the gap between passing primary examination and joining service.

Out of twenty-five class IV employees, fifteen were educated upto primary level. Four of them were matriculates and three have not even passed class Vth. The matriculates realised that they were under employed, and wanted as well as attempted for clerical jobs. The gap between school leaving and joining service was between five and seven years. The primary pass candidates has worked as casual labourers on roads, buildings and agriculture farms. The gap between school leaving and joining service was between eight and twelve years. The situation of non-primary candidates was even worse. All these people and joined service because they had no other alternative to earn their livelihood.

Out of the sample of twenty-five constables, twelve were non-primary, six were primary, four were non-middle, two were middle and one was matriculate. The gap between school leaving and joining service in their case was also between eight and twelve years. Almost all of them had done some job or the other before joining the police department.

The survey analysis establishes that through minimum qualification for public services is primary, attraction of people to join the same continues even after a gap of eight to twelve years of non-academic, non-working and unproductive period. It is, therefore, required that primary level should not be made an eligibility for getting public employment. People having primary education, if necessary, should be provided with some avenues of private jobs on shops, factories and agriculture farms. They should also be encouraged to start their own work after getting requisite financial help from the government. This scheme may help in absorbing the educated people. in varied private jobs leaving the primary level to be an exclusive level of improving literacy rate and its quality, Prevailing pardoxical situations, academic and administrative, will also be resolved to a great extent in this manner.

REFERENCES

1. Illustrated Encyclopaedia of the Modern World, Vol. 6, p. 11.
2. Encyclopaedia of Social Sciences, Vol. V & VI, p. 403.
3. Some of these key points are:
   (i) Free and compulsory education up to the age of 14.
   (ii) Improved status, emoluments and training of teachers.
   (iii) Three language formula and development of regional languages.
   (iv) Equalization of educational opportunities and promotion of science and technology.
   (v) Development of education for agriculture and industry.
   (vi) Improvement in the quality and production of inexpensive text books.
   (vii) Investment of six per cent of national income on education.
   (viii) Spread of literacy, adult education and promotion of games and sports.
   (ix) Search for a uniform pattern of education.
   (x) Establishing closer links between patterns of education on the one hand, and the needs of development and emptoyment market on the order.
   (xi) Improvement of the quality of education.
   (xii) Involvement of the academic community in the task of social and economic development.
4. These universities are the Aligarh Muslim University, Banaras Hindu University, Delhi, Hyderabad, Jawahar Lal Nehru, North-Eastern Hills and Visva Bharti.
5. Primary education is also free for children in the age group of 11-14 in all states except Orissa, U.P. and West Bengal. In almost all states education for girl students from communities is also free.
6. See:
   (a) Mehta, Prayaa, Opinion about Standards. New Delhi: NCERT, 1965.

(b) Mukerji, H. Barrow, A.E.T., Kripal, P. Samuel, Kapur, M.N. Sen, S.C. Bhattacharaya, S. and Goswami, P.C., Age Educational Standards Falling.

(c) Mangla. L.R., "Falling Standards in Education: Causes and Remedies, Propers of Education, Vol. XII No. 7, February, 1967.

(d) Narain Raj, "Falling Education Standards: An Analysis, Indian Educational Review, Vol. 4 No. 2, 1969.

(e) Trivedi, Shankarlal "Falling Standards in Education." Teacher Today, July-September, 1976.

11

PRODUCTIVITY IMPROVEMENT IN EDUCATIONAL ADMINISTRATION —SOME EXPERIMENTS

B. MOHAN AND S. PARKASH

Education plays a significant role in the development of human resources of a country. It paves the way for building up its economy and thereby helps in improving the quality of life. Although education is as old as organised society and the first teacher would have also been an administrator of some sort, management of education, as we know it today, is a recent development. In India, it has emerged as a significant activity only after independence when the government assumed greater responsibility for education and training.

The fact that educational administration has become a challenging task is indicated by the rapid expansion of education and the considerable rise in literacy during the past 35 years. Student enrolment which was 17 million in 1947 is now estimated to be over 10 times that number. A large amount of public funds is being invested in education: the current plan outlay for education is Rs. 5750 crores. The number of educational institutions at the school and university level has also increased at a very rapid rate.

With the expansion of education and the sea change in the social environment in which schools and universities have to operate, the problems of educational administration have become highly complex. They need to be tackled in a spirit of scientific inquiry for the optimal utilisation of available resources, maintenance and improvement in the quality of education, reduction in the burden on the tax payer, improvement in the image of the educational institution and enhancement of productivity, all around.

Although problems of education have been examined by several committees and commissions during the past three decades, the application of productivity techniques to this area is a recent phenomenon and that also in a limited sphere. This is due to lack of adequate appreciation of the potentials of productivity techniques by teachers and educational administrators as well as the lack of expertise and experience of practioners of productivity techniques in the area of educational administration. With the increasing emphasis on professionalism in administration, there is a growing awareness of the fact that productivity techniques can help in bringing about remarkble improvements in the planning and control of activities in a non-traditional management area like education.

In this paper, it is proposed to summarise the findings of a number of studies in the field of administration in three universities. Most of the recommendations outlined in the succeeding paragraphs were, however, evolved by using Work Study methods, the basic productivity technique; very limited use was made of the more sophisticated techniques drawn from the field of mathematical, engineering and social sciences.

The Administrative Office of a University: Its Organisation

The university which was established after the independence of the country, developed over the years into a major educational institution with a modern campus and a number of highly developed faculties. Quite naturally the work load in the Administrative Office, headed by a Registrar, also increased significantly. As changes in the organisational structure and the staff strength were effected only on an *ad hoc* basis just to cope with the growing workload, the organisational design developed certain weaknesses and showed signs of wasteful use of available resources in certain areas.

A broad survey of the set-up indicated that the major activities of the Administrative Office could be classified into the following five categories:

(a) Constitution and deliberations of various university bodies,

(b) Affiliating colleges and other related matters,

(c) Conducting examinations and declaration of results,

(d) Personnel administration, finance and accounts matters, and

(e) House keeping jobs relating to general administration like management of the estate, transport and stores, etc.

The existing organisational set-up of the administrative office of the university indicated that there was neither a clear-cut demarcation of activities nor was there any rational grouping of activities in some areas. For example, the "Stores and General Branch" had been assigned heterogeneous activities like the constitution and deliberation of various university bodies, purchase of stores, handling of inward and outward mail and reception/enquiry services. Similarly, the head of the Administration branch was looking after the activities relating to affiliation of colleges and matters relating thereto, in addition to management of the estate, personnel and accounts.

After a comprehensive productivity services study, the following recommendations were made:

(a) The administrative set-up of the University be organised into the following branches:

Meeting branch
Academic Branch
Administration Branch
Finance and Accounts Branch
Examination Branch;

(b) The allocation of work among the various branches should be made clear cut and overlap should be avoided by laying down activity lists for which specific proposals were made;

(c) The staff structure of the Administrative Office should be designed, keeping in view the current factors in the external and internal environment like the following:

(i) Correlation of span of control to the nature of the work that a supervisor had to perform; the qualifications and qualities of the subordinates under his control; the degree of public contact involved; the geographical dispersion of the work; the corresponding span of control in other institutions in the public service as well as professional bodies engaged in educational activity;

(ii) Provision of adequate career prospects to the staff with a view to reducing stagnation which had caused considerable erosion in the morale of the employees and had resulted in some unrest among them; and

(iii) The need for cost-effectiveness in administration made imperative by the fact that the university was going through a period of considerable financial strain, which even increasing assistance from the Central and State Governments could not fully relieve on a continuing basis.

The implementation of the recommendations of the study resulted in making the administrative set-up more rational, expediting the decision making process in academic as well as administrative matters, reducing the intensity of staff unrest and creating opportunities for bringing about significant financial economies.

Study of the Organisational Set-up and Methods of Work in the Office of Dean, University Studies in Science

The office of the Dean, University Studies in Science, controlled and supervised the work of six post-graduate departments, each under a Head of Department. In addition, it managed the under-graduate Wing of University Studies in Science.

A productivity services study indicated *inter alia* the following:

(a) Multiplicity of command over the staff in the Dean's Office;

(b) Lack of clear demarcation of responsibilities of the various functionaries;

(c) Inadequate delegation of powers;

(d) Duplication of certain types of work between the Central University Office and the Dean's Office;

(e) Cumbersome and time-consuming producers for maintaining records of financial transactions, particularly with regard to collection of fees from students, resulting in considerable inconvenience to the students and employment of a number of clerks; and

(f) Uneven distribution of workload in the office.

The study team made a number of recommendations relating to the organisation structure, staffing pattern and simplification of procedures with a view to increasing efficiency and effectiveness of the existing system. Some of the significant recommendations were:

Rationalisation of the organisation structure to achieve unity of command over the various sections;

Clear demarcation of work amongst various sections and amongst the staff members within the sections;

Delegation of appropriate administrative and financial powers to the Associate Dean and the Administrative Officer;

Definition of the duties and responsibilities of the Accountant and delegation to him of adequate authority to finally dispose of certain items of work;

Simplification of the procedures for payment of fees by the students to enable them to do so without missing their classes;

Simplification of the procedure of work by reducing the number of steps in the process;

Simplification of forms and elimination of unnecessary registers; and

Determination of the staff strength for the different sections in the office on the basis of scientific work measurement.

Implementation of the recommendations which involved an additional recurring expenditure of Rs. 20,980 led to an annual saving of over Rs. 45,400/-. The non-finnncial gains were also significant as the proposed system provided more effective administrative control over the work of the staff and significant reduction in the time that the students had to spend for depositing fees, or obtaining other services from the office.

Study of Records Management in the Office of the Registrar

The existing records management system, based on instructions of unknown antiquity, was found to be a major impediment to effective decision making and generated a large volume of clerical work.

Keeping in view the need to reduce the bulk of files, make retrieval of information quicker, reduce the storage load and improve sccurity of information, a comprehensive productivity services study was carried out. This resulted in the development of a records manual which, in addition to giving general instructions on the subject of records maintenance, contained detailed guidelines regarding the following:

(a) Design of the file covers,

(b) Sccurity classification of files (as secret, confidential and routine),

(c) Opening of new files,

(d) Maintenance of files by various functionaries,

(e) Method of filing papers,

(f) Physical arrangements for storage or files,

(g) Control over movement of files,

(h) Closing of files after abstraction of important information,

(i) Record retention and control,

(j) Maintenance of a "Precedent book".

(k) Weeding of unwanted papers,

(l) Setting up of a Central Record Centre, and

(m) Development of a Record Retention Schedule covering a large number of documents relating to various administrative and academic matters.

The implementation of the recommendations of the study was expected to bring about major economy in clerical/cost and significant expedition in decision making at various levels of administration in the university.

Study of Office Layout

The layout of the office covering five floors of the Administrative Block of the university was studied in detail and a comprehensive plan for reallocation of space and modification of the pattern of seating of the staff was developed.

The implementation of the study, which did not require any structural change to the existing buildings, was expected to bring about the following:

(a) Removal of congestion in a number of branches,

(b) Streamlining of the flow of work,

(c) Saving of approximately 2000 sq. ft. of space which at current cost of construction was valued at over Rs. 3.00 lakhs. (Incidentally, the university was considering allocation of additional space to the Administrative Office before the study was undertaken.)

Studies of Service Matters

A number of studies were carried out with regard to "establishment matters" handled by the Administrative Office. The main recommendations made are outlined in the succeeding paragraphs.

Service Matters—Non-teaching Staff

It was recommended that:

(a) the rules for *ad hoc* appointments be standardised on the basis of certain guidelines developed during the course of study;

(b) *Ad hoc* appointments should be made after proper determination of essentiality and for a specified period related to the need justifying such appointments;

(c) Promotion of non-teaching staff be based on certain objective criteria, evolved during the course of the study;

(d) Greater delegation of authority to various officers in respect of service matters;

(e) Grant of honorarium to administrative officers for the performance of work outside the prescribed range of their duties.

Implementation of the recommendations brought about simplification/rationalisation in the existing system and contributed to greater satisfaction among the staff members.

Salary Administration

The study of the functioning of the Salary Section of the university indicated that the redesign of the Establishment Check Register (ECR) which was used for making entries regarding emoluments due/paid to the staff would radically improve the existing method of calculating the monthly emoluments. With the introduction of the redesigned form and the modification of the procedure, it was possible to:

(i) eliminate approximately six registers;

(ii) bring about a major reduction in the clerical effort involved in maintaining the registers;

(iii) facilitate recalculation of entitlements for any past period.

(iv) expedite answering of staff enquiries regarding salaries, etc. Study of the procedure for preparation of the salary bills indicated that there was no need for preparing individual salary bills for the superior staff.

The implementation of the recommendations resulted in economy in the use of forms as well as reduction in the clerical effort involved in filling up and processing the same.

Income-tax Statements

The Salary Section was supplying to staff members a large statement indicating their liability for payment of income-tax, details of salary and deductions therefrom, etc. This involved considerable amount of clerical effort in preparing the statement and in typing the same. A study of the procedure in consultation with the officials of the income-tax department resulted in the development of a simplified form for the statement and reduction of 85 per cent in the number of entries in the form, in addition to saving in the cost of the form itself.

Maintenance of Provident Fund

After a study of the existing system it was recommended that:

(a) The entire establishment in the university be arranged in a definite order and every staff member be allotted a permanent code number;

(b) A provident fund deduction schedule be prepared;

(c) A provident fund pass-book on the lines of a savings bank account pass-book be introduced and be updated once a year for the information of the subscriber;

(d) The procedure for grant of loan out of the provident fund be simplified.

It was expected that the implementation of the recommendations would make for improvement in the accounting system, lower clerical costs, quicker response to enquiries by employees and saving in stationery items.

Studies of Procedures in the Examination Branch

Redesign of Examination Admission Forms

The university was receiving, processing and storing approximately 1,50,000 applications for admission to various examinations. The forms which had come in vogue over the past many years and catered for a variety of requirements felt from time to time were inconvenient to fill, difficult to process and awkward to store. A comprehensive study undertaken in consultation with the heads of the various sections of the Examination Branch of the university resulted in the development of a set of redesigned forms which had the following salient features:

(a) Elimination of unnecessary columns and instructions;

(b) Modifications of the headings and size of various columns;

(c) Provision of cages for recording essential information in a manner convenient for processing;

(d) Reduction in the size of the form from two extra large foolscap sheets to one A4 (quarto) size sheet;

(e) Use of different coloured forms for different examinations.

The redesign of more than 40 forms resulted in costable recurring annual saving of Rs. 2,020.00 in cost of production of forms, and brought in economy in clerical effort/time involved in processing them in addition to savings in postage cost. The reduction in the size of the forms was expected to reduce the record storage load by 50 per cent thereby releasing 40 steel cupboards valued at Rs. 48,000 and 350 sq. ft. of space valued at a construction cost of over Rs. 50,000. The college authorities and students also expressed great satisfaction with the design of the new forms which were comparatively easier to fill and process prior to submission to the University.

Verification of Qualifications

Some of the foreign institutions were requesting the university for verification of qualifications of individuals who had passed their examinations from the university. The statement was being sent in a closed envelope. The use of an aerogramme in a revised form suggested by the productivity services study resulted in saving in postage, in addition to improving the look of the communication and making the document more authentic with the stamping of a post mark on the aerogramme.

Use of a Consolidated Statement Instead of Admission Farms for College Candidates

In accordance with the existing procedures, a candidate for admission to examinations who is a regular student of a college, fills in an individual application form which is received in the university after due certification by the college authorities. A productivity services study of the procedures recommended that the individual admission form be eliminated and, in lieu thereof a statement of particulars of all the candidates from a college be submitted by the Principal of the college. Implementation of this recommendation, which is being discussed with the heads of colleges, is likely to result in a major reduction in the volume of paper work in respect of college candidates. This will bring about considerable economy in the processing of information at the university level and will also substantially bring down the record keeping cost.

Compilation of Results

The forms used for compilation of results of various examinations conducted by the university were the subject of an in-depth study carried out with the assistance of the sectional heads of the operating staff. The revised formats which were welcomed by the staff and immediately brought into use resulted in a costable savings of Rs. 25,000 in printing and processing cost, in addition to ensuring greater accuracy in the compilation of results.

Declaration of Examination Results

Early declaration of examination results is a major requirement of a university and can reduce the large incidence of queries from anxious examinees.

A study of the work of the Conduct and Secrecy branch of the university resulted in the submission of the following proposals:

(a) Target dates for printing of the required stationery and of the question papers may be decided after due consideration of the work involved in different elements of the process;

(b) A marginal increase in the staff strength of the conduct branch to balance the staff structure and reduce bottlenecks;

(c) Reduction in the number of scripts for sub-examiners;

(d) Restriction on evaluation work by examiners; and

(e) Payment of remuneration for evaluation at standard rates.

While implementation of the proposals involved some additional expenditure, the invisible economy resulting from reduced number of queries by examinees and significant improvement in clientele satisfaction were expected to be significant.

Result-Cum-Detailed Marks Card

As per the existing procedure the result of an examination was being communicated to private candidates through the medium of a result-cum-detailed marks card despatched in a closed cover. The size of some of the cards was as big as 20″ × 5″.

The redesign of the card of an inland cover resulted in a saving of more than Rs. 10,000 per annum in processing cost, postage and stationery, besides making the document more compact and authentic.

Study of the Accounting System Concerning Examinations

Maintenance of Fee Accounts of Private Candidates

The procedure for maintaining accounts of fees remitted by private candidates was studied in detail and the form used for maintaining the accounts was redesigned with a view to making the size more manageable. The redesigned form resulted in considerable economy in processing time, and made for more effective accounting.

Refund of Excess Fees Paid

The university was receiving thousands of refund claims for

excess payments made in respect of registration fees, examination fecs, etc. As the procedure for processing the refund was rather complicated, there was considerable delay in processing the requests. More than 5,000 cases of refund were usually pending at various levels at any point of time.

The study of the procedure resulted in a recommendation for a simplified design of the form for claiming a refund and remittance of the amount by cheque instead of money order. This resulted in an estimated saving of Rs. 25,000 per annum in addition to greater clientele satisfaction.

Refund of Security Deposits to Students

On a suggestion from the Dean of Student Welfare, the Vice Chancellor had constituted a committee to suggest ways and means for early refund of security deposited to a student leaving the university.

The study of the problem in depth resulted in the formulation of detailed procedure involving introduction of a few new forms. The proposed procedure met with the approval of the committee and it was expected to eliminate a source of irritation among student community.

Submission of Bills by Examiners

In accordance with the existing procedure, examiners were expected to submit bills for various types of claims. At this involved a large number of examiners and the bills were also not submitted properly in many cases, considerable delay in payment of remuneration was occurring, resulting in complaints from the examiners.

A study of the procedure followed by the university resulted in a recommendation to the effect that no bills need be obtained from the examiners. Insread, the Secrecy Branch could send to the Accounts Branch a consolidated list of examiners to whom payment was required to be made. Implementation of this recommendation is expected to reduce correspondence with the examiners, expedite payment of remuneration and reduce the processing time and cost in the Secrecy Branch as well as in the Acconnts Branch. The costable savings are likely to be of the order of Rs. 12,000 per annum.

Studies of Administrative Matters

Identification of Job Opportunities far the Physically Handicapped

Rehabilitation of physically handicapped persons in the stream of normal life is a duty of all organisations, both in the Government and outside. Instruction issued by the Central Government provides for reservation of 1 per cent of the vacancies for each of the categories of handicapped candidates *viz.*, blind, deaf and orthopaedically handicapped.

Analysis of a number of jobs in the university in the prescribed categories resulted in the identification of a number of posts in the office of Registrar where the handicapped could be accommodated in a suitable manner. The implementation of the recommendation will meet one of the social obligations of the university without any adverse effect on its working efficiency.

Evolution of a Staff Suggestion Scheme

A well-structured Staff Suggestion Scheme can provide a very useful device for motivating the members of an organisation to participate in an effective manner for the improvement of productivity.

An in-depth study of the requirement in respect of the university resulted in the formulation of guidelines for inviting suggestions from university employees and processing them at appropriate level with minimum of delay. The scheme also proposed the type of incentives which could be given for suggestions of an acceptable nature.

Computerisation of Office Work

The large volume of work handled by the university in connection with the conduct of examinations, the need for reducing processing time and minimising the incidence of errors indicate that gradual introduction of computerisation in the examination work was an inescapable requirement.

A study of the systems of work in the Examination Branch with a view to standardising the procedure and evolving necessary forms is being currently carried out by the productivity services team. The result of the study is likely to form the basis for major modifications of the examination work at the university and the gains in time can have a highly significant impact on the educational system. Financial as well as non-financial implications of computerisation can be far-reaching. The need for quickening the process of work gradually according to a well thought out scheme is too obvious.

Introduction of Modern Office Equipment

The productivity studies of various aspects of administration in the university have resulted in the identification of areas where mechanisation of office operations can be beneficial. Two items of equipment which have been introduced are:

(a) A paper shredding machine for disposal of waste paper which cannot be sold intact;

(b) Calculating machines in some of the branches of the university.

Identification of Training Needs and Design of Training Programmes

Realising that the greatest gains in productivity can be achieved through people, the university decided to conduct in-service training programmes for different levels of staff.

A survey of the training needs of various categories of staff was carried out after preparing comprehensive job descriptions and work distribution charts in various branches of the university. Training programmes were designed for officers as well as the subordinate staff. Some of the subjects covered were as follows:

Programme	*Duration*
Improvement in office skills in the university	3 days
Improvement in filing systems	2 days
Form design and Control	2 days
Accounts management	3 days
Effective writing techniques	2 days
Workshops of the functioning of various branches of university	2-3 days each

The salient features of the training effort made by the university on the basis of the recommendations of the productivity services team were as follows:

(a) The programmes were organised partly on holidays to make it possible for the participants to benefit from the training with the minimum possible disruption in their normal work;

(b) Different levels of staff were brought together in the programmes to provide for greater interaction between members of the work team and thus promote better understanding of common problems;

(c) All programmes included sessions on action planning which involved identification of areas where the knowledge and skills developed during the course of training programmes could be immedlately applied for bringing about improvement; and

(d) Some of the training programmes were followed by project work by small groups in selected areas of activity of the office and the project reports were reviewed in follow-up sessions. These project studies were found to be extremely useful in formulating many of the suggestions for methods improvement.

Performance Appraisal

Sound assessment of the performance of employees is an essential requirement for a good personnel management. Study of the performance appraisal system followed by a university resulted in the redesign of the existing from which enabled the reporting and reviewing officers to evaluate the work of their staff members in the light of specific well considered criteria. The revised system made it possible to identify the strengths and weaknesses of the appraises and thereby enable the management to take suitable action to help their staff members to perform more effectively in their existing assignments and to equip themselves for their future role in the functioning of the university.

Management of a University Library

The library of a new university, with multi-disciplinary schools of studies as its basic units, started functioning with a collection of meagre 2,400 books. The number grew to more than 2 lakh books on different subjects within five years. The average annual intake of books in the library ranged between 20,000 to 30,000 books. The library had reading facilities for 275 persons.

A Productivity Services Team was invited to look into the procedure adopted for processing of books from the stage of their acquisition to the stage they were ready for use by the readers with a view to reducing unnecessary routines and eliminating avoidable delays in the process.

The team found that after a book had been received, 67 difierent activities were performed in four different units, *viz.*,

Acquisition Section, Classification Section, Cataloguing Section and Maintenance Section. The book would also travel on an average 338 metres before it was placed on the display racks. Books were being transported from unit to unit on hand trolleys causing disturbance to the readers as the messenger with books passed through the reading hall. The division of work between the Classification Section and the Cataloguing Section was also not based on rational grouping of activities.

The team came out with a revised procedure which reduced the number of activities to be performed from 67 to 42 and the distance to be travelled from 338 metres to only 176 metres. The team also recommended re-grouping of the Classification Section and the Cataloguing Section so that unnecessary movement and location of the books under processing in different sections could be avoided. It was also recommended that disturbance to the readers should be avoided by using ordinary lifts and trolley service.

The implications of the recommendations in financial terms were a recurring expenditure of Rs. 1500 per annum. But the noncostable gains were many: easier location of books under processing, reduction of unnecessary movement of books, minimum disturbance to readers, speedy flow of books from one point to another and reduction in manual effort by optimum use of trolleys.

Conclusion

The studies summarised above are simple attempts at applying productivity techniques to the design of organisational structure, formulation of operating procedures and development of human resources in universities. The scope for improving educational administration is wide and demands commitment of considerable resources in time and money for improving an "industry" which is of vital significance to the country. To make use of the full potential of multi-disciplinary approach of productivity techniques, they need to be applied both at the micro level of administration in the universities and at the macro level of national planning of educational facilities. This will provide the student community with better services at a lower cost and help them prepare themselves for a richer and fuller life.

12

EDUCATION AND WORK: MANAGEMENT OF LINKAGES

K. SUDHA RAO

Just as circulatory and respiratory functions are necessary preconditions to the biological existence of an individual, education and work are essential for his social and psychological normal living. Education may be formal; non-formal or informal; and work may be in the form of wage employment, in organised sector or in non-organised or unorganised sectors—both, education and work, are the two inevitables in an individual's life. In the beginning, there was no demarcation between the two. Both education and work were intermixed and each was supported by the other. However, an artificial line of demarcation emerged between them; over the years, causing significant harm to development and progress of both the sectors in particular, and national development in general. The damage done by this sectoral approach to the system is beyond anybody's comprehension. Fortunately, planners and administrators are now keen to develop proper linkages between the two. An indepth analysis of both the sectors can help us in visualizing the right type of linkage and aspects of their management.

Education in the 'Gurukuls' and 'Maktabs', in the early days, did not have any dichotomy between education and work. In fact, the first type of education that had existed in our country was a model in which education was through work and work through educatien. It was education for life and through work. Be it the learning of Sanskrit or the learning of Archery. With the emergence of formal schools and expansion of education, both horizontal and vertical, the role of management became more and more important. Alongwith the management, sectoral approach entered into the planning, administration, and implementation of programmes in these two sectors. In other words, it would not be wrong to say that the sectoral approach gained a priority over others in the formal education system. Over the period this kind of sectoral approach has become more of a convenience to the planners, administrators and implementors rather than a required ingress to our countrys development. With the passage of time, individuals, in the system, are now habituated to this kind of approach. As a result, theoretical knowledge has got separated from the manual work and education got identified with the white collar jobs. Each sector started planning, designing and implementing its own activities, without even taking note of the needs of other sectors. As such there has been a great mismatch between the output of one sector and the input of the other sector. Hence, we find a large amount of country's financial and human resources being wasted in mere duplication and replication.

Historical Background

Though education and work have been progressing as two distinct streams, each one's dependency on the other is getting increased day by day. It had been recognised as early as 1835 by Lord Macaulay in his well known minutes under British rule in India, and approved by Lord Bentick in Woods Despatch of 1854. Later, Wood Abbot, in 1937, stressed the need for manual activities in education, for the sake of a harmonious development of personality.

Indian Education Commission, under the chairmanship of Hunter 1882-83), Diarchical Administration (1921-1934), Hartog Committee (1929), Mahatama Gandhiji, Sargent Plan (1944), University Education Commission (1948-49), Secondary Education Commission (1952-53), and finally the Kothari Commission (1964-66) all realised the importance of linkages between education and work. The working group under the chairmanship of P. Sabanayagam and the Review Committee under the chairmanship of Malcom S. Aidseshiah identified the merits and demerits of the envisaged education system and suggested remedies for strengthening the linkages between education and work.

Though Ravindranath Tagore had already deplored the ineffectiveness of mere book-learning, and emphasized the need for (manual) work for a total education, it was Gandhiji who spelt out clearly the imperatives of a new integrated education system to meet the needs of Independent India. With his usual clarity of vision, he categorically said that "any scheme of education designed for Indian children will, in some respects, radically differ from that adopted in the West",. and suggested an alternative scheme popularly known as "Basic Education." The Wardha National Education Conference of 1937 formally approved the scheme of "centering education around some form of manual and productive work" and integrating all other developmental activities of the child around one central handicraft.

The scheme of basic education raised controveries in the minds of elite particularly in its productive aspect, its relation to the other areas of the curriculum, and the position of text books. In 1951, the Ministry of Education and Culture issued a clarification related to these issues. Gandhiji's aim was to involve the child in work and activities that would prove developmental as against mere emphasis on book learning.

The Education Commission report under the chairmanship of Prof. D.S. Kothari (1964-66) introduced work experience as a curricular component of education at all stages of school education. Further the objectives were strengthened by Ishwaribhai Patel Committee in 1977. Then came the introduction of Socially Useful Productive Work. As a result, a new dimension, the social dimension of work education, got highlighted. Adisheshiah Committee and later the National Conference (1977) recommended that 50 per cent of the total school time ought to be devoted to productive, creative and recreational activities, and at least half of this should be focussed on socially useful productive work of various kind.

Present Status

In spite of all these efforts, there is a strong bias against work education today. It is rather rooted in the experiences of people. In India people who do the brain work are considered superior to that of manual workers. Hence, people see education as something preparatory to brain work through which one can attain the status and prestige of society. Due to this kind of perception even the vocationalization programme designed to cater to the needs of the society are not willingly accepted by the people.

Socially useful productive work is another such programme which has remained only on papers for a large majority of schools. In spite of such feelings still here and there we some times find schools which have really implemented the programme of work education with full sincerity. In such schools it is a pleasure to see the young boys and girls growing with awareness of individual responsibilities towards society.

Work in the past had been something simpler than what it is today. Production was based on the availability of raw material in the vicinity and the amount of manual work individuals could put to that item. Similarly marketing system was something like exchanging goods. Slowly and slowly, man started exerting his mental energy more to make his living much more comfortable. He invented means and mechanisms for production, consumption, communication, transport, and what not. We had industrial revolution, green revolution and are probably in the period of information revoluation. All these aspects have their roots in work. With this arose the need of the management of work, research and development of work, planning of work, monitoring and evalution of work. Thus, we have work in the organized, non-organized and unorganized sectors, work in the form of wage employment or in the form of self employment. We have work as a means to living, work as a hobby, work for pleasure, work as a social service.

Work which had started from one individual, has today become a group activity. Contribution of many individuals put together brings the product. Work has become modernized and sophisticated necessitating certain preconditions to the success of work itself. One such precondition is the knowledge, understanding and conceptualization of work theory and work practice. And this aspect is provided by the education sector. Hence, the basic requirement of success of both education and work is to develop proper linkages between the two sectors.

The present article focusses its attention on analysing the existing pattern of work and education in the country, its merits and demerits, and the type of linkages that work and education can and should establish between the two for the benefit of the society. The methodology, its implementation part, and merits and demerits of such linkages are discussed in the following paragraphs.

The basic assumptions that underlie such linkages are as below:

(a) Education and work are mutual to each other. Each is complete without the other.

(b) Education precedes and succeeds work.

(c) Invariably work education is given after the completion of general education and before the beginning of the work.

(d) We have those involved only in work, those only in education and those in both education and work.

(e) Inter and intra education and work linkages alone cannot suffice the requirement of the society, but can definitely contribute to solving major problems of the society like educated unemployment, uneducated under employment, educated mal-employment, educated under-employment and educated over-employment.

Following are the four major type of linkages that have been visualised between education and work:

(a) Education for work

(b) Education to work

(c) Education through work

(d) Education and work.

Education for Work

Education for work encompasses the set of linkages that need to be established for making the system of education geared to the needs of employment market. Such education, it is assumed, caters to the manpower need of the society and hence visualizes education as a preparatory ground for preparing individuals to meet the work demands of the society. In India, we have a relatively well developed network of such education and work oriented programmes offered in the following categories of institutions:

(i) Polytechnics

(ii) Industrial Training Institutes

(iii) Industrial and Technical Schools

(iv) Junior Technical Schools

(v) Crafts and Handicrafts Schools

(vi) Agriculture Schools

(vii) Forestry Schools

(viii) Veterinary and Animal Husbandry Schools

(ix) Nursing, A.N.M. and Health Visitor's Schools

(x) Other Paramedical Schools

(xi) Pharmacy Schools

(xii) Schools for Training in Co-operation

(xiii) Commercial Training Schools

(xiv) Schools for village Level Officers

(xv) Fishery Schools

(xvi) Schools for Music, Dance, Drama etc.

(xvii) Schools for Drawing and Painting

(xviii) Other Schools

As per the IAMR report, there are 5098 institutions (1981-82) with a all enrolment of 7,12,680 in the formal system alone. So far exact number of persons educated through non-formal and informal system for work is not drawn. But a commensence analysis reveals that it should be definitely three four times more than the size of the formally trained people in India though the formal sector.

Distribution of Technical and Vocational Education Training institutions and their enrolment in the year 1981-82, is given below:

Categories	*Number of Institutions*	*Enrolment*
Polytechnics	359	1,69,880
Industrial Training Institutes	356	1,43,413
Industrial/Technical/Arts and Crafts Schools	2,296	2,35,793

Agricultural and Forestry Schools	78	6,707
Nursing, ANM and HW Schools	639	33,306
Pharmacy Schools	101	4,545
Other Paramedical Schools	129	4,059
Schools for Music and Fine Arts	386	49,648
Other Schools	754	65,299
Total	5,098	7,12,650

The above table indicates the institutions other than professional three institutions like the institutions for preparing engineers, doctors, chartered accountants, architects, etc. We have large number of engineering colleges, medical colleges, teacher training institutes etc. in the country. All these are in the public sector. Private sector also runs a large number of courses like computer courses, TV technology courses, women polytechnic courses and other tailor made courses geared for jobs. As private sector is more sensitive to the demands of the job market, from time to time, new courses keep emerging and old courses keep vanishing from these institutions, a solid test of the quality of these courses is the employability of their products in the employment market. The very origin and survival of such institutions depend on course content suiting to the work needs. It is not necessary that a well designed course given to an individual is sufficient enough to make the individual to suit job market. In addition to cognitive skills, job sector requires affective as well as psychomotor skill.

The cognitive factors include knowledge, comprehension, application, analysis, synthesis and evaluation facilities. It is necessary that in the fast changing technological society courses should be so designed that individuals be trained for a group of skills rather than a particular skill. This requires a strong base of conceptual clarity which can only be strengthened by the cognitive factor.

The affective factor deals with individual's affect, which is supposed to be the steering wheel of any activity. Concepts like interests, attitudes human relations, work ethic, values, adjustment etc. fall under this category. These aspects are equally important, may be at times much more important in an organisation where group of people work together for achieving the goals and objectives. Education geared for work should also include activities meant for developing affective domain of the individuals.

The analysis of history of education reveals that so far the education that has been planned, designed and implemented in both private and public sectors has kept its main focus on the work in the organised sector and that too for wage employment. It is high time that programmes are developed and geared for the work in non-organised, unorganised sectors and for self employment purpose. The clientele analysis, going for educational programmes geared for work, indicates the following two groups:

(i) among fresh students coming from different levels of education, too meritorious and advantaged groups going for professional courses, and the rest opting courses meant for education, and

(ii) persons already working yet desireous to improve their performance in a particular area.

There is also a third group (small in size) which has neither the experience of education nor the work but come for such courses with an ambition that they would be able to get a job after completion of the course. But this group is not there in the courses organised by the formal sector due to certain eligibility restrictions laid down by the later. However, we do find some courses organised by the Ministries of rural development, and small scale industries meant specially for them.

It is obvious that education that is geared for work should keep in few the requirements of the first two groups. Curricular, co-curricular and intra-curricular activities designed for these groups should cater to their needs. Those who are coming to these courses, after having worked in the held, require inspiration to work in addition to other contents like motivation, practical solutions for political, structural and, individual problems in the work environment. Having gone through the drudgery of work, they know the difference between theory and practice, between what is good as a course and what exactly, out of that course, could be implemented. Hence, there is a need for field oriented courses rather than classroom oriented courses. Courses designed for first group require role playing, simulation exercises etc., to make the students visualise the work environment.

In the context of education for work, socially useful productive work, and vocationalization of education programmes are worth taking note off. The creativity of teachers, leadership of the institutions are challenged by these programmes. Linkages are to be established at different stages of programme planning, programme designing, programme organising, programme implementation and programme evaluation. It is necessary that the functionaries working in different capacities be trained for an integrated approach in working.

Education to Work

The preposition 'to' indicates the transitional phase from one sector to the other. Each individual has to undergo this phase of life sometime or the other. Hence, an awareness about the world which one is going to enter helps an individual in preparing oneself for better adjustment in the later.

It is obvious that products of the education sector are being absorbed as inputs in the job sectors. In other words, an individual as a product of the education sector has a feeling of content, confidence, and achievement as far as education is concerned, but a novice in the work sector is relatively less confident. In the education sector, during training period, individuals find an atmosphere where teachers protect them, give a kind of parental treatment, make avenues for their progress and feel proud and concerned about their students. Curiosity, questioning, skill and confidence are inherent in the learning system. This kind of feeling has contributed to the openness and free atmosphere of the education sector, at each level.

In the job sector, at each level employees feel their subordinates' work needs to be supervised, checked and controlled, otherwise they will not work. There is invariably a kind of unhealthy competition, jealousy, suspicision inherent in the employees. This has either taken roots in the very structural design of the organisations or in the rules and regulations laid down by the institutions for the management purposes. Questioning the boss is somewhat unheard in the system. The atmosphere in the job sector is less free, somewhat closed. Each employee is found busy in saving one's own skin, guarding own interest. As a result, in majority of the institutions we do not find anything new, except maintaining the status quo.

As a matter of fact, the main task of the education sector is to prepare people to initiate, accept and adjust constructively to the economic, social and political changes which are both conditions and consequences of modern development. Similarly, the task of the job sector is to prepare people to perform effectively the hundreds of occupational roles required in modernising economic, social and political systems. Achievement of these two tasks depends not only on the knowledge and understanding of the area, but essentially in producing new attitudes, outlooks and motivation by both the sectors which help in proper adjustments to the work atmosphere.

The kind of preparation that is made in the education sector, makes the individual feel less confident. Hence, he always looks for wage employment. The number of uneducated getting into self-employment is much higher than those of educated. Once educated, individual looks for a white collar job in an organised sector. This can be rectified only by proper pre-work education to the products. The pre-work education at the end of the each level of education should be properly planned and given as a package to each individual during their training to facilitate the adjustments to the employment sector. Some of the important tasks of pre-work education should be to provide each student with:

(i) information about occupational opportunities,

(ii) assistance in discovering his own aptitudes and in relating these to occupational possibilities,

(iii) a set of basic skills, knowledge, and work habits pertinent to some family occupations, and sufficient to make him employable at the beginning level,

(iv) a set of personality characteristics to make him confident enough to start self employment, and

(v) techniques to learn faster and better while on the job.

Of late, vocational guidance and counselling programme have been educated and implemented in the schools for facilitating pre-work programmes. For this, counsellors are also appointed in the schools.

In India, teachers generally follow the "Chalk and Talk" method of imparting education. It has been found convenient under the lack of sources condition. According to the Fourth All India Educational Survey, (NCERT, 1978), 9.18 per cent of primary schools in rural areas function in open space; only 58.02 per cent of rural schools have blackboards; 28.2 per cent of such schools have their playground. These figures clearly depict the picture of resource structure in our education sector. Education through work demands resources. As work requires, equipments, machines, raw materials, trained teaching, workshop facility, and contingency amount for maintenance of the facility, implementing work education has got the last priority in spite of the fact that the need and importance of such education has been long recognised. Education

State/Union Territory	1977	1978	1989	1980	1981	1983-84	1984-85
Andhra Pradesh	Nill	Nill	22	77	82	107	108
Gujarat						66	54
Karnataka	13	45	76	82	95	109	132
Maharashtra	Nil	33	107	155	206	250	314
Tamil Nadu	Nil	709	911	944	1014	N.A.	N.A.
West Bengal	69	63	62	62	53	N.A.	N.A.
Delhi	17	17	17	15	16	15	22
Andaman-Nicobar	Nil	Nill	Nil	Nil	1	Nil	N.A.
Pondicherry	Nil	5	5	5	5	7	N.A.
Kerala						21	71
Assam						16	N.A.
Haryana						22	29
Goa, Daman & Diu							3

through work demands properly trained teachers, who are generally the professionals and have large incentive packet available to them in the work place than in the education sector. As a result, the education sector is finding it difficult to get the right persons to teach courses through work (teacher's scale in the professional colleges is higher to that of other colleges). To facilitate education through work, Tamil Nadu government has made several relaxations to attract the professionals to the education sector under its vocationalisation scheme.

Another major problem today is that common man's definition of education is limited. Education generally means learning through books, teaching and library and not beyond that. Parents do not send their children to field for learning. It is necessary to make common man understand through media the real meaning of education, its goals and objectives, means and ways of achieving it, and its merits and demerits:

Vocationalisation programme (the one which is aimed for education through work) is still not gaining momentum in spite of its introduction ten years back. The following table depicts the number of institution running vocational courses at the Plus Two stage:

Education and Work

In order to work out a proper methodology to develop linkage between work and education, identification of common elements between the two sectors, alongwith charting a proper linkage programme is essential. Following diagram depicts the commonalities and distinct features of education and work sectors:

Common Element	Education	Work
Employer	Management	Management
Employees	Administrators Academicians	Administrators workers

Goals	To produce good citizens	To produce goods and products
Raw material	Living human beings	Lifeless raw materials
End products	Human beings	Finished consumer products
Site of education	No specific placed but generally schools colleges/NFF centers	Factory/ industry work site
Time of function	Before work begins (no specific time can be fixed for learning)	After education ends (done during the specific hours (in the work)
Method	Instruction and self study	Supervision of labour
Materials used	Teaching aids and equipments	
Assessment	Teachers judgement	Supervisor's judgement
Criteria	Performance of other students	Social utility of users
Rewards	Grade and qualification	Economic and social benefits

Management of Linkages

Primary condition to have any type of linkage between education and work is to nurture collaborative climate including culture of openness, mutuality, trust, empathy and inter-departmental sensitivity. With this as a pre-condition, let us try to identify the ways and means of establishing linkages between the two sectors and its management. Linkages in education and work sectors could be visualised on ideological, structural, and operational bases, and at national, state, district, block, village, and institution levels.

Though these levels are indicated as units for the purpose of dividing them into managable geographical units, they form vertical linkage with each other besides having horizontal linkages with the organisation/associations/individuals involved in education and work activities.

Coming to the ideological linkages there is no need to go into the details as we know that both education and work are aimed at providing an individual with certain competency certain basic amenities with which an individual may lead a good living and thereby contribute to the national development.

Structural linkages are nothing but developing/establishing organisational, structural linkages which would take care of developing linkages and maintaining coordination between education and work sectors. At the central level, Ministry of Human Resource Development and Ministry of Labour and Employment should continue to play central role in coordinating the provision of all the employing sectors and the production (education) sector.

Possible Linkages between Education and Work

Linkages and coordination that need to be established amongst various levels and organisations could be of two types:

(a) intra-sectoral linkages and coordination, and

(b) inter-sectoral linkages and coordination.

(a) Intra-sectoral Linkages and Coordination

Many a time, programmes of work and education suffer from lack of coordination among central, state, district, block, village and institutional units. It should be the essential feature of a programme to initiate and forge proper mechanism at all levels —from institution to village, village to block, block to district, district to state, state to centre and *vice veras*. Progress made at each level should flow to the other levels and in turn should get feedback to imitate, improve, modify and innovate the actions required for achieving the goals of work and education programmes.

Discussions should be held involving members working in these two sectors to bring individuals working at different levels face to face, so that problems at different levels could be discussed and strategies to overcome those problems could be evolved. Discussion of this sort would be an important input to decision makers at various levels.

While the government policy towards education and work may be supportive, important functionaries and decision makers at various levels may sometime not be fully committed to or interested in the programmes charted by the education and work sectors. As a result of it, the mechanism established to promote institutional linkages and coordination would remain unutilized. Hence, it is essential to promote interest and commitment of the members working at various levels. Involving members from all levels, in planning the programme, decision making etc. makes them feel responsible and committed to the cause.

Short duration orientation programmes could be organised involving members working at various levels to renew their interest and sustain commitment. Mass media should be eegagsd to bring awareness and create public interest in the programmes. This in turn would contribute towards stimulating interest and commitment to the cause in the functionaries.

All programmes irrespective of their nature and specialization should have an inbuilt mechanism of monitoring and evaluation. Evaluation should include its implementation at each level of the information and resources received from the source and their dissemination to the lower levels. Evaluation in necessary at the beginning, middle, and at the end of the programme. Since these programmes have started long back summative evaluation of these programmes might have only restricted meaning of application at the end of the particular time period. Formative evaluation should be conducted from time to time, and the report should reach various levels without much loss of time Necessary action should be taken immediately to rectify the loopholes.

Research projects should be promoted for trying out different approaches to linkages and coordination to effect systematic efforts to improve linkages and coordination. This can be done in the manner that wherever research and evaluation units are attached to the education and work programmes, they should be encouraged to promote research in the areas of linkages and coordination. Wherever such sections do not exist, other research institutions should be approached to take up action oriented research projects in this area. Necessary resources should be made available to encourage people to take up research in this field. Innovations tried at various levels and research findings be disseminated to other levels, so that they in turn could disseminate horizontally for better implementation of the schemes at various levels. Newsletters, bulletins providing information and data to strengthen coordination at various levels may be published. The existing units at various levels should be strengthened by making provision for suitable personnel to undertake qualitative measures to improve coordination and promote linkages.

(*b*) *Inter-sectoral Linkages and Coordination*

Different departments, organisations government, semi-government and voluntary organisations are involved in the process of planning and implementing education and work programmes at each levels. No doubt, these agencies have their own priorities but by establishing proper linkages among these agencies, and by instrumenting proper coordination at planning and implementing stages of these programmes, one can save time, energy, and money. For example, we have lot of courses in education sector. The degrees today have only cosmetic value. Job sector might find this product out of date after some time. Obviously, such a situation is to arise mainly due to the insensitivity and lack of understanding of the two sectors.

We have formal and non-formal systems of education, and number of work sectors with sub-sectors. Each sub-sector is having a number of programmes. As there are several agencies having earmaked resources for a particular activity, if proper planning and coordination linkages are established and mechanisms are devised to make use of these resources both the education and work sectors may benefit to a great extent.

Coordination committees can be established at national, state, district, block and village levels. These coordination committees should develop plan for implementing these programmes and spell out the role of different agencies to ensure effective implementation, and avoid overlapping, and duplicating of services and wastage of resources. Wherever the agencies are involved in similar activities, and resources are limited, coordinating committees should be entrusted with the responsibility of distributing the work.

The most important task of coordinating committee, at any level for that matter, is to develop and establish strong working links between the education and work sectors and the implementing agencies. Periodic evaluation and involvement of local leadership in these coordinating committees are essential requirements for the successful implementation of programmes. These committees should decide upon, sharing, lending, using, witholding, extending, and pooling of resources (money, men and material) for effective implementation of the scheme.

Mechanism of coordination and developing linkages gets strengthened provided the staff members are professionally and technically qualified, and a proper system of information flow, from centre to local level and *vice versa*, is established.

13

CRUCIAL IMPORTANCE OF URBAN PLANNING

JAGMOHAN

"For a variety of reasons, the subject of cities has assumed great importance. There is an urgent need to look beneath the surface and review the policies and programmes currently in vogue.

The 20th Century has been called the Age of Urbanization. In 1900, about 8 per cent of the world population lived in urban areas. By 2000, this percentage will rise to 50, and about 3 billion people will be living in the cities of the world.

India is no exception to this process of urbanization. Though our rate of urbanization is comparatively low, the size of our urban population is very large. According to the 1981 Census, it is 157 million—fourth largest urban population amongst the countries of the world. In number, only three countries have more urban population than India. These are the USA, the USSR and China. By 1985, India will outpace both the USSR and the USA, and will have the second largest urban population in the world, next only to China.

During the last decade (1971—81), in particular, the urban population registered the largest increase (66 per cent); in absolute terms this decadal growth almost equalled the addition to urban population during the 60 years between 1901 and 61.

By 2000, India will have 350 to 400 million people living in its urban areas. There will be 20 cities with more than a million population each, and 600 cities with population ranging from 50,000 to 5,00,000. Four of our cities—Calcutta. Bombay, Delhi and Madras—will be amongst the 30 largest cities of the world, each with a population of more than 10 million.

The metropolitan centres play a significant role in generating income and production. The GNP of any large Indian city—region is as great as the national GNP of countries like Sri Lanka or Nepal.

Undoubtedly rural development is necessary for our progress. But it is no substitute for solving the urban problems. On the other hand, rural prosperity depends upon what happens to our cities—how will be organize and manage them. The cities afford the opportunity for those who come as well as those who are left behind.

The dramatic increase in the size of our metropolitan cities has not reduced the pressure of population or poverty in rural areas. We are facing problems not only of 'teeming cities' but also of 'teeming countryside'. During the last 30 years, our rural population increased by 74 per cent, while during the same period rural areas lost 15,000 square kilometers of land to expanding cities. The per capita availability of arable land has declined from 0.46 hectare in 1951 to 0.30 hectare is 1981. More than 28 per cent of the rural population is landless. Millions of poor people, both in the cities and the villages, are groaning under the spatial tryanny. This is specially true in the case of metropolitan owns. The metropolitan cities with a population of more than 1 million, particularly, face acute congestion. The average space (0.15 hectare) occupied by one inhabitant is 1/40th of the average national space available to an individual (0.6 hectare).

The problems confronting our cities are similar to the problems which are being faced by other developing countries. What we do in India to solve these problems is of special interest to them. Any innovation provided by us will bring us closer to the developing countries most of whom are non-aligned. The developing countries, by the turn of the century, will together hold about 75 per cent of the world population.

World peace, to a large extent, depends upon what happens to the cities of the developing countries. For the story of these cities is also the story of exploitation of one part of the world by the other. Unless the nature of the underlying forces that operate, both at the national and international levels, is clearly understood and new relationships built, the tragic element in the horizon of our cities will continue to loom large, Our cities have slums primarily because the power to clean or prevent them has been taken away from us. The cities of the Third World from a part of the world economy, but their population do not share the resources of the world.

By itself, the study of the city is of fundamental importance. Its all-pervasive character was aptly brought out by Spengler when he observed in the Decline of the West; "World history is the history of civic man. Peoples, states, politics, all arts and all sciences rest upon one prime phenomenon of human being, the town". The city is the most imposing creation of man. It is the cradle of civilization. It has many facets. As an economic entity, it is a seat of business and industry; as a social organization, it is a creator of community and collective action; as a political unit, it is a centre of power and government; and as a cultural force, it is a repository of old traditions, a fountain-head of new ideas, an instrument of intellectual advancement, and a moulder of attitudes and thoughts.

Urban planning, ideology, patterns, administration, linkages, and resources are all issues of fundamental importance—

not only for the individual countries, but also for the international community. The issue really involves the vision of the future.

The City in History

For a depeer understanding, it is necessary to take a long-running start in history and to view the city in historical perspective.

Cities are symbols of the settled life that began with permanent agriculture: a life created with the aid of permanent shelters and utilities.

The role of the city in shaping human civilization has been a mixed one. On the one hand, the city has freed man from the conservatism of the village and enriched his life by imparting urbanity, civility, and diversity to it. On the other hand, the city has bred poverty and dehumanized and depersonalized its citizens and engulfed them in traffic snarls and crime waves. As Alexis de Tocqueville described Manchester of the 19th Century:

> In the city, humanity attains its most compete development and its most brutish; here civilization works its miracles, and civilized man in turned back almost into a savage.

In the West, the industrial and technological revolution has been accompanied by an equally significant urban revolution. Millions of migrants have moved from rural areas to urban centres, and towns have grown into cities, cities into metropolises, metropolises into megalapolises. In the USA, for instance, two-thirds of the total population are now concentrated in about 10 per cent of the total land area, and 90 per cent of the city population in 1 per cent of the nation's territory. With the increase of congestion in the heart of the cities, the affluent classes have stated moving out and 'strip cities' and 'conurbations' is the Washington-New York-Boston strip, extending for about 400 miles, almost entirely built-up.

Thirteen such 'strip cities' now contain half the population of the U.S.

The growth of such large settlements has resulted in what has been termed as 'socially-retarded civilization'. It has made life more mechanical and artificial. It has been significantly remarked that the modern western citizen, stops when it is red, goes when it is green; sees what he is supposed to see, thinks what he is supposed to think. His personal contribution, like income tax, are deductible at sources.

The western city, according to Rene Dubes, has become 'a symbol of the fact that man can become adapted to starless skies, treeless avenues, shapeless buildings, tasteless bread, joyless celebrations'.

Of late, however, there has been great awareness in the West of the need for ensuring healthy environment. Public movements have stated on large scale. Governments have taken effective measures to clean the air and the waterways and eliminate noise. It has been made compulsory for the industries to adopt anti-pollution devices. The new technological revolution in telecommunication and computerization is making it possible for the manager or businessman or even public and private enterprises to function from residences or small offices or small settlements. The need to travel long distances in the city is getting gradually diminished. Life is becoming more agreeable.

Whereas, the western cities have been instruments of economic advance of the country, the cities in what are now known as developing countries had mainly served as basis for exploitation by the colonial rule, and their growth was not accompanied by industrialization. It was through the cities like Bombay, Calcutta and Madras that the raw material was taken and manufactured goods brought in, thereby denuding the countryside and impoverishing the people. Now these cities are being overwhelmed by the problems of poverty and over-urbanization. 'The city of the developing world faces today one of the most awesome tests in our history'. Whereas growth of cities in the West took place over a sufficiently long period of time, the cities of the developing world are expnding rapidly, and that too, against the background of larger population growth, lower income and fewer opportunities from migration abroad. Life in the city is perhaps better than in the village: yet it is very oppressive. And we are impelled to ask: 'Did we come here to laugh or cry? Are we dying or being born?'

The Present State of Our Cities

Since Independence, considerable progress has been made in regard to planning and development of our cities. For about 600 cities, we have now well-formulated master plans. There are 60 statutory development authorities functioning in various cities and regions. From 1972 to 1980, 7 million people have benefited from the slum improvement schemes alone. Another 10 million slum-dwellers are likey to benefit during the Sixth Five Year Plan. A public sector undertaking, the Housing and Urban Development Corporation, has been set up and it has helped in the construction of 1.4 million houses. To ensure equitable distribution of urban land, the Urban Land (Ceiling and Regulation) Act, 1976 has been enforced.

In Delhi, a dramatic improvement in the cityscape has taken place recently. It won applause from thousands of visitors during the ASIAD, NAM, and CHOGM. It has enhanced India's prestige abroad and given new self-confidence to the nation. Delhi also saw successful implementation of a historic scheme of resettlement in which about a million squatters were resettled in planned colonies with basic environmental and community facilities. Under this scheme, which has rightly been termed as one of the biggest socialist schemes undertaken in any developing country, about 3,000 hectares of land, the market value of which exceeds Rs. 2,000 crores was allotted to the lowest sections of the urban poor. New measures of public health and family planning have been introduced on a large scale. The life expectancy has increased from 30 to 54 years in the urban areas and the city's birth-rate is now 27.8

per thousand as against the all-India average of 33 per thousand.

Notwithstanding these significant achievements, the general picture of our cities is one of concern. In every aspect of city life—density of population; availability of land; housing; slums and squatters' settlement; municipal services; the scale and character of migration; employment; transport; civic sense, and general environment—the current conditions are far from satisfactory.

Density

There has been a simultaneous growth of population in our cities and rural settlements. India's population of 658 million is spread over 329 million hectares and is concentrated in 575,936 rural settlements and 3,245 urban settlements. It is one of the most densely populated countries in the world. It accounts for about 15 per cent of world's population in a land area constituting only 2.4 per cent of the world's total. As such, the per capita availability of land in the country comes to 0.43 hectares in 1981, as compared to 4.14 hectares in the USA, 8.43 hectares in the USSR, 1.91 hectares in Burma and 0.98 hectares in China and Pakistan. Under the impact of growing population, per capita availability of land in India has progressively declined over the past decades: in 1981 it was nearly half of the per capita figure for 1951. The overall density of population has gone up from 77 persons per kilometre in 1901 to 221 persons per kilometre in 1981.

Quite a sizeable portion of this urban population lives in 12 major cities. In these cities, 27 per cent of the urban population is concentrated. They have the highest gross, density—85 persons per hectare—as compared to 43 persons per hectare for the cities with population ranging from 1 to 5 lakhs, 32 persons per hectare for cities with population ranging from 50,000 to 1,00,000; 21 persons per hectare for cities with population ranging from 20,000 to 50,000; and one person per hectare for cities with a population of less than 20,000. An analysis of the urbanization process during the period 1901-81 shows that while the total urban population between this period increased six-fold, the number of cities increased by only 80 per cant, thereby indicating that most of the urban growth has taken place by enlargement of the existing cities.

Land Availability

There is an acute scarcity of developed land in all the metropolitan cities. To meet the requirement of population that would be added to our cities during the period 1981-2001, over two million acres of urban land would be required.

In our cities, the land speculation lobby is extremely powerful. An analysis of data for 19 years (1963-82) in Delhi reveals that in residential colonies, the land price increased from Rs. 15/75 to Rs. 2,000/4,000 per sq. metre, *i.e.*, 40 to 60 times. According to another survey, the prices of undeveloped land within the municipal limits of Calcutta increased by 900 per cent during the period 1950-65; in the outskirts they increased by still higher margin—1300 per cent.

There are pronounced disparities in urban income. 40 per cent of the urban households get only 16 per cent of the total urban income. 30 to 45 per cent of the households live on income of Rs, 300 per month or less.

Housing

In the sphere of housing, there are acute shortages. Of the total housing shortage of 23.5 million dwelling units in 1981, 18.3 million was estimated to be in the rural areas and 5.2 million in urban areas.

About 44 per cent of the families in the urban areas live in one room only. This percentage increases to 67 in the four largest cities, and reaches the fantastic figure of 70 in Calcutta excluding, of course, thousands who live on the pavements. We have the highest congestion rate in the world—16 to 19 per cent of Indian families live in less than 10 sq. metres of space.

In Kanpur, a recent survey shows that 58 per cent of the households have only one room and another 26 per cent have only two rooms. Three-quarters of the houses have no windows, and 80 per cent have no latrines. In heavy rain, 66 per cent of the households become waterlogged.

Paucity of resources and low levels of income are major handicaps. A World Bank study of five typical cities of developing countries—Madras, Ahmedabad, Nairobi, Mexico City and Bogota—reveals that it is only the richest 30 to 50 per cent of the urban population who can afford to live in the cheapest tenements bui't by public authorities. And this calculation is based upon the optimistic assumption that poor people can afford to earmark 15 per cent of their income for housing. Actually 75 per cent of the income of such people is spent on food and 19 to 23 per cent on other basic necessities like clothing and medical care. Only 6 to 10 per cent is left for housing. Thus, even a smaller percentage than what has been worked out by the World Bank can afford to buy the cheapest tenements for low-income groups. Recent surveys of public housing projects in northern India also indicate that out of every ten houses being built for the poor, seven to nine are actually used by the better class of people.

What is worse, instead of abating, the shortage is increasing. It is estimated that 61.16 lakh houses costing about Rs. 19,662 crores will have to be constructed during 1983-87 to shelter the net increase of population in our cities and during the period 1988-92, 75.33 lakh houses, at the cost of Rs. 24,218 crores will be needed. Clearly, physical and financial resources of this order will not be available at all, and the position of housing in our cities will worsen. Actually, financial outlay required for additional construction will be much more than estimated here as the cost of construction is bound to go up. During the first three years of the Sixth Five-year Plan, the cost of construction increased at an average rate of 15.6 per cent.

Municipal Services

The position in respect of availability of municipal services is equally depressing. Only 40 per cent of our cities have protected water supply, and that too, of inferior quality. In respect of sewerage, only 8 per cent have underground system. About half of the inhabitants of the cities have no access to even public lavatories. The standard of open spaces in our cities is distressingly low—it is only 0.83 acres per 1,000 population against six times that proportion in the American cities and fifteen times the British towns.

Slum and Squatters' Settlements

The slums and squatters' settlements have become the most serious problem of our cities. At present, about 30 per cent of the cities' population live in these settlements. About 8,000 acres of Bombay's land is slum where 3.5 million live in a density of 400 persons per acre.

No site is too slushy, too filthy and too dangerous for the precarious huddle of huts to be put up and for human beings to dwell in them.

Calcutta and its attendant towns and districts now stretch like a rotting narrow ribbon for six miles along the banks of Hooghly river, and in every possible way that a city can go sour, this has gone sourer . . . . an estimated 600,000 sleep in the streets every night. Almost half of the suffocating populous area is totally without sewers, and moderate shower floods the shallow kutcha channels which act as drains, and sweeps the filth and effluent through thousands of bustee basements.

Dharavi of Bombay is now the biggest slum of the world. It has hardly any road, and in most places the width of the lane is less that 2 feet. If the present trends continue, 75 per cent of Bombay population would be living in slums by the turn of the century. In Kanpur, between 1961 and 1976, the slum population increased by 133 per cent.

It is not only the congestion or the absence of civic amenities but also the unclean way of life and utter disregard of civic obligation that make our settlements extremely filthy.

Japanese cities are extremely congested and their streets, and lanes are crowded with people; yet they are remarkably clean. Even in other developing countries, where the flood of squatters from the rural areas continues unabated, the cities' slums are better than those in India. In the words of Prof. Marshall, a noted scholar of sociology, 'The city slums in Ceylon, Thailand, Hong Kong and Lagos reveal nothing like the insanitary conditions prevailing in the slums of Calcutta and Kanpur'.

Village Slums

Here, it needs to be noted that in our country most of the villages are also without adequate facilities, although the crippling effect on the body and soul is somewhat mitigated by open atmosphere around. About 90 per cent of the village houses are made of mud. 40 per cent of the families live in one-room houses, 29 per cent in two-room, and 14 per cent in three-room houses. About half of the villages do not have any pucca structure at all. It is estimated that to provide rudimentary shelter or house to rural population during 1983-87, 70 lakh additional houses at the cost of Rs. 12,316 crores need to be constructed in the villages and for the period 1988-92, 63 lakh houses need to constructed at the cost of Rs. 11,060 crores.

The green revolution, though it has made dramatic contribution in increasing the country's food production, has increased rural disparities and made it more difficult for the poor to stay in the villages. About 75 per cent of the rural household have only 10 per cent of agricultural land, while 3 per cent of the rural households have cornered about 50 per cent of the agricultural land.

Rural and Urban Misery

For the poor, the quality of life in both the cities and the villages is virtually the same, the same shortage of living space, the same insanitation, the same phenomena of people without clean water supply and sewage facilities. A sizeable portion of the migrants to the cities merely exchange urban for rual misery.

The analysis of 1981 Census of India shows that in the poorer states like Orissa and Bihar, where the percentage of urban population is 12, it is the 'push' factor that swells the population of the cities; while in the comparatively rich state like Maharashtra, Gujarat and Tamil Nadu, where urbanization has gone up to 30 per cent, it is the 'pull' factor that accounts for migration from villages to the urban centres. Thus, it is the peculiar combination of 'push' and 'pull' factors that a accelerating the migration and determining its characteristics. And, as is evident from the 1981 Census data of major metropolitan centres and their hinterlands, the growth rate of hinterlands has been sustantial. For instance, the growth of Delhi Metropolis, during the period 1971-81 has been 4.6 per cent, while its hinterland has at the same time grown by 5.8 per cent. Simiiar is the position in regard to Bangalore and its hinterland.

The problem of simultaneous growth, and the peculiar combination of 'push' and 'pull' factors, bring us face to face with one of the gravest dilemmas of our times. If we do encourage substantial migration from villages, these will be swamped with unemployed farmers and labourers. If, on the other hand, we step up migration, our big cities will grow at a disastrous rate and will be overwhelmed by the squatters. At present, on an average the squatter population is increasing at the rate of about 10 to 12 per cent per annum in our cities, which is more than double the general growth rate of the population in the city.

Contrary to the general impression, a sizeable number of migrants remain unemployed or underemployed in the cities. A recent study, sponsored by the International Labour Organisation, reveals that about 20 per cent of the slum-dwellers in the city of Bombay are unemployed, and a third of them have been unemployed for more than five years.

In the rural areas, the rich peasants and farmers are cornering all the agricultural surpluses. This, coupled with migration without real and dynamic industrialization, is causing acute hardship to certain sections of the urban and rural poor.

Both our cities and villages have really two social economic and cultural levels. At a higher level, our cities suffer from the extravagance of European urbanization and our villagers from the hang-over of the feudal era. At a lower level, both suffer from acute poverty and deprivation. In the cities, only a few get jobs in the industrial sector. Most of them are under-employed in the tertary sector as hawkers, domestic servants, rickshawdrivers, etc., and they are too disorganized to constitute an effective pressure group. In the rural areas too, the landless and the deprived lack articulation and organization to make their presence felt.

If the present trends and attitudes persist, migration and squatting will change the very structure of our cities. It will subvert the pattern of living, It will give rise to new civic and cultural distortions.

Urban Indiscipline

Unfortunately, the problems are being further compounded by unauthorised encroachments and illegal constructions on public lands. These encroachments and constructions are being done not only by the poor but also by the better-off, and even by the affluent. Urban indiscipline is creeping imperceptibly into our civic set up like a cancer, and large-scale violations of civic laws are taking place with a view to securing pecuniary benefits at the expense of public interest.

Taking advantage of the weaknesses of urban institutions, the illegal builders have perfected a cunning technique—obtain stay orders from the courts, buy time, and then plead that illegality is old and the only practical way is to regularize it. More often than not, the plea for regularization has succeeded, and this has encouraged more and more people to adopt the same technique and get away with huge illegal benefits.

These illegal builders are ruining the city. Any firm action taken against them, though warmly welcomed by the law-abiding citizen and general public, is termed as excess through a propaganda machinery that is assiduously set in motion. Pressure groups come into play, crowds are gathered and 'human considerations' are summoned and action is frustrated.

What is worse is that this urban indiscipline is being abetted by the legal system and its various components, including the attitude of litigants. The manner in which this system is operating in the civic sphere demonstrates in a classic why that, apart from the structure of the institution, it is the spirit with which the institution is run that really matters. In the absence of proper spirit, the institution intended to serve a particular cause happens to serve exactly the opposite cause. It is, indeed, 'paradoxical to have justice object to such steps as endeavour to bring justice into an injust situation'. The vested interests are able to exploit the system, and this is causing incalculable harm to the city, the people and the rule of law itself. For instance, one court issued as many as 1833 stay orders in a year or so against the notices issued by the civic authorities and this covered almost all the cases in which action was initiated by the authorities against the illegal acts.

Then there are unauthorized constructions which are done under the smoke-screen of religion. Self-styled leaders of religious communities or groups occupy public lands with impunity. The interest of a caucus is described as the interest of a religious community and even legally correct and morally perfect action is described as hurting the sentiments of the people.

Urban Transport

Most of our cities lack efficient transport system. Four major cities account for one-eighth of the 16,000 annual road fatalities in our country. This is the highest motor casualty rate in the world. In Bombay, 3 to 4 persons die every day on the suburban trains, and two are killed on the road. In Delhi, 982 persons died in road accidents in 1982.

Congestion and traffic jams are rempant. More often than not, half the metalled road is encroached upon. Traffic staff is inadequate. For instance, in Delhi, there are 35 lakh commuters every day, and there are only 1,200 policemen to man traffic Primitive and modern modes of movement exist side by side. The bullock-cart, the car and the heavy truck have to compete for the same limited space causing speed stagnation, pollution and commercial bottle-necks. For instance, in Delhi there are twenty kinds of vehicles. There are 6.25 lakh registered motor vehicles and 13 lakh non-motorized vehicles.

Relationship of work, residence and the structure of the city is rarely well-conceived. The distance between work and home is lengthening. The average for Bombay is 17 kilometeres and for Delhi 11 kilometers. But lakhs travel anything between 50 to 120 kilometres, spending 4 to 6 hours a day in buses and trains. On Bombay's local trains, over 5 million tickets are sold every day. In most big cities, trains and buses have increased only by about 33 per cent of the additional demand.

There is little appreciation of the fact that the movement of the vehicles has several important implications—the energy it consumes, the space and raw material it requires, the pollution which it causes, and the environmental and ecological problems which it raises.

General Environment

Extreme congestion and high densities and use of inferior quality of charcoal and fuel wood by majority of the people to meet their needs of energy cause a high degree of air pollution. Contrary to general impression, concentration of suspended particulate matter—especially carbon monoxide—in our cities, is many times more than in the western cities at its worst. These cities had at one stage acquired notoriety for air and water pollution due to emission from automobiles and industries.

Noise is another factor that lowers the quality of life in our cities. According to the survey conducted by the national Physical Laboratory, Delhi, Bombay and Calcutta are the noisiest cities in the world. Another study of the Society for Clean Environment reveals that even on non-festive days, noise level in the city is 77 decibels as compared to WHO standard of 19 decibels.

It should be obvious from the above facts that the general state of our cities is not encouraging, and in many areas we have taken a wrong turn. There is inadequate understanding of the forces at work and we seem to have few ideas to prevent the situation from reaching a point of no return.

Conditions of the Cities in Other Developing Countries

Before proceeding further, it may be useful to have a look at what is happening in other developing countries. This will enhance our understanding of the underlying forces and help in exploring solutions to the problems. These forces are similar in origin and impact.

It is estimated that by the turn of the century 66 per cent of the world urban population will be living in the cities of the developing countries. The world's major metropolises are now found in the developing countries: In 1950, only 23 cities in these countries had more than 1 million population. By 1975, this number increased to 90, and by 1985 it is expected to be 147.

At least one-third of population of the cities of the developing countries live in miserable shanty towns and they are doubling in size every four and a half years.

They are not only swelled by population growth but by the greatest migration in history—a ceaseless tide of people leaving the countryside.

The United Nations estimates that, in the Third World cities, up to 80 per cent of the population live in slums, shanty—towns and other uncontrolled settlements. In Africa, squatter settlements constitue 90 per cent of Addis Abada, 61 per cent of Accra, 35 per cent of Nairobi, and 30 per cent of Mourovia. In Asia squatter settlements from 29 per cent of Seoul, 31 per cent of Pusan, and 35 per cent of Manila. In Latin America, squatter settlements from 30 per cent of Rio de Janeiro, 50 per cent of Rocifs, 60 per cent of Bogota, 72 per cent of Santo Domingo, 46 per cent of Mexico City, 40 per cent of Lima, and 42 per cent of Caracas. In Tunisia, squatters live in "caves dug out of hill sides". In some south-East Asian Cities, there are floating squatter colonies in junks, boats, and half-sunk ships. Near Mexico City, occupation of public land by squatters is so rapid that they have earned the name of 'squatter parachutists'.

History has recorded the birth and growth of many lawful slums. The earliest slums, the Jewish ghettos, were labelled as nauseous and deadly'; the Irish and Chinese slums earned the notoriety of being 'most fearful'; and the English slums of 19th Century were called 'frowzy dens' by Dickens. Quite a number of city slums of the developing countries are no less deadly than the Jewish 'ghettos', no less 'fearful' than the Irish and Chinese slums, no less 'frowzy' than the slums of Dickens's England.

The policies and programmes so far evolved to meet the critical situation have proved wholly inadequate. The site-and-service schemes supported by the World Bank have made little impact. A study made by International Institute for Environment and Development concludes that even if all of the World

Bank's financing were allocated to basic housing amenity, excluding acutal construction, these poorest elements of global society would have at their disposal about US $ 232 per person per year to upgrade their shelters.

If one accepts the World Bank's conservative estimate that there are 200 million urban people living in inadequate shelters, then all its agencies would be spending only about $ 8 per person for ameliorating their conditions.

It has been estimated that over half a billion houses have to be constructed before the year 2000 to provide shelter to the people of the developing countries. The average rate of construction in these countries is only 1.8 per one thousand people per year as against the requirement of 8 houses per one thousand people per year.

According to the study made by International Institute for Environment and Development, a continuing problem is that inflation, the cost of land and building materials devalues a houseowner's repayments on his loan. Funds cannot be effectively recycled, and housing finance becomes a 'bottom-less pit', continually needing more money.

What do these common conditions reveal? How is it that not even a single city of the developing countries has been able to solve, or even to contain, the problems of its slums and squatters, of its land and housing, of its transport and social services? And why are the conditions deteriorating?

The answer to all such questions is that the city of the developing world is still-in the grip of the same forces which made one part of the world rich and the other poor, which concentrated the ability to exploit and manipulate all resources in one section of the international community and deprive the other of the same.

'The wretched, humiliated, despised, insulted and oppressed of the human race', wrote American novelist Richard Wright, who attended the Bandung Conference, 'left their calling cards on the table of history, announcing their arrival on the international scene'. Arrive they did. But with all the past burdens of inequity and injustice on their head and their vision blocked by old reflexes and models, they remained powerless to take a new turn and chalk out a new path towards economic emancipation, both externally and internally. What was earlier taken by erstwhile colonial masters and their collaborators through political and military domination began to be taken through trade and exchange-rate manipulation. And within the city community, old elites, who were beneficiaries of the colonial rule, were replaced by new elites who kept the same system going, the only difference being that the latter were more powerful and articulate than the old ones.

Process of urbanization in the third world continues to be controlled by external forces and mode of production in which both the urban and rural poor continue to subsidize the local elites and the erstwhile colonial rulers by way of cheap goods, service and labour. In essential ingredients, the plot of the drama remains the same, through the actors now wear different masks, speak different languages, and act in a more subtle and refined way.

The State in the developing countries—in most cases unwittingly, perhaps—is strengthening the powers of elite both in the rural and the urban areas. The trickled-down effects of economic growth have not materialized, the millions are now living and working in what is called the informal sector, a twilight zone between the formal industrial and rural sectors, without any hope of ever getting absorbed in the formal industrial sector.

Looking at the conditions of our cities and the cities of other developing countries, the following lines of T.S. Eliot come to mind:

> Shape without from shade without colour
> Paralysed force, gesture without motion...

What are the roots that clutch, what branches grow
Out of this stony rubbish?

Strategy for the Future

History of the urban literature of past thirty years shows that authors are usually convincing while analyzing the current situation. but when it comes to laying down a practical programme of action, they are rather imprecise. The remedies suggested have usually proved unworkable and incapable of yielding definite results. Even the resolutions of UN besides are usually couched in generalities and seldom indicate how resources in concrete form will be made available for implementation of the recommendations.

Undoubtedly it is difficult to predict the future, particularly when the world is moving so fast and social, economic, political, and international issues of far-reaching consequences are involved in giving a new shape to our cities. Nevertheless, an attempt is made here to indicate a clear blueprint, a precise agenda for action, and also to provide some food for thought for working on new lines. The planks of this agenda are:

(i) technology adaptation for our cities, particularly in the sphere of public utilities and informal sector of our economy;

(ii) a new approach to urban lands and housing;

(iii) a new policy for migrants coming to the cities;

(iv) a new attitude towards old and historic portions of the city;

(v) a new design for our urban institutions; and

(vi) a new pattern for distribution of resources.

Clearly, this is a tall agenda, and looks like a grand design. But our problems demand such a design. They call for a new vision of the society. A great society alone can give birth to great cities. After all, the city is the spiritual workshop of the nation. Manifest in its landscape are the inner beauty and compassion as well as the inner ugliness and brutality, of society. Reform and reconstruction of the cities are not isolated items; they involve the larger issue of reforming the society and giving a new direction to its social and spiritual forces.

Reprinted from "The Challenge of our Cities" by Jagmohan (Sardar Patel Memorial Lectures 1983—Vikas—New Delhi—1984. pp. 1—23). Reprinted with the written permission of the author.

14

URBAN STRATEGIES IN RURAL DEVELOPMENT

The concept of urban strategies usually pertains to the subject of urban development: how policy makers, planners, official bodies and urban dwellers react to the challenge resulting from uncontrolled urban growth, particularly in sprawling metropolises. We believe however, that a second type of urban strategy does exist: a type which encompasses the strategies elaborated in towns and cities and which is directed, not towards the urban sphere itself, but towards the countryside. If the legitimacy of state and government is founded upon the votes cast by the entire population exercising its franchise—and this population is predominantly rural—the seat of power is predominantly urban. It is in cities that decisions are taken on policies affecting the fate of villagers and it is mainly in local towns that the policy implementation machinery is at work. It is in these towns that the state[1] has traditionally established its antennae towards controlling the countryside in the domains of law, order and revenue and it is in these towns, as well, that economic and market forces have established the bases from which exchanges with the rural sector and conducted, or at least supervised.

In this context we propose to analyse here the means by which the state machinery, which is urban at the decision making level, conceives the implementation machinery of rural development policies in the countryside. This paper will thus be an attempt at some understanding of the nexus between urban-rural relationships on the one hand and state policies for rural development on the other.

The full range of urban-rural relationships will not come under systematic scrutiny here, though it must be emphasised that only a comprehensive view of the problem would be capable of doing justice to the complexity of the facts. However incomplete the following attempt may be, it is believed that its focus is not irrelevant to a better understanding of the dynamics of change in Tamil Nadu. A set of related questions may best express this focus: how, explicitly and implicitly do rural development policies conceive of urban-rural relationships? What network has the post-independence state established for controlling its territory, as far as development policies are concerned or, in other words, how does the state development machinery penetrate the rural sphere from its urban centres of power? When urban controlled bureaucracy and urban functions go rural, how can rural feedback reach the towns from the villages?

The limits determining the scope of this paper have purposely excluded a thorough analysis of the effective results of rural development policies. However, since spatial dynamics are nothing other than a particular expression of social dynamics, we shall try to assess the significant social change expressed by spatial strategies and, in so doing, will come to question the extent of the validity of the 'urban-rural divide' concept.

The field study upon which this paper is based was carried out in early 1985 in South Arcot, a coastal district of Northern Tamil Nadu.

I. RURAL DEVELOPMENT AND THE IDEOLOGY OF URBAN-RURAL RELATIONSHIPS

Prior to Rajiv Gandhi's recent decision to link Rural Development and Agriculture again at Central Government level in a single ministry, Rural Development, as such, was under the responsibility of a fully fledged ministry. At the outset, a brief analysis of this Ministry's latest annual report (1983-84) may provide an important clue as to how the makers of policy at the highest level integrate rural development into the vital framework of urban-rural relationships.

A. Urban Sphere, Rural Sphere: A Great Divide? Disagreegated Perspectives in General

A clear answer to the above question can be found by going through the Annual Report (1983-84) of the Ministry of Rural Development, Government of India[2]: at the highest level, rural development policy makers simply don't take urban-rural relationships into account. The 155 page report finds room for comment upon the progressive increase in the use of Hindi in the Ministry, the reconstitution of Hindi Salahkar Samiti and the new Gramin Vikas Sahitya Puraskar scheme (total 11 pages) but makes no specific statement on the positive or negative roles towns may play when interacting with their rural hinterland. An incidental remark to the effect that, "all towns with a population of one lakh as above..." might possibly become "eligible for central assistance for terminal markets for fruit and vegetables" (page 63) certainly does not substitute for a theory of (or programme on) the influence of towns on rural development.

Whilst it is true that theories of development might not normally be set out in ministerial annual reports, such theories might nevertheless be expected from the Planning Commission. 'The Mid-Term Appraisal' of the Sixth Five Year Plan[3] does not bring much solace in this regard. It refers implicitly to urban rural relationships in paragraphs dealing with agricultural marketing, agricultural credit (p. 35), "flow of bank finance" to the Village and Small Industries Sector (p. 56). The priority given to the Urban Development programme is, however, explicitly referred to, as follows: "The thrust of the urbanisation policy during the Sixth Five Year Plan (1980-85) is to give greater emphasis to the provision of adequate infrastructural and other facilities in the small medium and intermediate towns. The aim would be to strengthen these markets centres to equip them to serve as growth and service centres for the rural hinterland" (my emphasis). These statements, whether implicit or explicit, and which are inserted into a very densely printed report running to nearly a hundred and forty pages, cannot be considered as anything more than passing remarks.

No matter what may percolate from the Planning Commission theories of space and development to the Ministry of Rural Development, this fact remains that even a central body involved in research and training, as for example the National Institute of Rural Development, pays scant attention to urban-rural relationships, although, as stated in the Ministry report, "the focus of its Research Studies was on problems of implementation (my emphasis) of rural development programmes" (p. 78): on the list of 57 training sessions, courses, seminars and workshops, announced by the NIRP for 1983-84 not a single one was on urban-rural relationships and non were any of the 17 research studies conducted by the Institute between December 1982 and December 1983.[4] It is true that there have been a few topics which have opened up vistas on this subject (such as "Role of Bankers in Rural Development", "Cluster Planning" or "Structure created for Rural Marketing System)" but urban-rural relationships themselves never come under scrutiny in the nation's leading research institute which is under the control of the Ministry of Rural Development.

This is a significant lapse and one which testifies to the fact that, for the most part, policy makers continue to have a disaggregated view of the space they are supposed to be developing. In the real world the urban-rural disparities are great and the urban-rural divide is still greater to many minds. Clear cut categories are most convenient from the point of view of the state machinery implementing development policies; the departmental approach, which is the rule in bureaucratic practice, strongly supports thematic perspectives and tends to discourage any attempt to come to grips, not just with topics, but also with the relations between topics. Even planners elaborating plans at the district level chose or endorse a thematic approach to projects, angled towards the administrative order; an example, amongst others, is the district plan for South Arcot made twelve years ago. The District Planning Cell, composed of three officers and headed by the Collector, was at pains to define subregions, all of which had already established administrative limits, for the sake of easier data collection. Projects, in each subregion, were defined in such a way as to fit into the already established administrative set-up: agriculture, animal husbandry, forestry, water supply, health, housing etc. each project obviously coming under the umbrella of a specific government department. Since no department had urban-rural relationships on its agenda, no particular attention was paid to that question.[5] This disaggregated approach is very much in the ascendancy over a geographical perspective which would attempt at a more intricate and a more adequate understanding of spatial dynamics. It would, of course, be naive to infer ignorance, on the part of administrative and extension officers, of the constant interaction going on between the rural and urban worlds. These links, of which they must be aware professionally, the interaction they are themselves practising in their daily lives, are not the objects of an explicit conceptualisation, simply because these relationships have not been defined as a matter of enquiry, nor as a programme of action; those, in other words, who know more than anyone else in the field of urban-rural relationships, have such a disaggregated and categorised view of them that they have no definite answer to give an interviewer asking them how they perceive those relations in the block development where they work.

An exception may possibly be the Town and Country Planning Department which, along the Ministry of Works and Housing's guidelines, works out master plans for control of land use in urban settlements, and in the rural areas promised to urbanisation around towns and cities, which also takes into account those rural settlements which could be identified as future growth centres. Town and country planning as a whole, however, is such more focussed upon towns and towns-to-be than on urban-rural relationships as such. The Town and Country Planning Department, moreover, operates only at the State level and has no permanent cells in the districts themselves.

It may thus be seen that, whenever government departments and semi-government bodies involve themselves in the identification of growth centres, which are bound to play a key role in the field of urban-rural relationships, the very Ministry in charge of rural development is, somehow, left quite unconcerned. The same thing can be said when it comes to most academic research: geographers, economists, anthropologists, demographers and other social scientists besides, have written extensively on urban-rural relationships and their work may be consulted by the State Planning Board. Neither their findings nor their interviews have come to be common knowledge amongst those who, in the field, are responsible for controlling, altering and improving those very relationships. This is not to say that State representatives have no implicit or overt perceptions of the urban-rural dichotomy and relations, nor that state and government are taking no practical action in this regard but simply that these perceptions are, most often, individual and are not an administrative credo which could serve as a base for action; in that field practical action usually reveals unformulated policies. Our task now is the identification of these perceptions and the analysis of the policies.

B. Four Concepts of Urban-Rural Relationships

Amongst the wide range of theories on urban relationships in India, four main trends can be distinguished, four conceptual approaches which are sometimes divergent, or even antogonistic and sometimes not. Any one of them, when adhered to by an officer of the state machinery, has necessarily, implications for the design and/or implementation of rural development. In most cases, as has already been said, this adhesion is not a matter of theory, yet the general feelings of the government servants who work in the Rural Development Department can easily find a place for themselves in this four sided conceptual frame and especially in two of its components. We shall therefore begin with these two predominant concepts.

The Village as a Place Apart

One of these four principal concepts of urban-rural relationships derives, to some extent from Munro's view of the Indian countryside. Munro depicted the Indian village, of pre- or early-colonial days, as 'something of a little republic', a kind of geographical entity in itself, that is: a place apart. It was supposed that rural communities dwelt in some isolation, affected only by raids by armies on the move and by the visits of the tax collectors. However, unhistorical such a cenception may have been it has still left its traces on the minds of many people who still think of the urban and rural worlds of today as separate entities. Except in a few special cases, where areas were isolated from the mainstream of Indian evolution, as some of the most remote hill tribes may have been (up until the last decade, the Kalrayan Hills of South Arcot were just such a tract apart), this view is not sustained by any geographical analysis; economic exchanges as well as a whole range of relations not purely economic (migration, pilgrimage etc.) have always linked villages to neighbouring, and sometimes remote, towns, quite intensively.

The point here is not to agree or disagree with such a concept but rather to mark the liveliness of the ideology derived from this mistaken assumption. However small their own town may be, all urban dwellers who think of villages and villagers as backward places and ignorant fellows are the direct heirs of this cliche, no matter what the personal philosophy of Munro may have been. In taluk towns and small towns the government offices are coming to be staffed with such members of the lower middle class; it is only too easy to imagine how their misconceptions about village life and their scorn for rural folk culture obstructs the imaginative implementation of rural development programmes.

The Town as a Centre for Change

The second theory of urban-rural relationships complements the First one in several ways but can also stand on its own, since contempt for villagers is not a prerequisite for its acceptance. This theory sees cities, and to a lesser degree, towns as centres of change: places of innovative ideas, of concentration of finance, places of many facetted powers and places of initiatives. For instance, towns set up or stimulated by colonial powers in the region under consideration here, were genuine centres of change: Pondicherry and Cuddalore (with today 250,000 and 127,000 inhabitants respectively) as ports and administrative centres; Villupuram and Tindivanam as market places, growing faster than any of the other ancient towns in the district because of their location on the Great Trunk Road and the Southern Railway tracks; to say nothing of the Madras metropolis whose influence encompasses the whole of Tamil Nadu and beyond.

It should be noted however that, in a district such as South Arcot, where most of whose urban settlements are modest, a town is not always, *per se*, an active centre for change. Whilst Pondicherry, Cuddalore and Chidambaram governed over an immediate hinterland of fertile alluvial plains, only the first two acted for long as real agents of intense economic change in the surrounding countryside: the first was the pioneer place for pumpset irrigation in South India, the second the generative node for market-oriented sugarcane cultivation, thanks to the big sugar mill at Nellikkuppam (1981 population: 40,000) set up by the Parry's Company, solidly established in Cuddalore. That nothing similar happened for decades around Chidambaram (only 62500 inhabitants in 1981, despite its glorious past and the modern Annamalai University) can be ascribed to socio-economic factors rather than to geographical ones as such. The required class of innovative, small or large entrepreneurs simply was not there, nor the sort of sizeable administrative machinery which sustained the growth of Pondicherry, Union Territory Headquarters, and of Cuddalore, District

Headquarters, nor a significant Central Government undertaking such as the Railways at Villupuram or, more significantly, the Lignite Corporation at Neyveli which transformed a quasi-vacant site into a township of one lakh inhabitants in less than thirty years, which process, inevitably, had many consequences for the surrounding villages located on the dry and poor ferralitic red plateau.

Aside from their purely economic role and their traditional administrative power, all urban settlements were, anyway, intended to be centres for change, after Independence when the new policy of development from the top was launched with the overall experiment in Community Development. The urban hierarchy, from New Delhi to block headquarters—via Madras, Cuddalore and the taluk headquarters was, to a large extent, the backbone of the power hierarchy embodied in the new development administrative machinery.

At the implementation level, almost all the officials involved in rural development consider the town as a Centre of change and, for most of those officials with an urban family background (a fair amount of them coming from villages even so), this relationship is a powerful expression of a hierarchy of values. Although, at high level seminars, IAS officers and academics stress the need to educate the rural population in, for instance, matters relating to the preservation of the ecological balance towards the promotion of better development[6], block level officers have a cruder, if not a fundamentally different, view of what forward (urban) places offer to backward (rural) people. To draw a quotation from the field: "the more contact they come with the town, the better civilized the villager will become" (sic).[7]

The Village as the Key to Development: The Gandhian Idealization of Rurality

Opposing the urban conceit is the Gandhian concept of the village with its idealization of the rural as the key to India's future. The Gandhian view is too well known for any examination of it to be necessary here. It is certainly true that no real development can occur without the villages being directly involved but it is as clear now-a-days that such an involvement cannot be effective in isolation: Gandhian experiments may work here and there in some dedicated communities but successive Indian governments, no matter what they may have said in their speeches, have rejected the blueprint proposed by the Mahatama as a model for development. Gandhi may have been largely in the right when he depicted the evils that go along with towns and cities but towns and cities are here to stay, and to grow. Just as it is unrealistic on the part of urban policy makers to regard villages as places apart, so it would be equally unrealistic to see the villages alone as having the keys to their own development, if for no other reason than because the market forces are mustered in towns and cities. There is no need to justify the statement that Gandhian visions are a lost dream for those in charge of rural development: the process of policy making and planning, the structure of power, the economic framework, party politics and the promotion of urban values have seen to it, to say nothing of pervasive corruption.

Though the Gandhian view of the villages may have been idealistic, it rightly emphasized two essential points: that the motor power for development cannot be found in cities alone and that, in a genuine development process, economic activities and social evolution cannot be separated.

The Urban Bias

The last theory we shall make mention of here accepts the concept of the town as centre of change, without reservation, and goes still further, asserting that such change is not necessarily positive for the villages and that it is extremely unbalanced. This concept was best expressed by Michael Liption, when he exposed the 'urban bias' as the cause of the 'slow and unfair' development afflicting India, amongst many other countries: a bias, both from the efficiency norm and the equity norm, a bias which encourages an unfair allocation of resources to the detriment of the countryside, a 'dispositional urban bias', due to the state of mind of policy makers, products of their own urban backgrounds and affinities which cause them to identify modernity with the urban sector alone and to promote development policies which are in fact, "from, by and for people in cities."[8]

These ideas are not usually shared by the field officers concerned with rural development who tend to believe that the schemes conceived in New Delhi and Madras are correctly formulated. Moreover their disaggregated view of the development process causes them to leave the urban question aside as being irrelevant to their duty. Things are naturally different at the decision making, levels of the state power: when planning and budgeting the government has to opt strictly for priorities and to determine what share of the anticipated outlay will go to the cities and to urban dwellers and what to villagers and which group will receive the biggest per capita share. An analysis of these financial choices and the study of their spatial distribution would build up a financial geography which would throw much light upon some key elements in urban-rural relationships; there is a promising field of research here which is not however touched upon in the present paper.

Having evoked the ideological background of urban-rural relationships we shall now consider the ways in which the state conveys its rural development policies from cities to villages and how it obtains feedback from the rural areas. We shall not deal with here with the social aims of the development policies nor with the results as such, but only with the spatial instruments upon which their implementation relies. However, an analysis of the spatial network of the powers involved will naturally offer significant information on these points. We shall attempt just such an analysis here, with South Arcot District as a case study.

II. RURAL DEVELOPMENT, URBANIZATION AND RURAL GRID-MAKING: THE SPATIAL NETWORK OF THE STATE DEVELOPMENT MACHINERY

Many are the discussions on the contents and results of the

various development programmes[9] many too are the studies on the development bureaucracy.[10] In a perspective distinct from these two important fields of enquiry, we would like to analyse here another parameter of the implementation process of rural development policies. According to its official formulation, the major thurst of those policies is "on strengthening the socio-economic infrastructure of development in rural areas and alleviation of rural poverty".[11] To be successful, this twin process—physical and social-demands, amongst other requirements, that the creation and the strengthening of socio-economic infrastructures and amenities spread effectively over the countryside. Even though it is most often loosely formulated, there is a vital spatial application to be found in it. We'll try to investigate these spatial patterns, as observed in South Arcot District. Due to its size 10895 km and to its 1981 population, 4201000 inhabitants, South Arcot is a fairly representative, example of an average district.[12] Without any big city, it is less urbanized than the State as a whole, with only 15.1 per cent of its population settled in Census towns. The State figure is twice as large. A part from the efficient Neyveli Lignite Corporation, which built up a township which today ranks second to Cuddalore, the district headquarters, South Arcot is poorly industrialized: in 1979-80, it ranked 10th amongst the 16 Tamil districts for small scale industrial registered units, and 12th for factories. This modest urbanization affects the literacy rate, 40.9 per cent noticeably lower than the State average. Another factor, socio-economic deprivation, may also explain this low rate: South Arcot along with Chingleput is one of the two Tamil districts where the Scheduled Castes account for more than 25 per cent of the total population, a very high figure by all-India standards.

The district can hardly be labelled as backward however; with agriculture as the main activity, South Arcot figures equalled the State averages in 1980-81 as far as paddy, groundnut and sugarcane, its three leading crops, were concerned. Similarly, the area sown more than once (19.9% of the net area sown) was identical with the state figure (20.3%). Amongst its four main geographical divisions only one is really backward, the tribal Kalrayan Hills, which were left in isolation up to the late seventies. Not far from the sea, the red sandstone plateaux with their dry lands and ferralitic soils are more poor than backward. The backbone of the district, the large pediment area running along the foot of the Eastern Ghats does encompass poor tracks, but is fertile enough due to the dense network of tanks established by villages centuries old. The remaining type, the alluvial plains of the Lower Varahanadi, Ponnaiyar, Gadilam rivers, and the northern fringe of the Kaveri delta, are prominent examples of the fertile paddy lands in which the classic Tamil civilization blossomed, aronud high towered and prestigious temples such as Chidambaram Sri Nataraja Koyil.

Hence, on the whole, South Arcot appears to be a significant field of enquiry for assessing urban-rural relationships in an under urbanized but non-backward district.

A. Urban Grid and Urban-Conceived Rural Grid

The power of the government and its practical implementing instrument embodied in the administrative machinery, control, from the State capital and from District Headquarters, the territory they are in charge of, through a network of roads, railways and towns, which are also axes and places of trade. The sophistication of this network is one of the basic requirements for an efficient administration and a dynamic market oriented economy.

During the Raj the state therefore had "two main activities" to perform as analysed by C.J. Baker: "Firstly it had to collect enough revenue to maintain the army and the administration. . . Secondly it had to do the minimum necessary, in terms of state expenditure, to oil the wheels of overseas trade".[13] Such a policy required a two sided network. On the one hand, economic exchanges and transportation needs required a network instrumental for linear movements: roads and railways leading to the ports, were its main components. Towns were the main needs from where impulses were given. On the other hand, for the sake of revenue collection and social control, the network had to cover the entire area under administration. Its pattern was not only linear: it had to authorize as well the efficient collection of revenue from all settlements. Hence, the Revenue Department developed the most articulate grid linking the district headquarters and its collectorate to the entire rural area, through a four tier system of spatial units: divisions, taluks, firkas, revenue villages.

After Independence the first activity had to continue since the collection of revenue is essential for any state. The second one was greatly altered, as state expenditure for economic growth increased dramatically, with national production trade now having the highest priority. A new basic activity was added for promoting not only economic production but also (at least in official statements) development *i.e.*, the overall diffusion of better facilities, amenities and resources to the largest possible number of people, in the fields of education, health, nutrition, employment, communication, etc. in a much publicized anti-poverty drive.

When the Community Development policy was launched in the fifties, and extended to the whole of rural India in the sixties, the Government had to decide which grid it was going to adopt to cover the territory under its jurisdiction. Once again, but this time with regard to rural development and not for revenue purposes the problem was to set up an efficient spatial instrument, able to convey from cities to village a policy which was intended to leave no area untouched. But if the aim was rural, the conception and the implementation process were urban-generated and urban-controlled.

We are thus faced with two types of networks (closely related to one another in fact but functionally distinct and complementary): the network and the hierarchy of towns can be called the urban grid, while the way the urban centres of decision organize the area coverage in terms of rural development could be called the urban-processed or the urban-conceived rural grid: the formula does not imply that the grid relies upon towns alone for its coverage of the rural areas. It simply stresses the fact that the power to establish the rural grid lies in cities, that, in other words, not only the strategy of rural development, but its tactics as well are vested in urban authorities.

This distinction being made, a brief comment on the urban grid is a prerequisite for the analysis of the rural development network designed by the cities and towns in control.

B. The Urban Grid in South Arcot: What is a Town in Tamilnad?

Without elaborating too much on a point which was discussed in detail in another forum a few years ago[14] we feel it necessary to underline here the haziness of the concept of town as accepted by scientist relying upon the Census of India statistical data. The Census criteria are well known: are urban areas "all places with a municipality, corporation, cantonment board or notified town area committee", and all other places with" (i) a minimum population of 5000; (ii) at least 75 per cent of the male working population engaged in non-agricultural pursuite; and (iii) a density of population of at least 400 persons per sq. km".[15]

On this basis researchers frequently conduct studies on urban dynamics, and built-up urban networks modelled on central place theories. However, Census data does not give a totally accurate image of the background of urban-rural relationships, for a major flaw prevents the Census typology from giving the required clue in that field. "All areas which are not urban".[16] Such an assertion however logical it might seem, is in fact misleading, bscause all settlements which are not towns are not necessarily villages. Between full fledged Census towns and villages is a series of settlements which perform vital functions and are, in most cases, obligatory relays in the urban-rural relationships. Those modest market places that we have suggested to label more specifically "boroughs", are classified as villages by the Census. In fact, even if their lay out is still predominantly rural, they perform some of the functions traditionally imputed to towns: besides a bazaar, they usually offer at least three of the following services; administration, banking, secondary education, health and welfare amenities, and as a result, more than half the working population is employed in the tertiary sector mainly for the benefit of the surrounding villages. As data on employment is not yet available at village level for the 1981 Census, it is not possible to update the identification of such centres here, as we previously attempted to do on the basis of the 1961 and 1971 censuses.

Fortunately, we have an adequate substitute for that, as, with only two exceptions, all the centres we classified "large boroughs", "boroughs" or "borough in embryo" with 1961 and 1971 as referencc years, happen to be classified today as "town panchayats" by the Revenue Department, which thus labels any settlement of 5000 inhabitants or more[17] having an annual income of at least one lakh rupees. Without theorizing here on the exact nature of urbanization, we shall, for the sake of convenience, use the concept of "Semi-urban" when referring to those town panchayats identified in addition to the acknowledged Census towns (Census towns which are not municipalities or notified townships are also classified as town panchayats).

Having built up a map of the urban (and semi-urban) grid, we may turn our attention now from localities to areas, in order to analyse the manner in which the state has criss-crossed the countryside toward the implementation of rural development, and answer three questions: what role do towns perform in the process? How far the rural development bureaucracy goes rural? What lessons can be drawn from the spatial pattern set up by the administration? Significant in this perspective, will be the size-approach: if we compare the rural development grid with a fishing net, then what type of meshes have the urban policy makers selected for implementing a programme bound to concern all villages? The analysis of the territorial mesh-making process, if we may risk using this formula, is bound to throw some light on three correlated perspective: the geography of state power, the development endeavour, and urban-rural relationships.

C. From Town to Village: The Rural Development Network in South Arcot

Chart 1 provides a first perspective on the hierarchical set-up of the rural development machinery, from town to village, as it was in 1984. Let us concentrate first on the left side of the chart, devoted to the rural development grid. In pursuit of what is now our objective, we may briefly take note of the grid pattern at the urban upper levels, and pay more attention to the lower levels, which deal with the direct implementation of the rural development policy.

The upper levels include three tiers, all of which have urban headquarters, all control the implementation process, define it, budget it according to the general policy designed in Delhi and Madras and to the funds received from Delhi and Madras. Those three tiers are:

the District, with the Collector and his-team of district level officers, including two Personal Assistants, Panchayat Development, and the Project Officer, District Rural Development Agency all of them based at the Collectorate at Cuddalore.

two "Development Districts", North and South, which were planning areas when the district level planning approach was in vogue. The two P.As, Panchayat Development, are in charge of the Divisions included in these Development Districts.

five Development Divisions, each one headed by a Divisional Development Officer, based at Tindivanam, Tirukkoyilur, Vridhachalam, Chidambaram, Cuddalore (all Census towns).

Next comes the key administiative unit ot the rural development machinery: the Development Block.

District Collector

Panchayat and Rural Development Administration	Urban/rural Character	Revenue Administration
District level Officers, including two P.A.s, Panchayat Development in charge of	District Headquarters (pop. 127000)	District level Officers including one P.A. General and Revenue
2 Development Districts and one Project Officer, District Rural Development Agency		
5 Development Divisions (5 Development Division Officers: DDOs)		*5 Revenue Divisions* (5 Revenue Division Officers)
Tindivanam 7 blocks	Census towns	Tindivanam 3 taluks
Tirukkoyilur 9 blocks		Tirukkoyilur 3 taluks
Vriddhachalam 9 blocks		Vriddhachalam 3 taluks
Chidambaram 5 blocks		Chidambaram 3 taluks
Cuddalore 4 blocks		Cuddalore 2 taluks
34 Development Blocks (34 Block Development Officers: BDOs)		*13 Taluks* (tahsildars)
8 urban headquarters 16 semi-urban headquarters 10 rural headquarters	transition from urban to rural	8 urban headquarters 4 semi-urban headquarters 1 rural headquarter
		82 Firkas (82 Revenue Inspectors) 11 urban headquarters 19 semi-urban headquarters 52 rural headquarters
340 Rural Welfare Officers *Intervention Areas* Each RWO is incharge of a few villages (4 to 6)	rural	
1768 Panchayat villages		*2333 Revenue villages* One Village Administrative Officer for one, and sometimes two or three villages.

CHART 1. The rural development administration and the revenue administration: a comparison between their spatial networks in South Arcot District.

Up to January 1985, the first feature of the Development Blocks network was, in a sense, the gap it left in the Kalrayan Hills. A short lived attempt to set up a Tribal Development Block on the mountain ended in 1961, as the gram sevaks posted there, hailing from the lowlands, set up their bases in the towns surrounding the hills instead of setting permanently in the Kalrayans. Before 1976, date of the final abolition by the Tamil Government of the traditional rights of the jagirdar families controlling the South Arcot part of the Kalrayans, the land was not even surveyed and the population, strangely enough, not even classified as scheduled tribes. A major geographical divide was thus intensified by the administrative-cum-development machinery, as if for urban planners and bureaucrats a mountain lacking roads, market places and hill stations was really too rural an area to be worthy of a developmental endeavour.

Things are now changing however. Roads and welfare infrastructures are now penetrating the Kalrayans, which become in February 1985, a full fledged Development Block. Its specificity will naturally remain, and deserves a separate study as such, but at least the entire district is now encompassed in the rural development grid.

How far the rural development bureaucracy goes rural?

We have mentioned earlier that, out of 34 Block headquarters only eight are frankly urban. Five of them, are also in fact taluk headquarters, three are Development Division headquarters, and one is district headquarters. It would be wrong however, to conclude too hastily that towns are always taking the best, as far as the rural development grid is concerned. Interestingly, several taluk towns are not block headquarters: let us mention Tindivanam, Chidambaram, and even Villupuram, the third town in the district, which is not even headquarters of a Development Division. (Neyveli, the second biggest town, does bring about change in its immediate hinterland, but, as a township, is outside of the traditional rural development network). This is certainly a noticeable feature: as per the urban hierarchy,

Villupuram municipality (pop. 77000), or, as second choice Valavanur town panchayat (pop. 13000) ought to be block headquarters, but the function was assigned to Koliyanur village (pop. 4500). The same pattern may be observed in the adjacent Annagramam Block, where Nellikuppam (pop. 40000) is not the headquarters. More generally, in more than fifty per cent of the cases, the block headquarters is not the biggest settlement in the area under consideration. In eight cases the headquarters is a village, while the block boundaries encompass a Census town or a town panchayat, and in five cases, in purely rural blocks, the headquarters is not the biggest village, but rather a village better located on a main road, such as Vallam, Mugaiyur, Tiruvanalur. All of us know these settlements and their contrasted morphology: the old village, usually slightly away from the road, and by the roadside the series of yellow painted stereotyped buildings in which are located the Development Block Offices, and ultimately a primary health centre, a veterinary centre, a land development bank... This is the way in which, for the most part, the rural development bureaucracy goes rural and all the more so, since a few town panchayats which are block headquarters physically still preserve their rural atmosphere. Their tertiary sector—services as well as trade—has grown a great deal but these "boroughs" such as Sankarapuram, Vikravandi, Tiruvennainallur owe their relative dynamism and prosperity to the rural hinterland they interact with.

There is however a second criterion by which the rural involvement of the rural development machinery may be assessed: it is the staff incharge, its duties and its background.

Such an assessment is not easily conducted; to be really significant extensive interviews would be required. Nethertheless an enquiry conducted in a single block—Kallakurichi may provide some pieces of information. It will be noticed that out of 51 government servants working under the Block Development Officer, only 10 Rural Welfare Officers (ex-grama sevaks, ex-village level workers) live and work constantly in the villages, while the tend Extension Officers and the eight technicians, even if based in town, are obliged to visit all the villages of their block once in three months. The Block Managers and naturally the clerks and the subordinate staff don't on the other hand, work in the field. In the case selected, as the headquarters, Kallakurichi, was a Census town, 41 out of 51 staff members were urban based. The figure would naturally differ for purely rural blocks even though, when the headquarters is too small a village, officers may live in the nearest town. But on the whole, the most important point is not so much the base for work as the personal background of the civil servant, and his direct or indirect acquaintance with village life. Here, the staff is divided into two clear categories, those who have a rural background, and the rest. The first category includes the Rural Welfare Officers, who all come from villages. They may have spent a few years in an urban or semi-urban High School in order to pass their SSLC, plus a couple of years in one of the four training centres established in Tamilnadu for Village Level Workers, but they have definitely kept their rural roots. A noticeable feature is that Rural Welfare Officers may by promotion become Extension Officers based at the Block headquarters: this process ensures that at least a part of the officers implementing the rural development policy have a strong rural background. But the pace of promotion is not so fast as to enable those starting at grass roots level to become Black Development Officers.

Thus, most, if not all, the B.D.Os, and many of the managers have an urban background, and for those who have spent decades in Cuddalore or in the large district towns, it is not so easy to settle in a minor town panchayat, much less in a village. If the children are in the best rated high schools or in the few colleges established in only a handful of district towns, the officer will want to leave his family in town, and to commute twice a week to and from his semi-urban or village office. Even if devoted to rural development, he will strongly preserve his urban roots, habits and tastes: it is probably at the key level of the Block Development Officers—men of power and authority in their area—that the whole ambiguity of the urban conceived rural policies is most experienced, if not most publicized.

The dynamics of change rural development policies aim at, are not of course just the result of officers moods. All B.D.Os, while implementing state orders, have to deal with four fundamental features.

the nature of the area they have to develop;

the additional forces of change at work in their blocks;

the nature of the development policies themselves,

and the socio-political feedback emanating from the villages, and canalized through various channels to the urban centres of decision.

The first and second of these four points are still related to the spatial network we are trying to analyse here. The last two points, though certainly not divorced from spatial dimensions, will however be commented upon separately.

The Development Blocks Grid: Some Striking Disparities

A brief examination of the area and rural population patterns of the 35 block currently existing (see map 3) brings two points to our attention. Even if we put aside the Kalrayans block (the largest, but the least populated), the disparities between the block areas are wide. In other words, the meshes of the net are very unequal. Areas range from 164 km^2 (Annagramam) to 450 km^2 (Mangalur). The twelve smallest blocks are (in the class 150-250 km^2) all in the rich alluvial plains along the Ponnaiyar and the Coleroon Lower Vellar system. The largest blocks (in the class 350-450 km^2) are on the whole poorer than the average, and include either tracks of the ferralitic coastal plateaux, or the south Western border areas. Between the two, most of the blocks, 18, are in fact spread over the granitic pediment.

Secondly, the disparities in the rural population charges, even if not as large, are nothertheless very noticeable. The least populated block after the Kalrayans (taking into account the rural population only, as this population is the target of the rural development endeavour) was Bhuvanagiri, 66,674 villagers in 1981. With 134,793 villagers Cuddalore, the most populated block, had twice the inhabitants of Bhuvanagiri Block. Moreover, there is no correlation between area and population: the most populated blocks are of very different sizes and, generally speaking, the high population of a block is not necessarily compensated, as far as the development staff duties are concerned, by a small area. As all blocks have the same staff (except when a special project runs in selected blocks where an additional officer might be posted), the norm is that large size blocks and highly populated blocks are handicapped. Even if the pattern of allotment of funds may alleviate these disparities (and the study of the allotment pattern at division level suggests that per capital equalisation is far from being the rule[18] it is an evidence that the Block Development Officer and his staff, including the ten Rural Welfare Officers posted in each block, cannot devote equal time to each village and each family when they have 42 villages to cover (Panruti Block) or 66 villages (Vallam Block); when they have to raise above the poverty line 40,000 Harijans (Kurinjipadi Block) or 17,000 Harijans (Melmalaiyanur).

Here is a major flaw in urban generated strategies which were apparently satisfied with the fact that each block was in the hands of a standard sized staff, and not pay enough attention to the micro regional disparities.

Another flaw affects all the blocks, including those which are relatively the best supervised: they are two large and this sized defect reveals a great deal of the general philosophy of the state, and its limited development endeavour.

Is Rural Development an Easier Process than Revenue Collection

We stressed earlier that revenue collection was one of the two fundamental tasks assigned to the colonial administration. More than thirty years after Independence the revenue collection grid established by the British authorities is still the leading pattern of space subdivision; when we think of any place in a district we can locate it precisely through the taluk grid. More than thirty years after Independence the leading district officer is still called the Collector, as if the main task of the administration was still officially acknowledgcd as being the transfer of the taxes to the Madras Treasury.

When trying to assess the rationale of the urban-conceived rural development grid, we cannot but compare it to the most elaborate of all network, *e.i.* the Revenue system of territorial coverage and control. This yields significant results. Let us have a fresh look at chart I so as to compare the rural development set-up and the revenue set-up. At the urban upper level under the Collector's control the five divisions are similar. Discrepancies appear at the medium and at the grass root levels. At the medium level, the Revenue Department has a two tier grid, the taluks whose headquarters are the focal points of the life of the countryside as far as most of the trade activities, welfare amenities and official facilities are concerned, and the firkas tier constituted on much smaller areas than the block. At the medium level, the rural development machinery has only one grid, the Development Block network. In 1971, as in 1961, there were, in South Arcot, 8 taluks, 55 firkas, and 34 Development Blocks. Today, we have 13 taluks, 82 firkas and still 34 Blocks, plus the new Kalrayans unit. Clearly enough, the Revenue Administration, although enjoying the better territorial coverage system, still make it tighten and multiplies the meshes of its net: the promise of a better catch. On the other side, not a single block has been divided: the rural development grid sticks to its large meshes.

The contrast between the two grids is still stronger at the grass-roots level. On one hand, the Revenue Administration identified 2333 revenue villages, and posts frequently one Village Administrative Officer to one single village. When villages are small, the V.A.O. may be incharge of two or three revenue units. On the other hand, the Development Block Machinery identified only 1768 panchayat villages (a few hundred of them including two or three revenue villages), and posts only one Rural Welfare Officer for, an average, five or six panchayat villages.

The rationale behind such a discrepancy is to be found in the following alternative: as the power to control the rural space through territorial grids is in the hands of those who, in Madras, control the state, either this state power believes that rural development is an easier process than revenue collection—and thus requires less men no duty on the spot—or this power believes that rural development does not deserve more men and a more efficient grid, snatching at least that of the revenue set up. Nobody, I suppose, would believe in the first assertion and it is likely that the second better reflects the thinking in high places in Madras. Whatever may be the content of the official speeches and the financial allocations granted to the blocks, if there is any urban bias against rural development it is to be found here.

An overall partition of existing blocks would seem to be strongly indicated. Taluks have been divided. Firkas have been divided. The district itself will be divided according to an announcement in early April from a senior minister from South Arcot. In such a context, it would be unjustified to deprive the rural development endeavour of a better adjusted grid, with more extension officers and village officers.

The dynamics of rural change itself provide us with preliminary indications as to how the blocks could be efficiently divided. Let us examine these indications.

D. How Urban Functions Go Rural: Marketing, Finance, and the Dynamics of Rural Change

Be it expressed by the dynamics of economic growth sustained by expanding production and intensified trade, or aimed at more intricate development dynamics, through a (moderate) redistribution of assets and incentives to the weaker rural sections, the rural change as it manifests itself in Tamilnadu to day is not, and cannot be, the result of the combined action of the Rural Development Agencies and the Agriculture Department alone. Social movement, trade and finance are very much at the core of process of change as well. Trade and finance were never exclusively urban. Sandais, were villagers gather once a week, have always existed and still do, and the same is true of village money lenders. But the money lenders are normally approached for emergency succour and family special expenses rather than for productive purpose, and except perhaps for a new cattle fairs of repute, sandais usually cater for the regular needs of the surrounding villages, and do not market agricultural production as such.

Hence, despite sandais and village money lenders, towns are traditionally the central places where traders in agricultural commodities are based, where financial institutions are located, be they nationalized or private banks, credit cooperative societies or registered chit funds companies.

A significant development of the last decades, as far as urban-rural relationships are concerned happened previously in those fields of agricultural trade and finance. Without examining the topic in detail[19] we may mention two instruments used by the state for accelerating the dynamics of change in rural areas. One is the grid of the regulated markets, the other is the network of bank branches.

The efficiency of the regulated market as a tool benefiting producers, and particularly small producers, has been strongly denied by B. Harris.[20] But whom so ever the final beneficiaries of the markets may be, it is relevant to note how they have multiplied recently (in contradiction to "the current emphasis on the necessity to centralize trade geographically" emphasized by Harriss). Traditionally, traders went or sent their agents to the villages to buy crops. The first regulated markets set up in "large" Census towns (Villupuram, Tindivanam, Vriddhachalam are currently still the big three) reversed the movement, and brought the farmers to the town, in search of a fair price for a standardized and controlled commodity by way of bidding and with immediate payment. Even if defective, even if in some cases traders may turn to illegal collusion in order to lower the bids, the system seens not to be so unattractive for the farmers, if the Kallakurichi Regulated Market may be considered as a significant example: the day we visited it, 703 growers were offering their produce (it was in March, with groundnut crops very prominent) to 55 traders (an average number), and, on the whole, official estimates suggest that 90 per cent of the groundnut crop, 90 per cent of the gingelly crop, and 60 per cent of the paddy marketable surplus of the notified market area are auctioned through the local regulated market.[21]

The next phase was the opening of regulated markets in smaller localities. Many of them were, as per our criteria, identified as "boroughs" in our interpretation of the 1961 and 1971 Census data: Marakkanam, Tittagudi, Thyagadurga, Sankarapuram, Tiruvennainallur, Vikravandi. This strengthened their role as relay between full-fledged towns and common villages, all of them being headquarters of a Development Block as well.

Finally, regulated markets were opened in a few big villages such as Manalurpet (pop. 6092), Anantapuram (pop. 5300), Avalurpet (pop-5947), Sethiathope (pop. 5893). A basic function of the town, *i.e.*, trading with agricultural commodities, is thus, even on a limited scale, going rural[22]. A map illustrating the network of the 27 regulated markets existing in early 85 would show that on the whole half of the villages are today, located at least 10 kms from a regulated market.

The same is true for another fundamental urban function: banking. The difficulties faced by central and State Governments in their attempt to convince commercial banks to tap rural resources are well known. Nethertheless, the original reluctance has diminished. Most Bank branches are still urban, but a good number of them have opened recently in those small town panchayats we labelled as semi-urban, most of them being block headquarters. The movement actually goes for beyond the semi-urban (or semi-rural) network: branches are new open in villages which qualify as firka headquarters but which remain definitely small places such as Ariyalur (pop. 2154) Nagalur (pop. 2064), Kammapuram (pop. 2929); and in villages with no other qualification such as Thembair (pop. 2213), Thitanagiri (pop. 2801), Salamedu (pop. 1997).

Aside from and above village banks, banks in towns do drain rural funds and do extend loans to villagers. The leading bank of Kallakurichi is the State Bank of India; all transactions of the Block Development Office are managed by it, including the loans granted under the integrated Rural Development Programme, and the branch has on its staff one Rural Development Officer and one Field Officer. Many of those who benefit from a bank loan also open an account deposit. For the bank manager it is clear that the growth rate of his branch, noticeable over the last five years, is largely due to the expansion of its rural activities, as most of its 3500 deposit accounts and 2000 loan accounts are those of villagers.[23] Data available at the district level confirm the growing penetration of rural areas by the urban banks, as Table 14.1 shows: outstanding bank credit

TABLE 14.1

Rural and Urban Patterns of Scheduled Commercial Banks in South Arcot in 1981

	Number of branches	*Deposits (crores)*	*Advances (crores)*
Total	166	73.2	54.3
Urban	19	13.4	8.5
Semi-urban	71	44.8	28.7
Rural	76	15.0	17.5
Share of the rural sector	45.7%	20.5%	23.2%
Share of the combined semi-urban and rural sector	88.5%	81.7%	85.0%

Source: From Tamilnadu, An Economic Appraisal, 1983-84.

in South Arcot amounted in 1981 (for scheduled commercial banks) to 78.1 crores out of which agriculture, with 31.6 crores came a close second to industry, 35.1 crores.[24]

Clearly enough a good part of semi-urban funds are provided by the villages forming the bank hinterland. Still clearer as the fact that, while urban dwellers draw less loans than they deposit funds, patrons of the rural branches do the reverse and draw more advances than they lodge money in the bank. This does not mean that the extra loans are made good out of urban money since the semi-urban sector with its deep rural roots accounts in actual fact for a considerable deposit surplus deposit being the larger drawer of loans. The semi-urban localities (that we have often identified as block development headquarters) may hence be seen as transit places for money coming in from rural deposits, and going out as rural loans.

If we consider the growth of the number of regulated markets and the expansion of rural and semi-rural banking as some of the indices of the dynamics of change at work in the district, we may come up with some useful elements in the analysis of the apatial network set up by the rural development strategists and bureaucrats.

E. Towards a Better Rural Development Grid

While trade and finance percolate better and better from Census towns to semi-urban localities and to villages, while the revenue administration is well equipped at least spatially to control the countryside at village level, with the firka as a fairly satisfactory low range unit area, the rural development bureaucracy is not receiving from the state and its urban decision makers the remodeled network which could help it to carry out its duty.

A detailed examination of the various maps we have presented in this paper would suggest that the nodes of a more efficient grid do already exist. They are those localities—whatever their official status, be it village or town panchayats—which combine a set of facilities. Semi-rural and rural bank branches are frequently set up in first headquarters. In a few cases, such as Avalurpet, Manaluspet and Srimushnam, there is even a regulated market. An analysis of the health and education amenities which has not been attempted here, would provide additional crucial information on the spatial dynamics of change: a good number of the localities recently enriched with an upgraded school and a primary health centre or a rural dispensary would be find on the list of the villages or small town panchayats graced with a bank. Those are the new grass roots centres of change, the interacting points between fully fledged towns and common villages, and it is around them that new blocks would most suitably be carved out of the existing ones. The firka, with its three dozen or 40 villages, could provide a model of what a better staffed development block could be.

Evidently urban policy makers are perfectly aware of what spatial pattern of coverage permit and what they do not: when the Noon Meals Programme was launched and developed, the government knew how to do it. Apart from the Revenue Development, another Department, Education, has a man in each village: the school master. In Madras, a Minister in charge of the Noon Meals Programme; in the district headquarters, a Personal Assistant to the Collector; in the block, a special Manager; in each village, the school master: this is certainly a coordinated and multi-level attempt to ensure that directives from Madras can be implemented in each village, for a programme which looks like a clever mingling of educational and nutritional strategies, with, as an additional attraction, no risk of social tension. And all political observers acknowledged, in the recent elections, that the noon meal programme was a fine feather in the cap of the popular Chief Minister, and a good vote catcher device as well.

Once again the question arises: why don't urban policy makers pay much attention to the defective network of rural development blocks, when they were so eager to build up a strong grid for revenue collection or for the noon meals programme? Could it be that rural development policies pay less practical or political dividends? This question brings us to the socio-political field which will now be looked at.

III. SPATIAL DYNAMICS, SOCIAL DYNAMICS, AND THE LIMITS OF THE URBAN-RURAL DIVIDE

We have deliberately left untouched, in the above spatial analysis, the effective social contents of the rural development programmes, the social framework in which they are implemented, and the social feedback received from the vllages by the state power as well as by the urban based development bureaucracy. The limits of the present paper leave no room for a detailed analysis of these fundamental questions, but they certainly call for some attempt to consider them, at least within the scope of the urban-rural relationships.

A. From Village to Town: The Feedback through Elected Bodies

Under normal condition the implementation of a rural development strategy is not simply an exercise of urban privilege and authority. Local government—the much publicized panchayat raj—is supposed to give villagers a voice in their own affairs whatever bias towards clientelism and social pressure there may be. As far as networks and areas are concerned, the key fact here is certainly the territorial identity between the development block and the panchayat union. This spatial identity is also hierarchically functional, as it enables the Block Development Officer to act as Panchayat Union Commissioner too. In the standard scheme, a regular feedback is thus provided at from the village: the members of the village panchayats may convey requests and proposals to the Rural Welfare Officer covering the area, while the village panchayats' chairman, at the Union Panchayat level are in constant interaction with the B.D.O. Further along the axis going from village to town, the panchayat unions chairman sitting in the District Development Council are in regular touch with the Collector, who, ex officio, chairs the Council. (see Chart 2)

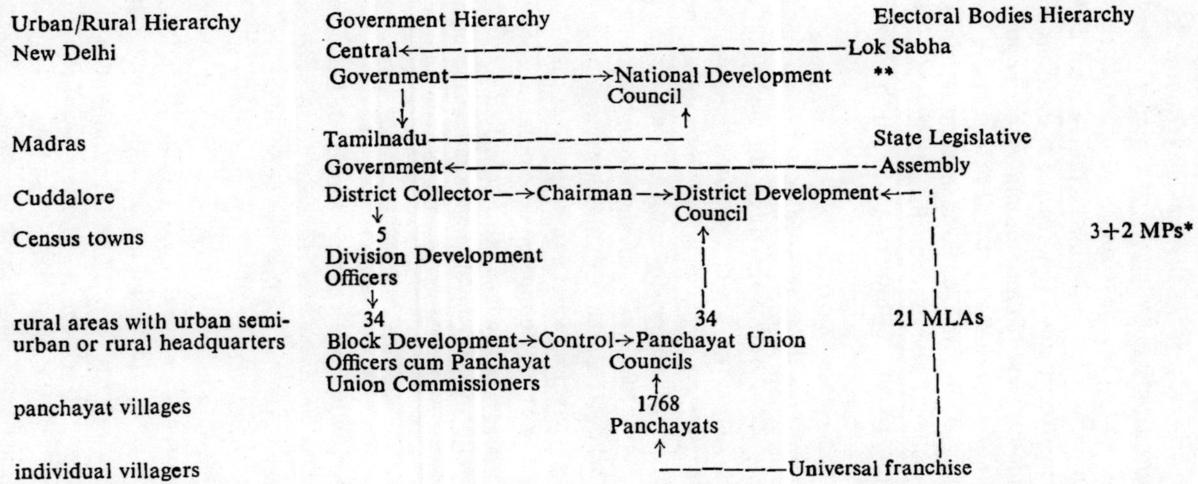

*2MP's constituencies extend mainly in other adjacent districts

**the Rajya Sabha and the State Legislative Council are not mentioned

Development Councils

Non functioning bodies

CHART 2. Urban/rural hierarchy, Development Bureaucracy hierarchy and Electoral Bodies hierarchy.

The point is that, in Tamilnadu, no regular feedback is authorized to flow upwards from the panchayat network, as the entire institution of elected village and Union panchayats has come to a standstill. The Government decision to reserve seats for women and scheduled castes and tribes in local bodies resulted in a Supreme Court stay. For years, no elections were held: villages and unions were simply administered by government officers. Mounting pressures for the reviving of the function of local bodies finally broke through, and elections to panchayats and panchayat union councils, announced at last by the Minister for Local Administration, will be held in September 1985.

We certainly do not take it for granted that the panchayat raj is *per se* a very efficient way for conveying the grievances and suggestions of the rural weaker sections to the policy makers. But the supersession of panchayats is not much more innocuous. Firstly, as far as urban-rural relations go in the development machinery, the power of the urban hierarchy is enlarged, as the Panchayat Union Commissioner who is none other than the B.D.O. has no elected counterpart at the Union level. At the end of the urban dominated development grid, the B.D.O. is thus both judge and judged. Rural feedback, the free comment on the result of the development policies is henceforth a self judgement, something of an urban-controlled mockery.

Let us go further, with reference to the recent Left Front rural strategies in West Bengal, where for years too, no local elections had been held; one of the first decisions taken by the Front after coming to power in 1977 was specifically to hold elections, and victory once achieved, to rely strongly upon local bodies, particularly gram panchayats and panchayat samitis, to break the traditional subservience linking the development and administrative bureaucracy to the powerful rural landed elite. For government devoted to reform the agrarian social relations, the political control of the local bodies—and the support at grass roots level of the party and of the Kisan Sabhas—was the way to bring significant change from Calcutta to the village. In

the Tamil context, a contrario, the case with which over the years the government held itself apart from the panchayat system can only be interpreted as a design of its reluctance to bring about radical change in the countryside. Not that the AIADMK is not eager to control the villages its political opponents tend to analyse the suppression of the hereditary village headman and Karnam, and the intronisation of the Village Administrative Officer, as a clear cut strategy of political control. The question, in Tamilnadu, in West Bengal, and everywhere else remains: control for which socio-economic purpose?

The temporary eclipse of the panchayat bodies has left open for the rural population, three ways to convey their grievance to town, *i.e.*, to the administrative or/and political powers. One is to spontaneously agitate for long due amenities. This is not a very common practice, but a few villages resorted to it recently, when they decided to boycott the elections in protest against the lack of response to repeated requests for a bus line, a bridge or a link road. A second line of action relies upon organised protest, and implies that lobbies or parties are at work. A recent example was given, in early April, when, with the backing of the Indian Farmers and Toilers Party, a procession of residents from Chengamedu village, Tittagudi taluk, went to the Development division office at Vriddhachalam, with symbolic empty pots in hand, and demanded "permanent relief in the matter of drinking water supply, repairs to roads from Chengamedu (...) proper functioning of overhead tank and opening of fair price shops in their village",[25] all matters normally dealt with by the panchayat representatives. The third way open for rural feedback is much more ambiguous and much more permanent as well. It consists in the upper level elected bodies, and the representatives who sit in them: MLAs and MPs. The ambiguity here is manifold, firstly, because, even when a representative of a rural constituency (and all the South Arcot constituencies are predominantly rural), a party-affiliated MP or MLA has to receive a preliminary urban and centralized sanction simply in order to be nominated as a candidate. Thus, he is both the representative of a specific area, and the representative of a State or All India party, which implies that he has to accept the directives of the Delhi and Madras headquarters. Secondly, because of the nature of his representativeness, a MP or MLA represents an area, certainly, but which social segment settled in this area does he predominantly represent? For which groups, which classes, which interests will he act, interfere, lobby and bring pressure to bear?

Here we come to a well known area of investigation and debate, *i.e.*, the relations between the local representatives and the development bureaucracy. Not unfrequently, those relations are summerised in one word by radical social scientists: collusion. In fact, it appears than such collusion, which is the rule more often than not, is largely the result of unequal power relationships. Studies of the bureaucracy (Kuldeep Mathur, V.A. Pai Panandiker) have underlined how different, and even anatagonistic, are the backgrounds of the leading IAS administrators and those of most of the MLAs. At the block level, the differences may be not so wide, but the uneven balance of power is more pronounced. First of all, an MLA represents a larger area than a block. Boundaries of constituencies and block-cum-panchayat unions are not necessarily adequate, but on the whole, a MLAs constituency encompass roughly two to three blocks. (South Arcot accounts for 21 MLAs versus 35 blocks), while a MP's constituency covers an average area approximately equivalent to ten blocks.

However, the power of the MLA is not to be found in the size of his constituency. It comes partly from the privileges and rights bestowed upon him. The MLAs, for instance, are ex-officio members of the District Development Council (as there is no Panchayat Union Chairmen now, the MLAs are all the better positioned to voice the grievances of their vote banks). Above all, the MLAs and the MPs are, in the case of the hierarchically subordinated development officers, men who have direct access to the urban centres of decision. Because of political affiliation, and besides their acknowledged role as representatives of the people, MLAs who have the ear of a ranking minister have to a certain extent the de facto power to transfer any one in the district, from the Rural Welfare Officer to the Collector himself. This relative instability in the administrative machinery, hopelessly subservient to the politicking game, shapes the actual background to the implementation of rural development policies. In most cases, collusion at local levels between the political strong man and the administration is unavoidable, be it spontaneous or not, and the changes in physical targets recommended by local representatives are just one common manifestation of it. This is also, we believe, one of the facets of urban-rural relationships as shown in the competitive spheres of political power and administrative power. The first takes the lead over the second for many obvious reasons, and also because the direct link between the rural constituency and the metropolis in command is much more efficient than the multilevel administrative and developments networks which compel men, as well as ideas and reports, to follow the hierarchical set up of authorities in going from the base to the top: a set-up which largely echoes the pyramid of the semi-urban and urban hierarchy.

B. The Limits of the Urban-Rural Divide and the Dynamics of Change

The urban-rural dichotomy is an effective reality in many fields; physical amenities, welfare infrastructures, rates of illiteracy, ways of life are noticeably different in the two spheres. In our opinion, however, these disparities are not such as to allow the urban world and the rural world to be considered as two separate and antagonistic entities. They are, on the contrary, closely correlated. The concept of urban-rural divide is henceforth valid only when we assign some limits to it. These limits result from, firstly, the constant economic, cultural, migratory, governmental relations established, directly or indirectly, between the countryside and the towns and cities, and, secondly from the nature of the state power. The idea of an "urban bias" is very relevant on many grounds, but it tends, to blur a basic fact related to the nature of the state in India, and to the power and choices of the rural dominant class.

We tend towards an acceptance of this common proposal: that the state power in India, at the upper level, sustains the interests of the two dominant classes of the India Society, namely the enterprising and industrialist class and the class of the big farmers; whatever may be the repeated complaints against the Government policies made by these two groups (too many controls said industrialists before the 1985 budget; agricultural prices too low, say the farmers). To accept such a view (extremely schematized here) is to agree with a basic point: that the leading rural class is not as cut off from the towns, nor as much despised by the urban sphere as a too rigid acceptation of the urban bias concept would tend to suggest.

A look at the dominant rural class as it is in the Tamil countryside will confirm this idea. Look at the mirasdars of South Arcot: two or three families for a standard village of 1000—1500 inhabitants, usually Reddiars, Mudaliars or Vellalas by caste. No one knows exactly what they own, for besides their registered landed property, most of it nanjai, they may control benami lands too. These assets give them power over tenants and over landless labourers families dependant upon them for their living, depending too upon the loans in cash or kind the landlord regularly extends to them. This wealth, and the deeply rooted socio-economic relations of clientelism, give the biggest landlords not only power, but status too. They are the benefactors of the local temple and the patrons of the village religious festivals. They are at the apex of the village social hierarchy. Because of this power over land and men, and because of their exalted status, landlords are usually not eager to leave the village. In a town, they would need much more wealth in order to enjoy an equivalent status, and their relationships with subordinate labourers would be of a very different kind.

It would however be unrealistic to believe that this rural power stands on its own. It stands because the rural "elite" has the necessary connections with the urban sphere.

The well-off farmers are those who know the men on the spot in the towns: the officers in the various Departments, those in charge of law and order and those who control the flux of finance, they know judges, police officers, advocates, bankers. Their surpluses are also for a part town oriented, not only for trade. Pretty often, they indulge in urban investments: they may buy property, set up a bus company, build a theatre, become partners, along with urban investors, in small or medium sized industries. A close relative may become an urban dweller and will then look after the urban interests of the family, sometimes on a full time basis, sometimes as an activity additional to the job he had chosen after passing a B.Com. or a B.Law. Last but not least, the mirasdars have useful political connections more often than not. The most influential amongst them are seen as vote catchers by politicians, in a spirit of give and take. Multifarious therefore are the intricate relations between those who have the village as their main base of power and those who exercise power from the towns. Here, we do believe, lies one of the crucial aspects of urban-rural relationships, and one of the key factors in rightly assessing the urban bias. If an urban bias drive the towns to grind down the countryside, the squeeze doesn't affect all the villagers. and works only because of the connections and the collusion between a section of the rural society and those who have some power in the towns, be it economical, political, or governmental in nature. Urban-rural disparities exist, but the urban-rural divide is not an overall reality. Beyond a certain point, the concept acts as a myth, masking—beyond secondary conflicting interests—a primary functional network of socio-economic powers which cuts across the urban and rural lines,

This picture. however, is somewhat fragmentary as social dynamics do not set it once and for all. One of the most interesting things to observe in India today is precisely the consciousness slowly transforming the social fabric of the village, a change strongly correlated with new urban-rural relationships. On the one hand, and we return here to the central topic of this paper, this transformation results from the rural development policy; on the other, it is the dividend of the spreading politicization of the rural masses. To summarize a complex evolution in a few lines, we may venture to distinguish three main phases in the general policies aimed at rural change in India. The fifties, and a good part of the sixties, were time of "Community Development" with emphasis given to the uplifting of the rural population as a whole. In the late sixties and in the seventies, the emphasis was shifted to agricultural growth and increased in production: the "green revolution" was supposed to benefit first the enterprising farmers, but also, ultimately the whole rural classes. Neither Community Development nor the "green revolution" succeeded in pushing the masses above the poverty line. Hence the approach selected for the eighties, with a twin emphasis on productivity on the one hand and alleviation of rural poverty on the other Phase II has resulted in an increase in the weight of an expanded class of medium-sized dynamic farmers (to the cost of those who could not match them and lost their land). In Tamilnadu, this class, on the whole, was largely sympathetic to the Dravidian movement. Phase I of yesteryear did multiplies physical projects, but failed to eradicate poverty. Phase III today may very well meet the same fate. Garibi hatao might be a piece of rhetoric. But rhetoric is also a factor in change, and if the results of the development policies did not come up to official expectations, they did however promote some decisive changes in the mentality of the villagers, whose perceptions of the town, of the urban power and of the rural relays of the urban power are noticeably transformed.

The contraction of land and labour availability in the villages was bound to increase a migratory trend to towns and cities (in the 1971-81 decade, urban population growth rate in South Arcot was twice the rural rate). The movement is the result of many correlated factors, one of them undoubtly being the diffusion of education, and, at a minor but complementary level, the diffusion of the cinema in villages. Both opened some vistas on urban values and urban dreams. Both speeded up contact to politics whose highest centres of power are urban:

the cinema, as a leading propagator of the Dravidian movement, ideology and rhetorics, and the education system, since the election of school leaders, even from the 10th standard, very quickly came to be decided according to political leanings. Thereafter, on the whole, the attitude of villagers with regard to the urban-controlled development administration underwent considerable change largely because, in one way, the urban centres of decision and power seemed to be less out of reach and alien than before, and sometimes less. Up to and including the fifties most villagers were rather subdued when facing the administration: for them submission to the goodwill of the bureaucrats was more or less of a rule. When the Community Development programme was really under way in Tamilnad, in the sixties, information on policies and projects circulated from town to countryside and upliftment was presented as the official aim of the governments in power, in New Delhi as well as in Madras. "Upliftment" (Munnetra) was also the key word for a young and very active party, the Dravida Munnetra Kajagam, and DMK propaganda contributed largely to a fresh awakening of the backward classes, and the lower forward classes, which account for the majority of the rural population. This conjunction between national goals and regional politics brought a change: facing the development bureaucracy, these classes of small and low medium peasants, knowing that urban rhetoric was now on their side, abandoned their age old submission, and started to request bureaucrats to act for them, and not only for those with traditional power and connections. Finally, after the DMK and the AIADMK came to power, their populist stands masked somewat the selective tendencies of the green revolution strategy. Politicization, more than ever, percolated everywhere, electoral promises and electoral compaigning aroused in many a feeling that after all, their voices counted, and that something was due to them, a reasoning further strengthened by the present emphasis on the weaker sections manifested in the Integrated Rural Development Programme. On the one hand, the movements having affected the Backward classes in the sixties gained momentum and spread over the Scheduled Castes, whose submissiveness diminished and whose demands were expressed in a stronger voice. On the other hand, and going a step further, the rural development bureaucrats were (and are now) faced with a new segment of villagers who not only ask to have things done, but also tend to order them, may to shrewdly threaten them. "I know my rights, who are you to delay action or to give me orders?" is not an uncommon comment in B.D.O.s' offices today: when expressed by a villager wearing a red and blackedged somin, the supposition is that the man may have the exactly right connection with the urban political power. "I'll have a word about it with the MLA" the peasant might say. "I'll have a word about it with the Minister" the MLA might say. It is important then to distinguish strongly the concept of "rural-urban gap", which refers to the widening disparities between the town and the village, as far as amenities and opportunities are concerned, from the concept of "rural-urban divide" which suggests that the two worlds are apart. In fact, the rural-urban gap—which itself deserves a thorough analysis—could very well result from a certain collusion between those in power in towns and the rural leaders enjoying both the benefit of their village, status and that of their urban connections.

Rural-urban Relationships, State and Society a few (provisional) Conclusions

A few (provisional) conclusions can be drawn from the here above analysis.

Firstly something of an ambiguity has to be clarified. On the one hand, the government machinery goes rural to a not negligible extent either directly, through the grid of the rural development administration, or indirectly, through its control of, for instance, regulated market and banking policies. On the other hand, the traditional ideology still holds good, that depicts the town as the authoritative centre of change, as the abode of education and knowledge, or even as the abode of civilization. The process of rural development is clearly expected to result from a descending pattern of hierarchized authorities, which is for the most part the copy of the urban hierarchy grid. To go rural is simply, in this perspective, to extend more efficiently the process of command from top to bottom. In the meantime, and secondly, this percolation of urban functions and powers to the countryside opens the way, along with current rhetoric on the eradication of rural poverty and the politicization of village life, for a new self assessment by the rural masses, who do not feel as alien from the town as before.

But, while rural people grow more and more acquainted with the town and its agents, the old prejudice (if not contempt) against villages and villagers still endures amongst urban dwellers and a good number of "rural developers". Those engaged in the battle for development with a theory of society and social change in mind how benefarious such an ideology can be. If these prejudices are not dispensed with one may wonder if the gap is not bound to expand between the urban men of decision, authority and action on one side and the rural weaker sections more and more conscious of their rights on the other. Politicians, in their own interests, know very well that the rural-urban divide is a fleeting and ambiguous reality with nothing simplistic about it: after all aren't they the very people who gain urban power through rural votes?

Thirdly, the increasing rural-urban mixture strategy departs positively from the past on at least one point: it testifies that the old disaggregated view of the urban sphere and the rural sphere is on the wane amongst policy makers. In contrast to the Sixth Plan philosophy (or lack of philosophy) of urban-rural relationships, the "Approach to the Seventh Plan"[26] recognizes, far more than before, the importance of urban-rural relationships with regard both to rural development and urban development. The Central Planning Commission now refers explicitely to "rural-urban disparities" (p. 8) and to the "widening of the rural-urban gap" (p. 13). The overall strategy currently rightly connects the future of the towns and the future of the rural tracks, hence the trend towards supporting a comprehensive effort in regional planning. A fresh and more detailed plea for district and block plans is the logical result of this integrated approach. Locating infrastructure in "the numerous towns with population between one lakh and 5000" and "in several small rural centres which would have to be selected in a regional planning approach or where economic growth is already showing itself" besides slowing down the population exedus towards large cities and metropolises, would "indeed make life worth living in smaller places": such are some of the recommendations emphasized in the Planning Commission document (p. 24).

Fourthly and finally, the two concepts of 'urban and rural' are evidently not the only parameters central to the challenge of rural development. The entire philosophy of the state and the nature of the political power presently in the saddle are crucial issues here, and what we have concluded from the analysis of the rural development grid, the looseness of a network whose meshes cannot match those of the Revenue Department, is just a clue amongst many others: that the Tamilnadu Government has no minister fully in change of rural development[27] provides us with another indication.

We do agree with M.L. Dantwala, when he qualifies the Rural Development picture in three words: "Investment without Organisation".[28] What can be added to his comment is that the lack of organisation also affects the spatial dimension of the development policy. Not that a finer grid would necessarily give a better result just as a finer plan is not automatically bound to fulfill the expectations. Whatever the grids and the plans are, the key questions remain: for whom do planning authorities plan? For whom does the implementation bureaucracy implement? Just as a more comprehensive plan would do, a more elaborated grid would only sharpens an instrument: the grid is necessary, not sufficient. In one way, the urban-conceived network of the rural development machinery expresses only the level of dedication of a state policy not the ultimate aim of that policy. Getting up and controlling spatial network is not an innocuous exercise, for spatial dynamics are, for the most part, a significant manifestation of social and political dynamics: in the field of urban-rural relations as in any field to which a geographical approach may be taken, space, state and society are always fundamental categories, as well as intricately interwoven realities.

REFERENCES

1. According to convention, 'state' which a small s, refers here to the state power, whatever its scale of application (from the national to the local level) may be, whilst 'State' with a capital S refers to the State of Tamil Nadu.

2. Ministry of Rural Development: Annual Report 1983-84 Government of India, New Delhi, 1984, 155 p (Hindi) and 155 P (English)+ two fold outs.

3. Planning Commission: Sixth Five Year Plan 1980-85. Mid-Term Appraisal. Government of India, New Delhi, 1983.

4. Ministry of Rural Development: Annual Report 1983-84, *op. cit. see* p. 78-85.

5. State Planning Commission: Towards an Affluent District Economy. A Perspective Plan for South Arcot. Madras 1973 Plan documents No. 20 and 21; pp 193 and 227.

6. This perspective was very prevalent during the three day seminar on the 'Kaveri Basin Ecodevelopment' organized in January 1985 by the Madras Science Foundation, little attention was given to the peasant and tribal rationales *vis-a-vis* environment.

7. An officer of Kallakurichi block development dixit, interview, March 1985:

   I leave to authorized linguists the care of commenting upon the Tamil inheritance one may decipher in the English rendering: after all, if I am not mistaken, there is a single word in Tamil for "inhabitants of a capital" and civilized persons (nakara-p-pati-valnar, in the Tamil lexicon transcription), and the word 'civilization' (nakarikam) refers also to "the manners pertaining to a city".

8. Michael Liption "Why Poor People Stay Poor" A Study of Urban Bias in World Development" Heritage Publishers, New Delhi, 1980. See particularly chapters 2, 3 and 4 p 44-141.

9. The most recent one has been launched by Nilakantha Rath: "Garibi Hatao"—Can IRDP do it? Economic and Political Weekly, Bombay, February 9, 1985 p. 238-246, and is going on thanks to the two following rejoinders: ML Dantwala: " 'Garibi Hatao': Strategy Options" EPW March 16, 1985, p. 475-476, and Indira Hirway

"Garibi Hatao': Can IRDP Do it?", EPW March 30, 1985, p. 561-564.

10. For instance: Kuldeep Mathur "Bureaucracy and the New Agricultural Strategy. New Delhi, Concept, 1982, and V.A. Pai Panandiker, R.N. Bishnoi, O.P. Sharma: Development Bureaucracy, New Delhi, Oxford & IBH, 1983.

11. Ministry of Rural Development: Annual Report 1983-84, *op. cit* p. 1.

12. But the "average district" features are fast evolving as the partition of old districts into two or three gains mementum.

13. C.J. Baker. An Indian Rural Economy, 1880-1955. The Tamilnadu countryside. New Delhi, Oxford University Press, 1984. See p. 422.

14. See J. Raeine: "Small market towns and small towns in South India: a critical use of the Census data in the field of urban geography. A case study of the Tamil district of South Arcot and of the Pondicherry Territory". Mimeographed paper presented at the *Indo-French Bi-National Seminar on Problems of Urban growth.* Centre for the study of Regional Development, Jawaharlal Nehru University, New Delhi, Dec. 1978.

15. Census of India 1981, Series 1, India. Paper 2 of 1981, Provisional Population Totals, Rural-Urban Distribution, New Delhi, 1981, See p. 23.

16. *Ibid.* p. 23

17. But Arakandanallur, a functional suburb of Tirukkoyilur, is classified as a town panchayat with only 4338 inhabitants in 1981. Other town panchayats not classified as Census Towns had in 1981 a population ranging between 5000 and 18000 inhabitants.

18. To choose an example on the maintenance front: allotment in 1984-85, under the maintenance grant for maternity centres: Vriddhaehalam Division: Rs. 41 per annum per hundred villagers Chidambaram Division: Rs. 87 (Source: calculated from "Details of allotment for 1984-85. expenditure and balance under various schemes as on 14-3-85" Unpublished. Collectorate of Cuddalore.

19. For a detailed assessment of trade aased on field survey conducted in a district adjacent to South Arcot, see Barbara Harriss "Transitional Trade and Rural Development". Vikas, Delhi, 1981.

20. B. Harriss: State and Market State intervention in Agricultural Exchange in a Dry Region of Tamilnadu: South India, Concept, New Delhi, 1984. See chapter 4 "Regulated Agricultural Markets, p. 71-116.

21. Interview with the Superintendent, Kallakurichi Regulated Market, 11-3-1985.

22. Occasionally for a time, as the concentration of decentralized activities tends to transform the nature of the receiving localities: Manalurpet, Anantapuram and Sethiatope have now received the status of town panchayats, as their annual income has passed the one-lakh line.

23. Interview with the Manager, State Bank of India, Kallakurichi Branch, 12.3.1985.

24. Government of Tamilnadu, Tamilnadu, An Economic Appraisal 1983-84, Madras, 1984, see p. 131-132.

25. "Assurance saves villagers' pots". Indian Express, Madras, 10.4.1985.

26. Planning Commission. The Approach to the Seventh Five Year Plan, 1985-90. Government of India, New Delhi, 1984, p. 32.

27. Besides the Minister for Housing and Local Administration, who deals also with Community Development, at least five other Ministers are concerned with matters related to socio-economic rural change.

28. M.L. Dantwala "Rural Development. Investment without organisation". Economic and Political Weekly, Bombay, 30 April 1983, p. 686-689.

15

RELATING METROPOLITAN PLANNING TO DEVELOPMENT—THE CASE OF CMPO & CMDA

K. Biswas

With the setting up of the Calcutta Metropolitan Development Authority (CMDA) which started functioning from October 1970, there have been occasions when questions have been raised regarding the relationship between Calcutta Metropolitan Planning Organisation (CMPO) and CMDA. An attemptis made in this article to bring out some salient aspects of their inter-relationship.

The task of drawing up a physical development programme for the Calcutta Metropoltan District, for what was then the Fourth Plan (1966-71) fell on CMPO. This programme was essentially based on the schemes prepared by it previously in the fields of water supply, sewerage, drainage, traffic, transportation and bustee improvement. There were additional schemes prepared by the other executing agencies, namely, the

Kalyan Biswas, formerly Director of Calcutta Metropolitan Planning Organisation, is now Deputy Secretary in the Ministry of Works & Housing, New Delhi.

Public Health Engineering, Irrigation & Waterways, Calcutta Improvement Trust, Howrah Improvement Trust, Calcutta Corporation, etc., operating in the metropolis. But no significant advance could be made during the period 1966-69 mostly due to a scarcity of financial resources, in spite of very serious efforts made by the Government of West Bengal in this regard.

In May 1970, during the second spell of President's Rule in West Bengal, the Government of India took the initiative in urban development in the metropolis and gave an indication of the resources likely to be available. At a very short notice, an item-wise programme was drawn up, largely consisting of the various schemes available, with an outlay of Rs. 150 crores for the revised Fourth Plan period of 1969-74. An amount of Rs. 44 crores out of the total outlay was to come from out of the State's Plan resources, with the balance to be met from market borrowings, proceeds of Entry Tax and grants and loans from the Government of India. The outline of the final programme consisted of 92 schemes (later extended and broken up into 112) including those continuing from the Third Plan period, to be executed by 17 major implementing agencies which were to spend Rs. 150 crores in virtually three years—a ten-fold increase over the average annual performance of the preceding five years. The socio-economic context and the political unrest both in the metropolis and in the State of West Bengal at the time this programme was launched gave an added urgency to what was essentially an "infrastructure improvement" programme of a rapidly deteriorating urban environment.

It was in this background that the CMDA was born. Its birthpangs were heightened by other crucial factors like the organizational weakness of the implementing agencies, scarcity of critical raw materials, lack of preparedness with detailed schemes in some cases, not to speak of the general law and order situation. But the fact that CMDA could at all get going in the first instance was almost entirely due to the tireless and productive planning work which CMPO had been doing since 1961.

It is useful to pause at this stage and note that the two basic issues, namely, (a) the necessity of creating a statutorily independent Development Authority, and (b) the pre-conditions for its success, are two separate but interrelated issues. For a task of such magnitude involving a number of agencies for successful execution including a large number of local bodies and local authorities within the CMD area, the creation of an all-pervasive high-powered body hardly needs any emphasis. It has been the common experience everywhere that unelss this is done, the necessary impetus and expedition may not be always available from within the existing apparatus of the state government where the paralysing routine hardly leaves any scope for getting new things done in a time-bound manner. All the same, unless (i) there are projects to implement (which means that adequate planning has gone before); (ii) definite funds are available on a long-term basis, and (iii) simultaneous adjustments have taken place in the implementing agencies to work in the given situation, such bodies can be veritable thorns in any state administrative apparatus.

To enable it to carry out its statutory functions the following tasks are envisaged for CMDA:

(i) Programming and allocation of work; supervision and coordination of work; evaluation of work in progress;

(ii) Financial planning and accounting;

(iii) Execution and coordination in specialized areas where the tasks may be new and organizational structures are not yet clear;

(iv) Communication and public information;

(v) Legal services and internal administration.

The first function identified in the legislation is the formulation of plans. Yet CMPO exists to formulate plans. Where is the line drawn?

The programming of projects by the CMDA and also its financial planning certainly represent planning activities. And in the more conventional sense of "planning" as a physical design, the bustes improvement and the low-cost housing tasks of the CMDA will also require plans.

The question is not a simple one of "who does the planning" but, "who-does what planning". An executing agency has to do a certain amount of its own planning. Plans generally have to be modified or revised on the spot as conditions arise. It is simple if the executing agency has this responsibility for plan revision.

Some plans must be revised to put them into workable form even before they reach the execution stage. To some degree this also is more simply done by the executing agency.

The establishment of the CMDA and an identification of its responsibilities require some new thinking about the most appropriate responsibilities of the CMPO and the most appropriate organizational pattern for carrying out this responsibility.

In separating the planning responsibilities, it is possible to identify CMPO's primary concern in the following way:

Advance Planning with Time Lag

The long-range as against the short-range. Thus, for example, the CMDA is concerned at this point with the first year of the Fifth Plan period, The later years and the Plans beyond, perhaps best fall within the purview of CMPO. Perhaps the CMDA should always be programming 4/5 years ahead, so that as it moves along in the Fifth Plan it begins programming for the Sixth Plan; and the CMPO constantly moves into the future 5 years ahead of the CMDA.

Planning for Spatial Integration

CMPO is primarily concerned with what one can call "spatially integrated planning" as distinct from individual project planning. The line here cannot be drawn as sharply as above. But the CMPO is concerned with all of the actions that must take place in an integrated manner in a particular area to achieve targets and objectives, whereas the CMDA is concerned with the specific projects in that area, particularly those to be executed by public agencies with public funds.

Conceptual Planning

The CMPO is concerned centrally with "conceptual planning" as against immediate, pragmatic planning. Once again, the line is hard to draw, but the CMPO should be concerned with idea-generation, ideas to be sure that must be realistic and meet the tests of logic and consistency, but ideas which need not take into consideration certain of the immediate political facts of life. CMDA, on the other hand, must be quite sensitive to these political facts of life. It seems desirable that there be a certain amount of tension between the two agencies working at these two separate ends of the scale. This tension lifts the pragmatists out of ad-hocery on the one hand and keeps the feet of the conceptual planners planted in reality on the other.

There may be some conflicts between CMDA and CMPO. But this is not necessarily bad. It is bad only if there is no resolution of the conflict. The conflicts may arise in two fields:

(a) A difference of basic policy. For example, CMDA might choose to emphasise central area renewal, whereas CMPO might choose a series of intermediate locations for renewal.

(b) Conflict in work priorities. CMDA may request, or even direct, CMPO to prepare plans which cause a significant revision of CMPO's work programme.

Short, well-reasoned debates can be useful; long, fostering arguments can be harmful. Therefore, the power to decide must be clearly identified. One would think that the State Government will have that power in its own right.

So far, we have sought to identify the basic characteristics of CMPO and CMDA based on their assigned or allotted tasks as expressed in the Government Resolution (for CMPO) and the Act (for CMDA). If the current debate were restricted only to this, one need not worry too much. But several other questions have also came up which require some examination.

For instance, the phrase "planning gap" has frequently been used by some in this context. This could mean, first of all, that for the schemes included in the CMDA fourth or fifth plans, not enough "projectising" has been done. In fact, it may be that many items have been included in the CMDA programme which still are or were at a notional stage. There are certain distinct stages in the process by which an idea or a concept gradually develops forward, the stage of per-tender engineering and architectural drawings. Such a process is by definition and nature an evolutionary one, and is also time-consuming. A situation might, therefore, have arisen where notional schemes were included in the CMDA programme, which, because of lack of follow-up planning activities, remained unimplementable. If CMPO were to take up these follow-up planning activities up to pre-tender stage, and if its failure to do so has led to the alleged "planning gap," several other questions become relevant. For instance, what is the level of planning activity expected from CMPO? If it be granted that conceptual planning is to be done by CMPO, is it also expected that detailed follow-up "projectisation" of the schemes arising out of such conceptual plans are also to be done by CMPO? Moreover, does CMPO have enough personnel to do justice to such a work-load? Apparently, a government planning agency cannot extend itself unlimitedly to take up such a load of work without losing its viability and effectiveness. Where then is the line to be drawn? Then again, it is important to understand that the pressures on CMDA are not the same as those on CMPO. If CMPO has previously done some projectisation especially of water, sewerage or traffic schemes, this was done in the "lull" period of the late 60s when hardly any of its schemes were being implemented. But in the 70s to expect

CMPO to give as much attention to the projectisation of its schemes as to additional concept planning, would be too much. The answer to the charge that there in a "planning gap" may have to be sought elsewhere, especially in the question, to what extent CMDA was realistic to include even notional schemes as part of their implementable fourth plan. But then, that is another matter.

However, "Planning gap" can also be interpreted to mean that CMDA is not getting enough schemes for implementation. In the normal circumstances, one would expect CMDA to get projects from four conceivable sources: CMPO, consulting firms, other departments, and its own organization. So far as CMPO is concerned, one would like to presume that there is no dearth of identifiable schemes for the fifth plan. The same may also be true to a great extent for other departments of the state government. One would however like to emphasise here that (a) not all such schemes need necessarily be of metropolitan significance or character and (b) all these schemes need to be inter-related area-wise to the extent possible so that their planning and execution can have some relevance and impact in a specific area within a reasonable time period. Such an approach however presupposes that CMDA would be concerned only with major capital investments of metropolitan or sub-metropolitan importance, leaving hopefully, the inevitable consequential "internal" or "fill-in" plans and schemes to be taken up by other agencies. If such a presumption be not correct, then the level of investment activity of CMDA (just as the level of planning activity of CMPO) would require detailed scrutiny.

It is however the role of the consulting firms preparing detailed projects (whether on "turn-key" basis or not) on behalf of CMDA, that has raised more intriguing questions than anything else. Unfortunately, this topic has always provoked emotive reactions, which has left the matter much less clear. While this is not the proper place to discuss the pros and cons one would nevertheless like to point ont the sterility of this debate so long as no attempt has been made to understand the basic issues involved. CMDA is virtually running against time to produce results and therefore it must have as many projects as possible ready on the ground if only to ensure arrest of further urban deterioration after a time. If for this purpose it utilises CMPO's or any other department's notional or functional plans for obtaining quick results, it gains in several ways: (i) it may have more implementable schemes off the shelves for the present or the future; (ii) it may help in developing an expertise and a core of technicians within the consulting firms involved in urban development project, which would be a good investment by itself for the metropolis; (iii) it may attract those young technicians who may be so roped in, to be our future planners of whom we are going to require a good many; and (iv) it can broaden its implementation strategy by employing such of the consulting firms as may agree, to work on a turn-key basis. One need not necessarily assume away the various pitfalls associated with such a system, but is it also not equally true that the system of employing private consulting firms on such a massive urban development programme has never been resorted to before, and that the various pitfalls arise due to inexperience on both sides? All our consulting experience in this country so far has either been on big steel and power complexes and the like or on specific industrial projects without any orientation whatsoever towords the multi-faceted urban projects with which CMDA is involved. Even in the cost element which otherwise does look prohibitive sometimes, one would like to think that there is room for adjustment, for mutual give and take, since the private consulting firms would be silly not to venture out on this ground alone on to such a technically and professionally challenging tasks as the CMDA programme offers. If CMDA can pay for the cost, there is no reason for it not to use the consulting firms as a matter of cautious policy, with professional ethics being shown on both the sides and the usual market chicanery eschewed.

Such a policy, if carried out well, will go a long way in setting the point earlier mentioned, *i.e.*, the level of CMPO's planning activity. One would expect CMPO in such an arrangement to play the role of the prime mover as also the final approver of the consultants' detailed schemes. It would be feasible to develop a working arrangement whereby the triumvirate of CMPO-CMDA-consulting firms could meaningfully cooperate even while continuing to function within their allotted spheres. In such an arrangement (a) CMDA need have no qualms that it would not get good, implementable and "as-desired" plans, and (b) CMPO need have no apprehensions that its planning prerogative would be whisked away by CMDA and the consulting firms. That this inter-relationship is not a mere hypothesis but has been duly protected under the law is evident from the fact that under the CMDA Act, the Government of West Bengal approves the schemes taken up by CMDA for execution. How does the State Government do this without the CMPO? One would like to presume, in the absence of any other evidence to the contrary, that the drafting of the CMDA Act was done in this fashion precisely because of CMPO's existence. Otherwise, this kind of government approval has little meaning, and would have been similar to the kind of approval provided for in the Calcutta Improvement Trust and Howrah Improvement Trust Acts where schemes approval is merely administrative and not planning or technical.

There is also the question whether metropolitan planning should also be organised under the single aegis of the metropolitan development authority. While one can cite instances where such an arrangement may have taken place successfully, the basic point for consideration is whether this would be effective in so large and complex an area as is covered by CMDA. At the cost of repetition we may point out that planning functions are long-range and radical, but operational and development objectives are short-range. If the two are mixed up, the latter invariably wins at the cost of the former. Yet there are other factors also which do not make it easier to conceive of such a "merger" of CMPO and CMDA. Firstly, not all of CMPO's work is relevant to CMDA. Although CMPO primarily exists for the CMD area, the way it has evolved over the last 12 years gives it a far wider range of activities than is possible for CMDA. The talent and experience associated with CMPO, suitably dressed up, can still be utilised to initiate state-level, subregional-level, and area-level physical planning. The list of works done during the last 10 years by CMPO in those fields is certainly impressive. Now that a State Planning Board and several sub-regional development bodies have been created in West Bengal, CMPO and the Town and Country Planning Department should be allowed to exploit the opportunities so thrown up. There is no other agency in the State to perform such a task, either on its own or in association with such other bodies as the West Bengal Industrial Development Corporation and the West Bengal Industrial Infrastructure Development Corporation. Secondly, increasing metropolitanization may eventually lead to a reformed local governmental structure where planning and development functions will have to be kept separate (but not de-linked). Planning is a prerogative of the government, but development can be carried out on an agency basis. CMDA, as at present, is not a local body which can impose and collect levies. In the event of a reorganised governmental structure for the CMD, the need for organizations like CMDA will have to be reassessed while that for CMPO will be re-assured.

The Basic Development Plan published in 1966 said very clearly: "The planning agency should assist Government in the critical area which lies between planning and implementation. A planning body in such a vast complex as Metropolitan Calcutta, cannot itself assume the tasks of implementation without risking a gigantism—an unmanageable growth of responsibilities—in which the planning function will be inevitably diminished and ultimately destroyed. Yet it cannot proceed on the assumption that good plans and programmes, because they are publicly attractive and socially desirable, will therefore be automatically implemented. Executive energy must carry the programme from the stage where it is informally proposed to the point where it is officially accepted, and from there to the point where a competent body, properly placed in the Governmental structure, will proceed to execute it." Nevertheless, what exists now with regard to CMPO and CMDA is not exactly what was envisaged in the Basic Development Plan. That document primarly thought of a statutory Calcutta Metropolitan Planning Authority acting mainly through two-tier statutory functional bodies as also area-wise (East bank, West bank) planning and development bodies. On the whole, one would be inclined to comment at this point of time that the detailed administrative organization for planning and development recommended in the BDP does no longer hold valid in the existing situation. Alternatively, what holds good today has not been made very clear, which perhaps smacks of inadequacy of due attention and analysis. The field for thought and action in this area therefore is of high potential and should be deeply rewarding for its existing possibilities.

16

ROLE OF AN ADMINISTRATOR AS A CITY MANAGER

M.K. Moitra

According to 1981 Census about 24 per cent of India's population are living in more than 3,000 urban areas. The total number of urban population is estimated to be 156 million, one of the highest in the world. Compared to a decadal population growth rate of 22 per cent for the country during 1971—81 the population growth rate for the urban area for the same period is 46 per cent. It is estimated that by the end of the Century one out of three Indian will be living in an urban area.

Urban administration is fast acquiring a specialised character and can no longer be considered to be an extension of the general administrative set up in a State or a District. With the expansion of urban areas, particularly urban agglomeration in and around metropolitan areas, the State Government's role in municipal administration has become more important and is not restricted only to ways and means advances or granting subventions for dearness allowances of municipal employees. Even the Central Government of late have entered the field of local Government through Centrally sponsored schemes for improving the basic amenities of the urban dwellers and are trying to influence the process of a balanced urban growth.

In the Constitution, urban administration is included in the State list of the 7th Schedule. The State Government is concerned with the smooth administration of the urban areas particularly in relation to certain basic amenities like public health, improved sanitation, supply of drinking water and shelter. The involvement of the Central Government in the urban areas is in the form of other utility services, telephone, telecommunication, Railways including sub-urban Railways, Posts and Telegraphs, Ports (wherever applicable) etc.

The urban Administrative system in the country follows two distinct patterns. Firstly, in the majority of the cases the urban areas, delimited by fixed boundary jurisdictions is considered to be an integral part of revenue Districts. Though the local representative take major decisions with regard to matters concerning the local municipal administration including the services, the District Magistrate has been given primary over the municipal authorities. Thus the District Magistrate is, under the Municipal Act, in many cases expected to look after the smooth and efficient discharge of municipal functions. Normally, his intervention is necessary only when the municipal elected representatives are unable to function or where, it is not possible for the elected representatives to function effectively as a deliberative decision-making body. The District Magistrate has, in such a case, been given the power to recommend supersession of a municipal body and the appointment of an Administrator. The Sub-Divisional Officer in some cases, where there are big municipalities, has himself at times to work as the Administrator of a municipality in case of supersession. It is estimated that roughly 50 per cent of the municipalities are in a state of supersession. In the case of small and medium sized municipalities the D.M., on behalf of the State Government, is directly responsible for municipal governance, though they may have full time Executive Officers.

On the other side of the picture, there are a growing number of metropolitan cities where Police Commissioners are looking after law and order. The other functions of the District Magistrate are being directly looked after by various Departments of the State Governments. In such a case, therefore, the responsibility of looking after the municipal administrative functions could be with the local Government (whatever other name it may be given) Department of the State Government. Let this be called Type II Municipal Administration and former Type I.

In the case of Type I the task of the Administrator, whether he is a whole-time functionary or part-time executive officer, is relatively simpler as it is possible for him to identify himself within the broad framework of the District Administrative set up and link the decision-action sequence emanating from the District Magistrate with relative ease. However, even in such cases, where the size of the towns are growing and are fast requiring the character of cities, looking after municipal administrative functions become full time tasks, which cannot be treated as a supplementary function. Very frequently, this creates a problem of non-availability of adequately trained personnel, through the primary bottleneck is the extreme inadequacy of financial resources. The District Administration which is essentially meant for development oriented activities in the rural areas and to respond to the needs of a predominantly rural society, often finds that its manpower resources are stretched to the maximum and are unable to cope with the additional problem of any management. Urban growth is as inevitable concomitant of economic growth, and industrialisation. Over the next few decades, therefore, the existing towns will gradually grow into cities and existing cities will become larger in size. In the case of Type I municipal administration, as stated, the difficulties of coordination can be overcome because of the in-built mechanism in the District Magistrate's office. It is nevertheless necessary for the chief executives of municipalities to efficiently manage the scarce resources available at their disposal for the purpose of delivery of services to the residents. This becomes specially important because the municipalities generally deal with essential services which are intimately connected with the day-to-day life of the residents. Discontinuance of water supply even for a day will cause much more hardship than the discontinuance of postal system for 3-4 days or for a week. This is also equally true in areas like conservancy, drainage, sanifation etc. A Municipal Administrator has, therefore, to be conversant with the tasks and functions of municipalities and the approach to problem solving in case of crisis situations. The management problems (both human and material resources) acquire greater magnitude, along with the growth of size and with the problems of distribution and management of multi-disciplinary teams of technical people. Every Administrator in the course of the first few years of his service is bound to come across some such crisis situation involving municipal administration. The number of urban areas (whether municipal or non-municipal) in a district is bound to increase in future and bring with it the problems of urbanisation and urban management. Unfortunately this background is not kept in view while training our future administrators.

The concept of complementary growth and mutual interdependency as opposed to the earlier idea of rural-urban dichotomy, is fast gaining ground. It is wrong to presume that the urban areas exist at the cost of rural areas and development efforts focused in the urban areas are likely to deprive the rural areas. The present chaos and confusion that prevails in the urbon areas especially in their fringes and in respect of land use can be prevented if a comprehensive approach of town and country planning with appropriate methods of land use controls are developed. It may not be appropriate to go into details of the complications resulting from automatic expansion of urban areas. It is however important to bear in mind that a predominantly rural society finds it difficult to adjust to a changed life-style in congested urban areas, where several obligations are imposed on them primarily due to restrictions of space and various competitive uses within the restricted space. The role of an administrator trained in urban management becomes extremely crucial in such a situation as the vital link between the people and the administrative framework. We are, however, considering so far the Type I situation where there is a clearly identifiable link between the rural and urban areas as both rural and urban areas form an integral part of a revenue district. Soon, however, urban areas within a district might acquire their own characteristics. This has been happening in many of the cities of U.P. and M.P. Efforts have been made in such cases to segregate the urban administration and the rural administration (Kanpur for instance). Whether such an arbitrary segregation is the best possible solution would be a matter of great interest to all concerned.

One should, however, be more concerned about the Type II situation in respect of metropolital administration where no framework of coordination or clear link exists. Mutual inter-dependability of various agencies, attending to multifarious tasks connected with serving a huge metropolis is extremely involved and complicated. Generally the Municipal Corporation in such a case is recognised as the central authority which should be in a position to coordinate and inter-act with the use of other agencies. This presumption is however not supported by any statutory backing. Problems of coordination also arise in respect of utility agencies like P and T, Telephones, Electric Authority and other utility services which have to make use of the same limited space for the purpose of their distribution system. Each, with its own notion of priority, tries to follow a different pattern of implementation system in operation. Different utility agencies disturbing the road surface to the annoyance and inconvenience of road users is a common sight. This is a simple illustration of the problem of inter-agency coordination. But the actual difficulty is in identifying a common authority associated with city Administration (compared to the easily indentifiable district administration). Consequently the decision-action sequence is hopelessly deferred and difficult to establish. The City Magistrate would have to be fully conversant with the diverse sets of agencies and difficulties of forming a common link between them.

With growing complexities of urban administration specially in Type II situation, new urban agencies are coming in the field in addition to existing ones, such as Improvement Trusts, Development Authorities, Housing Boards, Sewerage and Drainage Authorities, Water Supply Authorities. Each of these organisations are manned by their own set of technical experts like sanitary engineers, public health engineer, doctors, electrical engineers, civil engineers and many other specialists. Management of such inter-disciplinary teams needs very careful personnel planning and a thorough understanding of the duties and responsibilities of these teams. The total strength of metropolitan corporations vary between 15,000 to 35,000 employees and the type of specialist skills required to manage different service would be anywhere near 100. The City Manager often does not have adequate resources in the form of finance or trained man power to control such a vast machinery. It is necessary, therefore, that today's City Managers who would mostly be the administrators should have a through understanding of the obligations of city management and the problems involved in the working of municipal corporation with its multifarious functions.

Some of the important functions of municipal administration are municipal revenue, building by-laws, and sanctioning of building plans, water supply and sanitation, conservancy, primary education and public health. In addition trade licenses, roads, burning ghats, birth and death registration, management of municipal markets are some of the other important functions. The primary resources of municipal revenue are octroi and property tax. Very other the City Manager himself is the appellate authority in property tax and building permit cases. He should therefore have a good understanding of the principles involving property taxation, and the various issues connected with the sanctioning of the building plans. Similarly, town and country-plan-legislation for the purpose of coordinated planned development of the cities has been adopted in almost all the cities. This also calls for a proper understanding of the planning process and its proper integration with the other developmental activities. The City Manager of today is therefore expected to understand these processes and the inevitable linkage between different disciplines of urban planning.

An administrator as a city manager in a Type II situation would have a much more difficult task to perform. He would not have the back-up support of District Administration or statutory authority given to him for overall coordination and guidance; at the same time he would be expected to deliver the results for which he is accountable. Municipal Statutes impose a statutory responsibility of the municipal authorities to deliver certain services to the residents. With the increase in 'public interest' litigations, it is not unlikely that the tax payers would take the City Manager to the court for redressal of their genuine/imaginary grievances. A City Manager will find himself ill-equipped to react readily for redressal of grievances, unless he is in a position to control all the resources available at his disposal and understand the implications and functions of various branches of administration. He will otherwise find himself mostly at the receiving end without appearing to cope with the situation. Changing pattern of urban growth calls for constantly evolving institutional infrastructure. In our country today, particularly in the case of metropolitan cities, we are in the midst of trying to find an optimum balance between the integrated approach and that of working through a number of specialised functional agencies, for finding out the best available approach to the problem of city management. With further increase in the urban population, a new administration structure would, no doubt, emerge to cope with the changing scene; for the present, however, the administrators as city managers will have to work as the vital link between the core authority and a number of functional agencies. It is time, therefore, that training institutions and inservice training programmes start paying adequate attention to this important aspect.

17

TRIBAL DEVELOPMENT ADMINISTRATION

Introduction

The history of Man as a social being begins in small groups. These groups formed by a cluster of families, cemented by limitations of geography and communication, and reinforced by common factors like speech, dialect, and methods of hunting, developed into tribes. A tribe today, can be described to be a society with a clear linguistic boundary and generally a well defined political boundary. The tribe also has a cultural boundary, though much less well-defined.

Evolution of human society from the primitive to the present stage of development demanded a competition for scarce resources. This has left many segments of population behind others who progressed rapidly. Tribal communities of present day context are such groups left behind.

In India, the tribes constitute a fairly large segment of population. These descendants of some of the earliest inhabitants of the sub-continent have been pushed by the onward march of more economically developed sections, into geographical areas relatively less conducive for an easier life. And yet, the tribals have evolved a distinctive life style of theirs. In terms of quality of life and cultural ethos, the tribals stand out in sharp contrast to the general rural people of India.

The tribal areas are characterised by their aloofness, a lower level of economic activity and a closed social structure. Aloofness arises from a difficult geographical situation. However, insulation from the rest of the country has by and large never been total. This is especially true of the tribal belt of middle India. The Districts of Bastar (MP) and Korapud (Orissa) are an interesting example. Predominantly tribal, and with large area still inaccessible, these areas saw establishment of small princely States by Nalas and Vakatakas from the Andhra region, as early as in the 5th century. The Chindakanagas ruled Bastar in the 11th century. The Karkatiyas arrived from the Warangal Region of Andhra Pradesh in the 14th century and ruled uninterrupted till 1948. The Jagannath cult of the larger Indian society may be traced back to tribal eommunities of Koraput. The Jharkhand tract of Bihar and the tribal belt of Western India have also been similarly exposed to outside contacts and influences. The tribal communities of North East India are placed on a slightly different footing as their contact with other regions is of a more recent origin. But there also the traders in commodities, like salt for example, have been making visits from very early times.

This interaction with the outside world, has left deep marks of economic exploitation, social discrimination and political isolation, on these areas. With increasing awareness (which itself is a result of greater outside contacts, breaking up of isolation by better means of communication, and spread of education) this leads to a conflict situation, discussed at length later.

At this point two broad objectives of any tribal development administration become clear. First, economic development and end of exploitation in tribal areas, and second, an opportunity to the tribals to preserve their distinctive culture and way of life.

Evolution of Administration in Tribal Areas

In pre-independence India, the British Government sought to protect the tribal people from unregulated exposure to the competitive forces operating in the rest of the country by creating for them "excluded" and "partially excluded" areas. This isolationist approach deprived the tribals of the benefits of welfare measures and other development activities.

The situation changed significantly after India attained independence. The integration of the tribal regions with the rest of the country was an imperative for nation-building and there was no question of keeping them isolated from the rest of the Indian society. All sections of the society had to be equal partners in the development of the country and had to have their share in the benefits of progress.

The policy was, therefore, of adopting a middle path between the two extremes of complete insulation and opening up of tribal areas in an unrestricted manner. In the words of Pandit Nehru "We cannot allow matters to drift in the tribal areas . . . . In the world of today that is not possible or desirable. At the same time, we should avoid over-administration in these areas . . . It is between those two extreme positions that we have to function". This task according to Pandit Nehru, had to be performed through their own social and cultural institutions without overwhelming them with a maze of modern economic institutions.

Today, after thirty years of planning for and development of tribal areas, we cannot say with certainty that an ideal framework has emerged for administration of development in tribal areas.

This report goes on further, to examine the following:

(a) The needs of the tribals, their desire to develop economically and also preserve their identity and way of life.

(b) The national priorities that necessarily transcend into tribal areas, not merely in the objectives of the government of develop tribal areas, but also in fields like forest wealth, mineral resources and industrialisation.

(c) The conflict situations that arise when items (a) and (b) both have to be fitted into a national policy.

Further, we have a look at the efforts made in the last thirty years in the area of tribal development, and try to evaluate the performance in relation to the objectives listed at (a) and (b) above. Next, we try and examine the situation today keeping in view the conflict situations listed at (c) above. We also take a look at the tribal development administration in its administrative structure and personnel policies.

All through, the group tries to express its views on areas of failure and steps that can be taken to improve tribal development administration.

The Needs of the Tribal

(*A*) *Specific Problems of Different Regions*

The tribal population of India is by and large concentrated in three zones and in isolated pockets scattered around the country (please refer Annexure No. I).

(*i*) *North-East*: Tribals in North Eastern India are a conglomeration of small but proud tribes. Their contact with the rest of the country is of recent origin, beginning with the merger of their areas with British India in the last century. These are by and large hill tribes. Hunting and food gathering in the forest remains an important way of making a living. Agriculture is primitive and in large tracts jhoom cultivation is practised. Christian Missionaries have done good work in these areas and have been able to convert the tribals to Christianity. Level of education in this tribal zone is the highest for any tribal area in the country, thanks mainly to the zeal of the missionaries. This zone is strategically located on sensitive international borders. Communication links with the rest of the country, limited as they are through the narrow Silguri Corridor, are inadequate. This directly comes in the way of industrialisation and development of the region, placing sources of raw materials and markets for finished goods far removed from each other.

Limited communication links, stunted economic growth due to geographical distances on the one hand and high level of literacy and the resultant inadequate emotional integration, have thrown up problems like insurgency and a grave sense of insecurity.

(*ii*) *Western India*: Tribals of Western India, have been exposed to the cross-currents of Indian mainstream for a much longer period of time than the North East. This has led to a slow process of Hinduisation over the centuries. The tribals do still retain many of their distinct features, but assimilitation with adjoining Indian non-tribal areas is less painful than in the North East. This is because the Bhil Region has been in turmoil over centuries. Most acute of the problems of this tribal zone is that it is scarce in resources, creating a disequilibrium between available manpower and the natural resources. While the pressure of population has grown in these areas, the available resource base became smaller and smaller. "If one traverses the tribal tract of Jhabua in Western M.P., there are unending waves of bare hillocks ... This is the habitat of the Bhils."* Studies reveal this to be a clear case of over exploitation of resources, with growth of population and with the arrival of outsiders to take share in the smaller and smaller cake, over the years. But this immigration has also dwindled over the years as there is little to share.

The socio-economic scene in a sizeable part of this region can be briefly summarised as follows:

*Occasional paper on Tribal Development No. 12, Ministry of Home Affairs.

"1. The Forest land resources have been over-exploited and are fast becoming non-existent.

2. The growth rate of population has been increasing and there is heavy pressure on limited resources.

3. There is little immigration because there is little to share. However, the exploitative elements are well entrenched."*

(*iii*) *Middle India*: The third main zone is Middle India. This is the biggest tribal zone of the country in terms of area and population. This zone is in many ways different from other zones. The zone is rich in forest and mineral resources. Eightyfive per cent of mineral wealth of the country is located in this region.

In Madhya Pradesh alone the forest revenues exceed Rs. 100 crores from this region. This gives an idea of the availability and level of exploitation of forests of this region.

Middle India has been exposed to outside influences over the centuries. Only the deep interior was largely left untouched. In this region, it has essentially been a story of onward march of immigrant population and the tribals receding to hilly and difficult tracts. Now, even the last exclusive pockets sustain immigrant population, the exploiter section being a part of this. The Southern districts of Bihar, now collectively called Jharkhand are a case in point.

(*B*) *Common Problems*

The common problems faced by tribals in almost all regions in addition to the special features in the three main zones mentioned above, are discussed briefly here.

(*i*) *Land Relations*: Tribals in all the zones have agriculture as their main occupation. Agricultural practices are generally primitive. On top of this, the tribals have faced a constant on

*Occasional Paper, on Tribal Development No. 12.

slaught by outsiders in many exploitative roles. The money-lender is one such agents who has been able to alienate the tribal from his land. Another aspect of tribal-lands going into the hands of non-tribals is through the immigrant non-tribal who occupies forest lands.

Problems of Tribal Land Systems are slightly different in the North East and other areas.

North East: (i) The main problem is that of shifting cultivation. The need in these areas is to replace this practice of "Jhoom", which is a crude traditional method of land use. "So far hardly ten per cent of tribals practising this type of cultivation have been settled."*

(ii) The second set of problems arise from communal ownership of land. These are:

(a) In communal ownership the individual has little attachment to improve the land they operate on. A tendency for improvement of land is noticed in areas where land is individually owned and cultivated. In Meghalaya, soil conservation efforts for example have been more successful in the settled lands of individual owners than on community-owned lands.

(b) It is difficult to extend institutional credit and other facilities.

(c) Land ownership being vested in the community, land records are in a poor state.

The need in these areas is thus to go in a big way to settle tribals on individual basis for cultivation, employ conservation methods, improve the land records of State, and extend institutional credit to curb exploitative vices like practice of usury by both tribals and non-tribals.

*Perspectives on Tribal Development Administration, NIDC Publication, Page 203.

Other Areas: The main problems in other tribal areas are:

(i) Low rate of per capita land distribution and high incidence of landlessness. Incidence of landlessness among agricultural labourers of the country is more pronounced among the tribals who constitute 12 per cent of total agricultural labour force of the country (whereas tribals contribute only 7 per cent of the total population of the country).

(ii) Land alienation, inspite of measures by State Governments to restrict sale of land to non-tribals in the form of benami transactions.

(iii) Persistance of a widespread inferior land tenancy in the form of unrecorded share-cropping practised as for example in West Bengal.

(iv) Land records have been in a poor shape in tribal areas, though efforts are now on to carry fresh settlement operations in these areas.

The need thus is to strictly enforce action against benami transfers, improve the state of land records, and ensure that land is distributed to landless tribals.

(*ii*) *Forests*: Tribal economy is intimately connected with forests and their economy. The forest regions are sparsely populated, generally inhabited by tribal communities who are at one of the earlier stages of economic development compared to other communities in the country. These regions are comparatively under-developed though they have rich natural resources. The dependence of tribal communities inhabiting the richer tracts, ironically is the greatest on the forest for their sustenance. It is here that, agriculture is most primitive, and the tribals go for food gathering in forests. The tribal economy has subsisted on minor forest produce since time immemorial.

In this kind of situation, the need of the tribal is to leave forests which are his habitate and provide succour—in the hands of his community. The forests were once a property of the tribal, and he would like that relation to persist.

It is erroneously presumed that the tribals continue to live in a pre-monetised subsistence static State. Tribal agriculture, primitive as it is, is insufficient to provide for a year round living. Minor forest produce has thus become an important source for meeting the tribals' cash requirement, which has been increasing with the diversification of their wants.

(*iii*) *Liquor Policy*: Liquor has been an essential ingredient of tribal food and drink. This is by and large true of tribals all over the country. The tribals have over the centuries brewed their own liquor and tribal communities all over would like this ancient right of theirs honoured and protected.

(*iv*) *Employment*: Tribal areas suffer from inefficient practices in agriculture, lack of subsidiary occupations like animal husbandry and either a total lack of operations or a lop-sided growth in the secondary and tertiary sector. A large section of the populace is of landless labourers or marginal farmers.

The immediate need of the tribal, is to provide him employment and/or opportunities to make a living. This, according to the tribal mind, would point towards not only assisting him in development of his activities in agriculture and allied sectors, but also making available opportunities in new activities on the one hand and protection of his traditional sphere of activity like collection of forest produce, traditional crafts etc. In the sphere of employment, the tribal would like his interest protected from outsiders in his areas. This is essential to him, as an outsider is, more often than not, better equipped than the tribal to perform on jobs created in the tribal belt.

(*v*) *Protection from exploitative agencies*: Tribal population has over the decades seen the arrival and entrenchment of an outside exploitative class in its areas. The tribal would like protection and vigorous enforcement of laws against money-lenders, forest contractors and rapacious Government servants.

National Priorities and Conflict Situations

In the post independence period, we have been engaged in the task of development of the country. Whereas in general, all regions of the country with few exceptions, are under-developed and backward, the tribal areas fall in at the very end of the scale by any standards of economic development.

We have generally been able to identify sectors which need urgent attention for rapid growth. For example, exploitation of minerals for the benefit of the entire nation is one important aspect. In addition, we have recognised that economic growth has to be accompanied by distribution of gains to all sections, most importantly to the weakest sections of the Indian society.

Here is where the tribal areas need special attention. It is not merely calling for extra attention and additional financial allocation that is needed for the tribal areas. It called for an effective identification of the special features of tribal areas, their special needs, which may or may not mesh in exactly into a national objective. Also at no point of time has it to be forgotton that tribals have their own distinctive cultural and social values and that they by and large desire preservation of some of these, side by side as they work for a better standard of living.

Some of the important areas in which the national priorities and the priorities of the tribals may lead to conflict situations are as follows:—

(*a*) *Forests*: Forests have come to be recognised as a big source of revenue to the government. With the ever-increasing requirements of a developing society, this natural resource is diminishing rapidly. The objectives of a forest policy that does not have a tribal situation to compromise with, would follow a pattern that gives maximum returns in shortest possible time. This would mean exploiting the existing growth and planting species that are most helpful in catering to industrial and domestic requirements of an urbanising society (of course environmental considerations also increasingly weigh in any decision to exploit forest wealth, but that is not considered here, as it does not lead to a conflict situation, in so far as it is an unescapable reality).

Also, any large scale forest project means import of skilled labour to tribal areas to deal with sophisticated techniques and machinery. The controversial Pine Plantation Project of Bastar is a case in point. The project envisages the cutting of a naturally growing sal and mixed forests and planting of fast growing tropical pine, useful for manufacturing rayon-grade pulp and paper. But what of the tribals—their need to collect minor forest produce, like sal seed, and their requirement of wood, available in the village backyard.

The conflict arises out of the need of the tribal—and at the present pace of their development for many generations to come—to make a living from the forest, and the national priority to increase revenues on the one hand and make available industrial raw materials. Another area of conflict has emerged from the change in ownership pattern. Earlier, the forests were widespread and the tribals had enjoyed an unrestricted access to this immense bounty of nature at their very doorstep. Suddenly, the whole situation changed and the ownership, started vesting in the State, and restrictive and prohibitive regulations came in between the tribals and the forest. The Chipko Andolens in the U.P. Hills and the tribal belt of South Bihar are a direct result of this conflict situation.

The forest resources are richer in the more backward areas since there is lower pressure of population and modern destructive elements have also not found their way to these areas. "Ripe for 'scientific' exploitation, it is ironical that it is here that the tribal depends to the maximum extent on the forests and as in the early stages of economic evolution."*

(*b*) *Industrialisation*: Economic development is generally characterised by diversification of economy and sustained growth of its numerous facets. In India, as we try to diversify our economy it is but obvious that we look for mineral resources that are essential raw material for industrialisation.

*Forest Tribal Economy and Regional Development—Occasional Papers on Tribal Development No. 26.

Once again, as in the case of forests, the areas that boast the richest mineral deposits are the areas of tribal concentration. The tribal belt of middle India has more than 85 per cent of the nation's mineral wealth.

Exploitation of these minerals need a very high order of technical skill. The tribal is most deficient in this. He possesses a high level of traditional skill, which is of no use in this context.

The experience of the last three decades has been that "the industrial and mining complexes, established in tribal regions are inward looking and self-sufficient, having most of their linkages with more advanced areas. They do not depend on the local communities even for unskilled labour".*

The conflict arises in this case, as there is no meeting point between the industrial complexes, (juxtaposed though they are in these regions) and the tribal population. Therefore, the modern industrial sector expands at the cost of the rest of the economy and displaces local communities without much benefits accruing to them.

Industries by and large fail to establish normal linkages with their immediate hinterland. The new job opportunities in the service sector also get dominated by outsiders.

(*c*) *Prohibition*: Yet another area of conflict is the prohibition policy of the Government and the frequent changes made therein.

Tribal food and drink have liquor as an eseential ingredient. On the other hand the State Governments, in their need to increase excise revenues, and in the name of introducing prohibition on moralistic grounds, have enforced varying degrees of control over brewing of liquor by tribals. This has caused interference and resentment amongst the tribals.

*Planning for Industrial Development of the Tribal Areas—Occasional Papers on T.D. No. 7, Ministry of Home Affairs.

(*d*) *Employment and Immigration of Outsiders*: Any active policy of industrialisation of tribal areas necessitates immigration of skilled workers from other areas. Also the service sector gets manned almost exclusively by immigrants.

The tribal areas are less thickly populated than other regions and are in general resource rich. This also attracts people from densely populated parts of the country. North Eastern India is the most prominent example. South Bihar, entirely tribal not so long ago, today has 40 per cent non-tribal population.

This gives rise to conflict situations as education and literacy levels of tribals go up and there is competition for scarce job opportunities. The main cause of resentment arises when the tribal realises the exploitative character of a section of the immigrant populace.

Conflict situations also arise out of political awareness. It cannot always be said to be righteous and oriented towards welfare of the tribal population, but these limitations do not obscure the fact that even the smallest of communities can ask for a certain degree of freedom to shape their way of life.

Tribal Development Administration in the Last Thirty Years

The constitution envisaged a fast enough pace of development for the tribal areas, so that they could be brought to the level of development in the surrounding regions in the concerned State, fast enough. Special programmes for these areas therefore were taken up in the early fifties in the form of special multi-purpose Tribal Blocks (SMTBS).

Beginning with a few blocks, and extended gradually to others this scheme was essentially an exercise in development reconnoitring.

Working of these blocks was reviewed, and the team headed by Verrier Elwin recommended a more flexible approach. The

SMTBS were rechristening Tribal Development Blocks (TDBS). There were about 490 such blocks in various parts of the country.

Tribal Development Blocks

TDBs were given 100 per cent assistance by the Central Government. Centrally sponsored schemes till the end of the Fourth Plan period were in the fields of cooperation, girls hostels post-matric scholarships, and other special projects. In the States' sector education (pre-matric scholarships, stipend, hostels, supply of books and stationery, mid-day meals etc.) economic, development (subsidy for agricultural development schemes, cottage industries, cooperation, minor irrigation, soil conservation etc.), health, housing, and other miscellaneous items like aid to voluntary agencies, social and cultural activities were covered.

The impact of the programme was evaluated by the Shilo Ao Committee (1969) in the following terms, stated briefly:—

(a) Though the TD Block has brought about a change in the outlook of the tribals, particularly in the field of education and agriculture, the impact has fallen below expectations.

(b) There is an intrinsic limitation of TD Block due to smallness of its area. This becomes more pertinent if the following inadequacies are also borne in mind:—

(i) Fragmented approach to development planning.

(ii) Application of a large number of standardised schemes in the tribal areas.

(iii) Neglect of employment aspects of development.

(iv) The programme became in most cases the exclusive effort of the tribal sector, and the general sector programmes failed to reach the tribal areas.

(v) The benefit of the programme did not percolate below the upper sector of the tribal community in most cases.

Tribal Development Agencies

The TDB Programme brought into focus, the fact that all-sided effort resulted in its diffusion. It also indicated that more investment and a more intensive effort was needed. Consequently, Tribal Development Agencies (TDAS) were set up in relatively more backward areas. Investment was enhanced for intensifying the development effort. Protective legislation was further strengthened to prevent land alientation and relieve the tribal from the clutches of the money lenders. At the same time a programme for providing alternative institutional credit, with a liberal repayment and interest structure, was envisaged.

The result of all these efforts was that tribal areas were buzzing with a good deal of activity. Schools have been opened, primary health centres operate at all block headquarters, work on village roads is in progress, some minor irrigation schemes have come up etc. All this has made at least a section of the tribal community development conscious.

The limitations on the other hand were:

(i) Arousal of strong expectations and gap in fulfilment.

(ii) Defective implementation of programmes with benefit going to the relatively better off seetions.

(iii) The programmes were not flexible and a uniform pattern was followed under different conditions, that require different approaches.

Tribal Sub-Plans—Fifth Plan

At the beginning of the Fifth Plan, a new approach was adopted for tribal development, where all areas with more than 50 per cent tribal concentration were identified and special plans prepared. The new programme covered 65 per cent of the tribal population, by starting 155 Integrated Tribal Development Projects.

Formulation of sub-plans was a step in the right direction. Each sub-plan focussed attention on a specific area and gave details of its problems and priorities. It also earmarked the budgetary allocations in different spheres of activity.

One major constraint was that 35 per cent of tribal population was not covered by the initial sub-plans.

There were a number of ongoing schemes and programmes which very often were not the right answers to the problems of the tribal area and yet these could not be reviewed on time.

But the main advantage of planning at the project level is that it has thrown up a wealth of data, which has either supported the general presumptions about these areas in many cases, or, indicated the necessary change in perspective sub-plans in the Sixth Plan.

The basic objectives of the new task in the Sixth Plan have been given to be as follows:

(i) The entire tribal population will be covered by suitable development programmes during Sixth Plan period.

(ii) The gulf between tribal areas and the surrounding areas to be bridged by the end of Sixth Plan and in the case of more backward tribal areas in another five years.

(iii) Same as in (ii) above will hold true for scattered tribal communities.

The details regarding formulation of sub-plans are not being enumerated here. Guidelines have been given in Home Ministry Booklets listed at items 7 (xi) and 8 in the Bibliography at the end.

Some of the salient features are given below:

(i) Total financial outlays for tribal sub-plan areas are to be worked out independently and then fix the inter-sectoral priorities.

(ii) For each project, the inter-sectoral priorities will have to be fixed with reference to certain financial parameters to be fixed for each ITDP.

(iii) The sub-plan should present a greater appreciation of the qualitative aspect, indicating how the weakest sectors are likely to benefit.

(iv) Attempt should be made in the sub-plan document in each sector to bring into focus the accrual of benefit to the target groups in qualitative terms.

(v) The Advisory Committee at the ITDP level, should be associated with the plan so that the views of the peoples' representatives get incorporated at the programme formulation level.

(vi) Delegation of powers and procedures—especially financial—should be worked out for uninterrupted implementation.

(vii) A policy frame for working out personnel requirements should be presented in the sub-plan.

(viii) Training of personnel and village leaders.

(ix) A policy frame for the involvement of voluntary organisation should be prepared.

(x) The sub-plan may even give directions of efforts proposed to be made for attending to special needs of hinterland of mining and industrial complexes, forest rich regions, areas with large number of landless labourers etc.

(xi) The sub-plan should highlight special problems and resource potential of the concerned area.

Education, health services and a full-employment economy have now been given a specially high priority besides accepting the need for consolidating the protective measures already undertaken.

Advantages of Sub-Plans

Whereas, it is too early to evaluate this new methodology for the planned development of tribal areas, the group feels that the formulation of sub-plans would help the process in the following ways:

(a) The sub-plans area-plans and focus on development of specific areas. This highlights the special needs of a particular area.

(b) As budgetary allocation will be made based on the sub-plans, the allocations made to tribal areas cannot be transferred to other areas. Central Ministries are now directly responsible to ensure that funds rearmarked in their sectors for tribal areas are spent there. In Madhya Pradesh the Annual Budget now has separate allocations for tribal areas in each sector.

(c) Inter-sectoral priorities being fixed at the project level, it would be a step towards integrated development of the area.

(d) The sub-plans are to place emphasis on qualitative aspect. If this and not mere spending of money, is recognised as the main objective, impact on the tribal population would be greater.

(e) If the sub-plan can include proposals in areas given in item (x) above, it will go a long way towards protecting the interests of the tribal.

At the same time the group apprehends that sufficient results may not be achieved in the following areas, due to inherent limitations:

(i) Local participation in programme formulation.—The tendency would be to ignore and not encourage consultation with local people, who at least in the most backward regions are largely unprepared for the role. Pressure to include local participation should be put on officials.

(iii) Personnel policies should be more thoroughly reviewed. Any new programme is only as good as the people who implement it.

(iii) Actual delegation of powers to project level may not actually come about. Integrated development is best done by a coordinated approach at the block and district levels. Departmental interests, well entrenched as they are, would come in the way.

Administration in Tribal Areas

Administration in tribal areas falls under two different categories. The situation in tribal majority areas that constitute a separate political entity as in the North-East is different from elsewhere.

In North Eastern region, the case is more for strengthening the developmental agencies at the block level, whereas in other States in addition to the former, there is an additional requirement to protect the interests of the tribal district *vis-a-vis* other areas. In these States, the group feels that the move to place Tribal Development Commissioners (TDC) as overall incharge of development activities is a right one. This would ensure an integrated approach to the problems of the tribal areas. But for this it is essential that control over funds is exercised by the TDC.

At the district and project level, again, the group feels that an integrated approach can be best achieved by placing all activities under the supervision of a coordinator, be it the Collector or in case a district has more than one project—the Project officers/Administrator. The spirit of the sub-plan is to delegate effective power to project level authorities. Unless this is achieved in reality by administrative restructing, the effectiveness of the sub-plans would be impaired.

At the Block level, the main difficulty is due to lack of qualified and trained personnel. The BDO should have effective control over the officials at the Block level. It has been the general experience, that the work of the officers at this level suffers from the dual control of the BDO and the departmental superior. This would be minimised once the tribal sub-plans are effectively implemented. The same would be true at the Project level also, once sectoral allocation are fixed project-wise and expenditure sanctioned at the same level.

The office at the District/Project needs strengthening so as to make it more effective in formulation and monitoring of various schemes.

Personnel Policies

The policy followed in the selection, training and employment of personnel in tribal area has never been given sufficient importance.

The result has reflected on the working of the development agencies in these areas. Some of the main problems are summarised as below:

(i) There is a shortage of trained personnel for posting in the interior parts of the tribal areas.

(ii) Many of the newly employed personnel are on the look-out for job prospects elsewhere and do not take interest in their work.

(iii) Tribals area postings are regarded as punishment postings. Those posted either are indifferent towards their work, or keep trying to get themselves transferred. In this respect State Government have also contributed, in many cases by posting to tribal areas, persons unwanted elsewhere. In addition, the Governments have not been immune to pressures for ordering cancellation of transfers of people posted to tribal areas.

(iv) Infrastructural facilities are poor in tribal areas. This also acts as a disincentive. Housing accommodation, schools for children and medical facilities are generally inadequate.

Improvements

The Government should provide incentives to personnel working in tribal areas, so as to attract persons who are interested to work there; and most importantly to drive away the reluctance in the minds of people to get posted there. Incentives by way of special allowances for tribal area postings will go a long way toward attracting good people to stay and work in tribal areas.

Residential accommodation should be provided on a priority basis *vis-a-vis* other areas. Construction of houses at Block level and quarters for teachers in remote areas should be taken up on a large-scale.

Conclusion

The situation in tribal areas is well summarised in the following paragraph from "Approach to Tribal Development in the Sixth Plan":

> "The basic question in many of the tribal areas is not of property, as is generally understood in the more advanced areas. The resources are plentiful and the needs of the tribals are limited. The level of technology is in consonance with the plentiful resources and limited needs. The task, therefore, is to prevent effectively in roads on their resources, help the tribal in upgrading his skills, and finally to enable him to stand on his own in the new situation. Where he comes in contact with more articulate groups with a different value system."

ANNEXURE I

Areas of Tribal Concentration

The tribal population of India is by and large concentrated in three zones·

(1) North Eastern India.

(2) Middle India (comprising Eastern Madhya Pradesh, South Bihar, Northern and Western Orissa, Eastern Maharashtra and contiguous areas of Andhra Pradesh, Purulia district of West Bengal).

(3) Western India (comprising districts of Western Madhya Pradesh, Southern Rajasthan, Eastern and Northern Gujarat, and parts of Maharashtra).

There are isolated tribal communities in the aforementioned States, as well as in other States of the South, and the hill tribes in the Sub-Himalayan Region.

BIBLIOGRAPHY

1. New Deal for Tribal India—Elwin V.
2. Planning for Tribal Development—Gupta, Ranjit.
3. Integrated Tribal Development Planning—NICD.
4. Perspectives on Tribal Development and Administration —NICD.
5. Tribal Development; The Concept and the Frame—Sharma, B.D.
6. Conflict, Tension and Cultural Trend in India—Vidhyarathi. L.P.
7. Occasional Papers in Tribal Development—Ministry of Home Affairs, Government of India.

   (i) Perspective on Tribal Development.

   (ii) Role of Voluntary Organisations in Tribal Development.

   (iii) Education for Scheduled Castes and Tribes.

   (iv) Tribal Development: The New Strategy.

   (v) Growth Centres in Tribal Areas.

   (vi) Development of Small Tribal Communities.

   (vii) Planning for Industrial Development of the Tribal Area.

   (viii) Economic Development of Extremely Backward Tribal Region.

   (ix) Planning for Education Development in Tribal Areas.

(x) Economic Development of Scarce Resource Regions.

(xi) Approach to TD in the Sixth Plan.

(xii) Forests, Tribal Economy and Regional Development.

(xiii) Planning from Below with Special Reference to Tribal Areas.

8. Preparation of Tribal Sub-Plan 1978-83, Project-wise Annual Sub-Plan, 1979-80—Government of India, Ministry of Home Affairs.

INDEX

U

V

W

Z